MURDER
MAYHEM
FIRE & STORM
AUSTRALIAN SHIPWRECKS

MAX JEFFREYS

For my parents, Sid and Margaret

Other Books by Max Jeffreys
Wreck of the Sydney Cove

First published in Australia in 1999 by
New Holland Publishers (Australia) Pty Ltd
Sydney • Auckland • London • Cape Town

14 Aquatic Drive Frenchs Forest NSW 2086 Australia
218 Lake Road Northcote Auckland New Zealand
24 Nutford Place London W1H 6DQ United Kingdom
80 McKenzie Street Cape Town 8001 South Africa

National Library of Australia Cataloguing-in-Publication Data:

Jeffreys, Max.
    Murder, Mayhem Fire and Storm: Australian Shipwrecks.

    Bibliography.
    Includes index.
    ISBN 1 86436 445 9

    I. Shipwrecks–Australia.
    I. Title.

    910.4520994

Editor: Julian Dahl
Project Editor: Howard Gelman
Designer: Nanette Backhouse
Typesetting: Midland Typesetters Pty Ltd
Printer: Griffin Press, Adelaide

Cover: *Admella* by James Shaw

Contents

Shipwreck Incidents

TIMOR SEA

MELVILLE
ISLAND

Cyclone Tracey
devastates Darwin

DAR

Cyclones sink many
pearling luggers and
guano vessels

LACEPEDE
ISLANDS

Broome

Koombana

NO
TE

BARROW
ISLAND

Port Hedland

WESTERN
AUSTRALIA

A

HMAS *Sydney*
HSK *Kormoran*

Zuytdorp

Batavia
Zeewyk   Geraldton

INDIAN
OCEAN

De Vergulde Draeck

PERTH

SOUTHERN OCE

KEY

🚢 *sailing ships*

🚢 *steam- or oil-powered ships*

THURSDAY ISLAND • *Quetta*

Pandora

Cyclone Mahina
devastates pearling
fleet. 100 luggers lost

CORAL
SEA

Cairns

HINCHINBROOK ISLAND
Maria
Townsville *Yongala*
WHITSUNDAY ISLANDS

Mackay

QUEENSLAND

FRASER
ISLAND

Centaur

BRISBANE

PACIFIC
OCEAN

NEW SOUTH
WALES

Rodney

ADELAIDE

Newcastle
Cawarra
*Sovereign of the
Seas III*
SYDNEY
Wollongong *Dunbar*
Catherine Adamson

ANGAROO
ISLAND

VICTORIA

Storms wreck many
vessels off the
New South Wales coast
Ann Jamieson explodes

Admella
The Mahogany Ship *Schomberg*
Loch Ard
MELBOURNE

TASMAN SEA

Cataraqui KING
ISLAND
BASS STRAIT

Fire distroys:
Columbian
City of Melbourne
Protector
Habitant
Hilaria
Empress of the Sea
Winchester
Lightning
West Wind

Launceston
TASMANIA
HOBART

Catherine Sharer Fire and explosions
destroy *Thomas*

Acknowledgements

No book of this kind can be written without recourse to a wide range of earlier publications, reports, journal articles, newspaper extracts and photographic works. Now this also includes electronic data bases, each compiled or produced by others, both past and present. To all of these people I owe a great debt of thanks for facilitating my own research. My thanks must also go to the staffs of the Department of Infrastructure and La Trobe libraries in Melbourne, where much of this material is housed, for their willing assistance.

Many experts in the field of maritime archaeology helped in various ways in connection with sources, references and illustrative material. In particular I wish to thank the staffs of the Western Australian Maritime Museum, Fremantle; the New South Wales Heritage Office, Parramatta; the Queensland Museum, Brisbane; the Museums and Art Galleries of the Northern Territory, Darwin; the Department of Communications and the Arts Heritage Branch, Canberra; and the Flagstaff Hill Maritime Museum, Warrnambool. In connection with the Mahogany Ship, I received quite specific help from Dr John Stanley of Geophysical Technology Ltd., Armidale, while for HMAS *Sydney*, I was given valuable assistance by Mr Ian Smith of the Australian War Memorial, Canberra.

Finally, my thanks are due to Averill Chase and the staff of New Holland Publishers, who conceived the original idea for this project.

Max Jeffreys
Bacchus Marsh, Vic.

Preface

Shipwrecks have been a feature of seafaring for as long as man has sought to conquer the world's oceans. Journeys by sea have thus inevitably been fraught with tragedy and loss, sometimes on a massive scale, though mostly as isolated sinkings off storm-bound coasts or in little-known corners of distant seas. Such occurrences have never deterred mankind in his eternal pursuits of exploration, trade, or new land, however, nor in his wars and conquests. So, for hundreds of years, the losses of ships and their complements have mounted steadily, to quite unknown and perhaps unimaginable proportions. As late as the start of the 20th century, the risks in travelling by sea were accepted as part of the quest for new opportunities, and even today the conduct of peacetime commerce is not without its price in the regular disappearance of ships, their cargoes and crews.

Britain, for instance, is reputed to have around half-a-million shipwrecks lying off her coasts—which is not surprising given her long history, her position, her approaches, her weather, and the extent of her navies, both maritime and martial, over the centuries. As an island nation, much of her growth and economic expansion—indeed her very survival at times— has depended on ships and the sea. So, too, were Mediterranean and Scandinavian nations dependent on sea commerce, with all the associated storms and conflicts, and for just as long, if not longer. The world's oldest complete ship, a cedarwood vessel nearly 5000 years old, was found in a dismantled state within the pyramid of Cheops at Giza in the 1950s. The Mediterranean's oldest shipwrecks date from the Bronze Age, between 2000 and 500BC, the forerunners of many to be lost down the ages.

While large numbers of wrecks have been found in the relatively short history of maritime archaeology, which developed only after the Second World War, countless others still lie beneath the waves. Even though Australia has been dependent on sea trade and passenger transport for little more than 200 years, shipwreck numbers about our coasts are high. Authorities vary in their estimates, but there are reputed to be up to 7000 shipwrecks in Australian waters, including the outer-lying islands. Though many shipwrecks are known—Charles Bateson and Jack Loney, for example, have together described nearly 6000—fewer than a quarter of these have been located and positively identified.

In terms of all Australian shipwrecks, New South Wales can lay claim to around 2000 or more, including those in inland waters. This figure represents perhaps a third of the overall national total, though only 200 or so sites have been discovered. Western Australia is said to have between 1000 and 1500 wrecks, though again only 200 or so have been located and identified. Victorian waters cover some 700 shipwrecks, 200 of which are reported as lying within 10 kilometres of Port Phillip Heads. Tasmanian wrecks also number around 700, of which more than 60 foundered off King Island, and as many as 120 are reputed to lie around the Furneaux Group. Of the other States, Queensland has around 1000 shipwrecks, South Australia has more than 600, while over 200 are known to lie in the seas bordering the Northern Territory.

Good sea stories engender atmosphere, adventure, romance, nostalgia even. Often they are founded on mystery, as old and remote as the *Mary Celeste* perhaps, or as recent and as close to home as HMAS *Sydney*. It is the nature of such mysteries, especially those which tell of shipwrecks, to be perpetuated by the fact that they cannot be adequately explained— hence their perennial fascination. Thus do they maintain the wonder about what really happened, and the wish to learn more about the events, the experiences—indeed the very fate—of those involved.

In telling the stories behind some dramatic wreck incidents involving many ships lost off the Australian coast between the years 1629 and 1943, I have tried to capture or re-create something of the atmosphere surrounding these events. In addition, there are two chapters which explain the loss of many other ships in causative terms—some of which became the victims of fire, or sank as a result of violent storms. Where appropriate, I have used contemporary language, sea terms and nautical measurements in order to be true to the time in which these events occurred.

Many of these stories demonstrate the eternal pull of new lands and the challenge of new ventures. They also reflect the lure of gold, the promise of trade, and the escape from oppression that brought many migrants to our shores, as well as the conditions and privations that had to be endured, the dangers that had to be faced, and the unavoidable uncertainties of navigation and weather on their voyages—and the disasters and loss inevitably connected with the continuing quest for new horizons.

The frontiers of the world's oceans can be likened to the frontiers of space today—both have involved voyages over relatively vast distances despite incalculable risks. Because the moods of the sea are more familiar to us, however, maritime tales invariably generate more of a sense of 'being there'. Such tales stir the imagination and give us a feel for something of the ways and lives of seafarers and travellers from a bygone age.

Introduction

The distribution of the 6000–7000 shipwrecks along our shores largely reflects the history of Australia's discovery and development. The expectations of finding a Great South Land at the bottom of the globe had long been expressed by philosophers and geographers as early as the 2nd century AD, in order to balance what was known of the northern land masses. The geographer Claudius Ptolemy endowed it with the name of *Terra Australis Incognita* about this time, but its discovery and recognition by European sailors had to wait until the 17th century, and was then largely accidental.

For a number of years, Dutch and English traders of their respective East India Companies had approached their destinations in the Indies by way of the Cape, the coast of East Africa along the Mozambique Channel, and thence across the Indian Ocean, sometimes via India itself. This was a route pioneered by the Portuguese. Difficulties with the rival Portuguese as occupiers of Mozambique and navigational hazards in the Indian Ocean eventually forced a reappraisal of this approach, however, and a more direct course was determined. This lay to the east of Madagascar, but other problems of contrary winds and currents were soon realised, together with the danger of long periods when ships lay becalmed in equatorial waters, their provisions rapidly putrifying, and crewmen died.

The solution was found in 1610 with the discovery of the so-called Brouwer Route by the Dutchman Hendrik Brouwer, by which means ships sailed east on the prevailing westerly winds which blow between latitudes 35–45° South, as far as longitude 110° East, thence due north to their East Indies destinations of Bantam and Batavia, as Java and its capital Jakarta were then known. Using this route, which quickly became mandatory for all Dutch vessels, meant savings of up to six months on all outward voyages, as well as healthier crews and sounder cargoes. Even so, difficulties still existed at this time in calculating precise longitude, which would not be effectively solved for another 150 years. There was therefore an ever-present prospect of unknowingly sailing too far beyond the turning point of longitude 110° East, and fetching up on the unknown coast of the conjectural Great South Land, forced on by the gales and storms always likely to be encountered in the wild southern oceans.

A number of these early Batavia-bound ships suffered just such a fate. Australia's oldest known shipwreck dates from 1622, when the English ship *Tryal* ran aground on what are now called Tryal Rocks, off Barrow Island, Western Australia. Though several Dutch captains had found and noted the existence of a barren, low-lying and ill-defined coast hereabouts as a lee shore often guarded by rocks and hidden reefs, they paid it little attention except as a place to avoid and veered away quickly to resume their course to the Indies. Captain Brooke of the *Tryal* had no such knowledge, unfortunately, and so lost his ship and nearly 100 of his crew in the mishap. A number of Dutch ships were to come to a similar premature end, in spite of their awareness, over the following 100 years or so. These were the first recorded shipwrecks on Australia's remote coasts. Hundreds of others would join them as the pace of exploration and settlement quickened.

Dutch explorations continued sporadically throughout the 17th century, but more in terms of following-up earlier discoveries than in any serious attempt to gauge the true extent and promise of the unknown continent. The Dutch were not impressed by what they had seen of the country, even though they had succeeded in surveying and charting almost the entire western half of what they called New Holland by 1650. Few landings were made amongst the mangroves, desert shores, cliffs and reefs of the coasts they traversed. Where they did land, they were frequently rebuffed by hostile Aborigines.

It was not until the last years of the 18th century, when the colony of Port Jackson was established in 1788 to ease Britain's prison population and thwart French ambitions in this part of the world, that interest began to focus on the future possibilities of New South Wales. But so poor was the potential for self-sufficiency in the early years that nearly everything in the colony, from corn-seed to convicts, had to be brought in by sea from sources elsewhere. Ships were destined to be a vital link with the outside world thereafter. Transports, traders, sealers and whalers, migrant ships, wool clippers, steam ships and naval craft—many would leave their mark on Australia's seaboard. Large numbers were also destined to leave their remains on her ocean floor.

HMS *Sirius* was the first of these wrecks to occur off eastern Australia, blown ashore in a gale in March 1790 whilst landing supplies and 275 convicts from Port Jackson at the Norfolk Island farming settlement of Kingston. The *Sirius* had been the flagship and escort of the First Fleet which landed in Sydney Cove in January 1788. Since then she had been retained to service the colony's needs, bringing in foodstuffs, farm stock and other provisions from places as far away as Cape Town. Her sinking was viewed as a major catastrophe, leaving only the smaller vessel *Supply* to sustain upwards of 1000 people in the colony's critical establishment phase. Famine threatened the colony for several months as a result of the loss of so vital a ship.

Within the first decade, however, there was enough promise in the colony's trade potential to entice commercial enterprises to send their own supply ships. One of the earliest was the *Sydney Cove*, an Indian trader from Calcutta, Bengal. In November 1796 she was dispatched with a speculative cargo of rum and other goods but, almost sinking in the aftermath of a hurricane, she had to be beached on an island off the north-east coast of Van Diemen's Land (Tasmania) in order to save both crew and cargo. Later years saw an increasing toll amongst smaller coastal craft—schooners, ketches, cutters and sloops—carrying such items as wheat, meat, salt, sugar, coal and timber into Sydney, Newcastle, or Hobart.

Sealers and whalers soon became active in the early years of settlement, particularly after the discovery of Bass Strait and the rich resources reported there. Doubtless many of these craft were lost off south-east Australia before full records were kept, though the *Britannia, Active* and *Echo* were each noted as wrecks up to 1820. In the early 1830s, however, after local captures had declined, Australian-based vessels undertook extended voyages in pursuit of their quarry, often in testing conditions. In 1830–31, for instance, several ships were lost as far afield as New Zealand and the Southern Ocean, including the *Cumberland, John Bull, George, Elizabeth & Mary, Industry,* and *Harriet.*

Convict transports continued to leave Britain for Australia meanwhile, though not all reached their destinations. Four such ships were lost in the years 1833 to 1835. In 1833, the *Amphitrite*, Sydney-bound from London, got no further than the English Channel when she encountered a violent gale which drove her into Boulogne Harbour. There she broke in two, and only three of the 136 souls aboard survived. The *Hive* was lost in 1835 when run aground near Jervis Bay, New South Wales, through her Captain's faulty navigation. Her position was such that all her complement, including 250 Irish convicts, were landed ashore with only one drowning. However, two other transports, the *George III* and the *Neva*, were lost with 350 fatalities when they were wrecked within a month of each other in Tasmanian waters in 1835.

The number of emigrant ships leaving Great Britain increased as Australian settlement progressed, though not without incident. While the discovery of Bass Strait had given access to Melbourne and shortened the time to Sydney, it also introduced its own hazards. King Island, athwart the Strait's narrow western approaches, has claimed over 60 ships through fog and storm since 1800. Its worst disaster was that of the *Cataraqui* in

1845, when more than 400 souls perished. As late as 1878 the *Loch Ard* ran aground and sank in fog on the Victorian coast, with only two survivors. Meanwhile Sydney's narrow heads and seasonal storms continued to threaten shipping, in 1857 claiming both of the clippers *Dunbar* and *Catherine Adamson* with heavy loss of life. Adventure had its price, as many discovered.

Even with the advent of steamships and the installation of lighthouses on the coast, the loss of ships at sea continued. Inter-colonial and international travel increased as permanent settlements grew between Brisbane and Adelaide. The Victorian and New South Wales gold rushes added to this movement. The new steamships offered speed and comfort— but they were still open to the vagaries of sea, storm and human error. The earliest such loss was that of the paddle-wheeler *Ceres*, off New South Wales in 1836, though without loss of life. The screw-steamer *Monumental City* had just been first across the Pacific in 1853 when she sank off Gabo Island, Victoria, and 32 died. Over 100 people drowned when the Adelaide–Darwin mail steamer *Gothenburg* was lost on a coral reef near Townsville in 1875. Many more would follow.

In the later days of the sailing ship, the clippers came to represent the ultimate in sail perfection. Their designs and speed were intended to shorten voyages, reduce turnaround time and improve profits, but still some masters drove their ships too hard, with calamitous results. The captain's boast of a 60-day passage from Liverpool to Melbourne brought about the stranding of the *Schomberg* on Victoria's west coast in 1855, though without loss of life. Hard masters also gave rise to resentful crews who sometimes threatened arson in response. Two clippers burned in 1861 were *Sovereign of the Seas III* in Sydney, and *Empress of the Sea* at Port Phillip. Other clippers lost to fire during this decade include *British Merchant* in Sydney, and *Phoenix, Result, City of Melbourne, Lightning* and *Eliza*, all on Port Phillip Bay.

The 20th century introduced a new kind of shipwreck as a result of the two world wars: modern warships sunk by enemy action, and commercial vessels lost to mines and torpedoes. Warships of the Second World War represented the ultimate in both steam power and conventional fire-power, as well as the stealth of the submarine and the subterfuge of the commerce raider. Ships in Australian waters suffered the effects of German raiders in both world wars. The activities of the raider *Wolff* in 1917 claimed at least three ships, with at least three others lost to mines laid by the raider *Pinguin* in 1940. Submarines caused even more losses following Japan's entry into the war. The greatest loss to a submarine off the Australian coast was that of the hospital ship *Centaur* off Brisbane in May 1943, when 268 died. Worse still was the loss of HMAS *Sydney* and her entire crew of 645, as a result of her encounter with the raider *Kormoran* off Carnarvon, Western Australia, in November 1941.

───────────

Shipwreck incidents in Australia's early days tended to mirror the number of sailings to this country, the number of vessels operating in Australian waters, the shifting phases of settlement over time, and the vagaries of seasonal weather patterns. Though the earliest shipwrecks occurred on the Indian Ocean shores of Australia, the fact that this territory remained undeveloped—indeed unattractive and remote in the minds of many— meant that other shipwreck incidents thereabouts were relatively few in number during the first half of the 19th century.

Most maritime activity in these years was focussed on the south-east of the continent, first on New South Wales, then on Van Diemen's Land, and later still on the developing colony of Victoria. Towns of substance were few in number, however, being largely confined to Sydney, Newcastle and Hobart, with most settlement in their immediate hinterlands. Only after 35 years or so were Brisbane and Perth founded (in the 1820s), with Melbourne and Adelaide soon after (1835 and 1836 respectively).

Shipping levels increased as coastal craft and inter-colonial traders made longer journeys and faced the wilder, year-round elements at sea—and so did the number of maritime incidents and shipwrecks. Wreck statistics increased markedly in 1825, and again around 1835 as shipping losses reflected the increasing levels of maritime activity.

Much of the sea traffic approaching Sydney and Melbourne around this time did so through the notorious Bass Strait. Its discovery had removed the need to approach the mainland's eastern settlements by rounding Tasmania, but other hazards were introduced along the more direct route in terms of rock-bound coasts, scattered islands, shoals and narrow channels, uncharted reefs, and often adverse weather. In fact, the whole of Australia's south-eastern seaboard from King Island, round the south coast of Tasmania and as far north as Port Macquarie in New South Wales is prone to periods of wild and occasionally extreme weather. New South Wales therefore featured large in the numbers of our early shipwrecks, with possibly more than twice the number of Tasmania and Victoria combined.

This trend was to be maintained throughout the second half of the 19th century. The waters off New South Wales continued to claim the largest proportion of maritime losses, though after Victoria had surpassed Tasmania as a destination for shipping, its western 'Shipwreck Coast' and the rocky jaws of The Rip became a graveyard for ships which failed to reach Port Phillip. The number of wrecks off Queensland also rose markedly during this period, especially where coral reefs and cyclones claimed the vessels of the unwary. Shipwrecks off the coast of Western Australia became more frequent for similar reasons.

The numbers of shipwrecks have steadily diminished throughout the course of the 20th century, despite the volumes of shipping, the intensity of reciprocal trade, and the impact of two world wars—though 1942–43 did show an abrupt increase. Since the early 1900s sailing ships all but vanished, steam power steadily gave way to the diesel engine, and post-war sea freight has become dominated by large-scale container vessels. As the number of ships on the oceans decreased overall, aircraft development grew to take over passenger transport almost completely. The heyday of ships and the sea has undeniably passed, but their history and heritage continue to live on.

As part of maritime history, shipwrecks and shipwreck narratives in particular seem to be imbued with a perennial fascination. Rarely do their tales fade with repetition; indeed they are often the basis of today's under-water recreation activities involving shipwreck research, wreck-diving, marine photography, and maritime archaeology. Here in Australia many of our shipwrecks now have the status of memorials, to be preserved and revered, not only as tributes to individual ships and their stories, but also to the people who sailed in them, and to *their* efforts in building and sustaining this country for which, especially in the early days, many lost their lives. In total, they represent a substantial part of Australia's rich maritime heritage, which is an inestimable resource for those who seek to understand more of our country's diverse history.

Chapter I

BATAVIA
1629

The *Batavia*.

'They intended first to rid the islands of unnecessary consumers of the limited foods available and then to seize the rescue ship, murder the crew and afterwards set forth on a life of piracy.'

Monday, 4th of June, 1629. The night watch—two hours before dawn aboard the Dutch East Indiaman *Batavia*. Eastward-bound on the Brouwer Route, across the southern Indian Ocean toward the 'Southland' (as Australia was then known), thence north to Java, she is nearing the end of her long voyage from Europe.

The sea is relatively calm, the weather fair. The ship sails on in clear moonlight save for a slight haze. She is no longer in company with the six ships she sailed with from the Dutch port of Texel on the 29th of October last. They were separated following a storm after rounding Cape Agulhas on the southern tip of Africa, though all appears secure on board for now.

Francisco Pelsaert, the ship's Uppermerchant and Commandeur, sleeps fitfully below. Though plagued by a lingering bout of the malaria he contracted in India three years earlier, he is assured by the knowledge that they are still some 200 Holland miles (about 600 English miles) from the nearest Southland coast before needing to change course. Time enough on the morrow, in full light of day, to turn onto the final leg of their journey to Batavia, the Java headquarters of the *Vereenigde Oost-Indische Compagnie*, or VOC United East India Company of the Netherlands.

But all is not well aboard the *Batavia*. Her skipper, Ariaen Jacobsz, has been up on deck most of the night, brooding, resentful. Ariaen Jacobsz is a bitter, angry man. So angry, in fact, that he is prepared to oust the upstart Pelsaert of his landlubber's command and take over the ship himself. So angry that he has willingly conspired with some of his crew to create an incident that will give cause for a mutiny against their Commandeur. How long has he suffered rebukes and humiliation from this imperious Pelsaert, darling of the VOC's directors, the so-called 'High and Mighty Gentlemen Seventeen'! High and mighty—hah! Bunch of dolled-up, lace-trimmed, over-fed codfish, all of them! He spat his contempt over the side.

Stinging, festering rebukes from others after that first violent argument they had in Surat, India, eighteen months earlier—that's when the hate started. It intensified when they met again at the start of this voyage, and became unrelenting when Jacobsz was most recently reprimanded by the Commandeur after drunken carousing and quarrelling aboard other vessels in Table Bay. And now, as expected, his insufferable attitude over a practical joke. He spat again. Anyway, the snooty bitch got no more than she deserved.

The 'snooty bitch' was Lucretia Jansz, a fair young widow amongst the passengers to whom he had quickly taken a fancy. But gold, jewels and all his practised blandishments had failed to coax her into his cabin, and her own acid rebukes and refusals had only added to his simmering anger. Revenge he wanted and revenge he would have—on all of them, and soon! To ease his rejection he had taken up instead with Zwaantie Hendrix, Lucretia's maid, who had been an easier touch and comely, and willing to share his plans just as she had shared his escapades at Table Bay.

He had also schemed to rouse others to wilder ventures. First he had persuaded Jan Evertsz, the High Boatswain, to get some of the crew to black up Lucretia one evening—face, body and all, with dung, tar, whatever—to teach her a lesson and to set the spark for a mutiny. Then he found a willingness in Jeronimus Cornelisz, the compliant Under-merchant who had also joined his affray in Table Bay and shared the Commandeur's wrath, to take over the ship when Pelsaert tried to have the lads arrested and chained by the Provost and the Constable. Once rid of the petty tyrant, they then intended to turn pirates all, and anyone not with them would be summarily thrown overboard! All it needed now was the right moment, maybe tomorrow . . .

These were teasing, pleasing thoughts, and some he had relished throughout most of the dark hours. His preoccupation was such that he had given little attention to the running of the ship, nor to her course or position since he'd figured the nearest land was still several hundred miles away. It came as a severe shock, therefore, when a sudden lurch sent him staggering. The *Batavia* reared high onto a reef that had not been seen in the reflecting moonlight, and noisily ground to a stop. They had crashed into the reefs known as Houtman Abrolhos, which lie some 35 (English) miles off the Western Australian coast, a little to the north of present-day Geraldton. The *Batavia*'s last voyage was over, and the most bizarre tale in Australia's maritime history was about to begin.

Commandeur Pelsaert picked himself up from the floor of his cabin, where the impact had thrown him, and ran out on deck. Charges and recriminations flew in the darkness. Rowdiness grew in the silence that followed the grounding as many of the more than 300 passengers and crew emerged bleary-eyed from their quarters, some bewildered, some frightened, all demanding answers to a hundred fearful questions. Confusion reigned as the Uppermerchant sought to quell the rabble and bring some kind of order to their perilous situation.

Soundings round the ship found shallow water at the bow, and only three fathoms at the stern. They were well aground and knew nothing of the state of the tide. Their two boats were launched to take soundings further away, and a kedge anchor was readied to try to wind the ship off the reef. To lighten the ship, parties were organised amongst the crew and the troops sailing as passengers to heave all their cannon overboard.

By daylight, however, the tide had begun to fall, wind and surf were rising with the new day, and the *Batavia* began to pound on the reef. Movement became difficult as the ship rose and fell heavily on the surging waves. As the tide receded, the boats that had been sent out were unable to return through the surrounding shallows.

They soon realised that the weighty mainmast might be driven through the bottom of the ship, so they cut it down. Its fall caused major damage, and then they were unable to clear it overboard. Meanwhile, the hold had begun to flood, an indication that the stricken ship had at last been holed. Before long the *Batavia* was showing the first signs of breaking up. To add to their woes it began to rain, while the wind blew harder and drove waves across the wreck. The clamour of distress and rising hysteria grew in Pelsaert's ears. Their stay on board was quickly becoming untenable.

With some 315 souls to save, Commandeur Pelsaert was hard-pressed to know what to do. Fortunately skipper Jacobsz, his hatred shoved abruptly aside, was still lying off in the yawl, unable to return aboard. Pelsaert was thus able to direct him to explore two small islands not far distant, onto which they might land the passengers with what stores they could save. Jacobsz' positive response meant they could shift their charges off the wreck, albeit slowly on account of the ship's cant, and ferry them across to temporary safety. By the end of the day 180 people had been landed, with casks of bread and some small barrels of water, but their haven was still exposed and open to the deteriorating weather.

Adequate supplies of water were soon to pose a problem. Even on the ship, supplies were limited as seawater rose in the hold. On the islets, however, there was hardly any to be found, even by digging. Throughout the day after the wreck, the winds blew strongly, preventing access to the ship. Pelsaert had left the *Batavia* late the first day to establish the rationing of water amongst those on the islets, who seemed intent on drinking as much as they could. Being unable to reach the ship, he organised the transfer of a large group to the larger islet, while 40 remained on the smaller. Unfortunately conditions were such that sufficient quantities of water could not be similarly transferred, and so the unequal sharing gave rise to further dissent and bickering. For those on the boats, there was a threat that their craft might be seized by others demanding a wider search for the life-sustaining liquid, and all control lost.

On the *Batavia*, meanwhile, the situation of the 70 who had remained aboard was becoming critical as the wreck began to fall apart. Their leader, Undermerchant Jeronimus Cornelisz, sent word via the carpenter, who managed to swim between the ship and Pelsaert's boat, that they needed urgent help. At the same time Pelsaert himself was anxious to rescue the ship's 12 treasure chests, for which he was responsible. Neither help nor salvage was immediately possible. Water for all was the first priority, though Pelsaert himself was reluctant to search far. It was only under pressure from skipper Jacobsz, and the promise by crew members to ferry water from wherever they found it, even from the distant mainland, that he gave way on condition that he might first inform the island castaways of their intentions.

Even this was not to be. Pelsaert's effort to land on the larger islet and leave his message with more water was thwarted by his boat crew, who feared that both he and the boat might be detained by the islanders. He was thus forced to return to the smaller islet, from which he set out next day to explore a group of larger islands, one of which they called High Island, some six miles distant. The only water they found there was brackish, spoiled by seawater, which therefore meant they had to make a trip to the mainland in search of other sources. They stayed a day on the larger islands to build up the sides of their craft with planking to save being swamped on the open seas, but before they had finished 11 others arrived in the yawl, intent on taking more water back. When none of the wells they dug produced palatable water, a decision was reached, on oath, that both groups would sail to the mainland. They agreed that if no water was found there, they would continue on to Batavia, their original destination, to break the news of the disaster.

There was now a party of 48 people split between the two boats, including Commandeur Pelsaert and skipper Jacobsz, two women and a three-month old infant. One of the women was Zwaantie Hendrix, the skipper's consort. What Pelsaert thought of their proximity is not recorded in his journal. And what remained of the skipper's resolve to incite a mutiny appears to have dissipated in the wreck. Together they faced a likely passage of nearly 2000 miles to bring rescue if they failed to find adequate water on the mainland. Such a journey would demand the cooperation of all in order to succeed.

That they did succeed, without losing any of their number, is an achievement which parallels that of William Bligh, master of the *Bounty*, 160 years later. The Australian mainland, which Pelsaert described as 'a dry cursed earth', proved to be devoid of water, thereby forcing them to sail on to Java as anticipated. They left their last refuge on what is now West Wallabi Island on 8th of June 1629, and arrived in Batavia Roads on the 7th of July after a passage of 30 days. The most heroic part of the *Batavia* story was complete.

Back on the Abrolhos Islands, the events that were to mark the *Batavia* story with infamy, and most of their perpetrators with the utmost odium, were already under way. Like a festering sore that had to burst, pressure mounted behind the wiles of a small group of psychopaths under the leadership of Undermerchant Jeronimus Cornelisz. They intended first to rid the islands of unnecessary consumers of the limited foods available, and then to seize the rescue ship, murder the crew, and afterwards set forth on a life of piracy. It was an extra corruption of Ariaen Jacobsz' original plan, but with consequences even he might not have foreseen.

By the time Commandeur Pelsaert returned with a rescue vessel, 125 of the 268 people he had left on the islands had been murdered, while another 40 had drowned or died of privations.

Cornelisz had taken Jacobsz' proposals to heart, with more apparent conviction and enthusiasm than Jacobsz himself. Pelsaert's journals identify him as deceitful, lying, heretical, unscrupulous, self-seeking and vainglorious. His later conduct showed him to be cowardly in outlook, cruel in control, and paranoiac in facing retribution. By his own admission, he was an ardent follower of the beliefs of the licentious Dutch painter Torrentius van der Beecke, who eschewed all the canons of property, morality and religion. Possessed of a better education and a persuasive tongue, Cornelisz had little trouble in beguiling men of meaner attributes to do his bidding. Without other forms of control, and with heady promises of future wealth and splendour, his followers gave way to brute lust, greed and sadism, and quite literally ran amok.

When Pelsaert and Jacobsz departed for the mainland, they left behind 268 people on the two islands thereafter known as Batavia's Graveyard and Traitors Island—the latter arguably because it was the islet Pelsaert left when he 'deserted' the others only two days after the wreck. When the yawl party set out to follow Pelsaert soon after, in the only other boat, the two groups were left isolated without means of either communication or movement. Before long, however, the need to find water became desperate as people came ashore from the wreck and others started to die of thirst. Under the direction of Jeronimus Cornelisz, one of the last to leave the wreck, rafts were built and groups were ferried out to search the islands round about. In this way he had many of the soldiers transferred to the High Island where, believing it to be waterless following Pelsaert's abortive search, he no doubt expected them to die of thirst. Whatever their fate, they would not be able to interfere with his secret plans.

As the senior man present, and elected 'Chief' by the survivors, Cornelisz' conduct at this time was exemplary according to the *Batavia*'s Predikant or minister, Gijsbert Bastiaensz. To all appearances it remained so through to the end of June 1629. During this time the soldiers' group had managed to find water in natural wells on another of the larger islands, where they were able to live securely at a distance. Meanwhile a group of 45, who were to be far less secure, was moved out to Seals Island to ease the pressure on the one hundred or so survivors remaining on the islet they had called 'Batavia's Graveyard'. It was here that the first of many murders took place, on 4th of July.

Jeronimus Cornelisz had not forgotten Ariaen Jacobsz' plan. He imagined that the skipper would dump Commandeur Pelsaert overboard on the way to Java, and return with a rescue vessel which would then become their avenue to piracy. In the interim he saw a need to get rid of people of little use to him, and to preserve only the stoutest and some of the women. This notion he somehow felt had been reinforced by comment from the departing Commandeur, when he was told that the number of survivors crowding Batavia's Graveyard should be reduced—though by moving people to other sites as he started to do, rather than by the wholesale murder to be wrought by his accomplices.

The murders had to be carried out secretly lest others rose against him. His band of followers numbered less than 30, but of this number only 10 or so were his silent killers. Three of these—Coenraat van Huyssen (cadet), Jacop Pietersz (soldier) and Davidt van Zevanck (book-keeper)— he appointed as his councillors. He himself would not participate in murder, other than as decoy to particular plots. By using lies and deceit, missing people were said to have gone to other islands.

In the first week, in small then rapidly increasing numbers, 20 people are drowned, clubbed, strangled or put to the knife. The sick have their throats cut. Several people, their suspicions roused, tried to make off to join those on High Island by raft, but they are hunted down and killed by the murderers who by now have built a small boat.

In the second week the murders become public when Andries de Vries, himself a killer, is seen talking to Lucretia Jansz against the orders of Cornelisz, and is chased into the sea and hacked to death by three of the others. By now, with death being the only alternative, Lucretia has been forced to give herself to Cornelisz as his concubine. Some other women have been similarly treated, although those who had been transferred to Seals Island were killed about this time, along with 18 men and a number of ships' boys who had been sent to the island with them.

Cornelisz is the instigator of the murders, selecting the victims himself either carefully, or at random. During the third week his methods become devious and crafty, his preparations more elaborate. Predikant Bastiaensz and his elder daughter Judick are of use to Cornelisz—the former as messenger between the island groups, the latter as consort to his principal councillor, Coenraat van Huyssen. But the Predikant's family is not. On the pretext of the pair dining with Cornelisz and van Huyssen in the latter's tent, Cornelisz sends seven of his men to the predikant's tent where the other seven members of his family and their maid are dispatched with knives, adzes and axes.

Later, three boys who had escaped the mass slaughter on Seals Island are captured, then forced to draw lots as to which two will die and which one will undertake their murders. On another occasion a young boy is beheaded by Mattys Beer, a soldier, to test the sharpness of his sword. Cornelisz had blindfolded the boy, saying it was part of a joke, while another would-be murderer sobs in anguish over being denied the chance to behead the boy himself. Others are stabbed or strangled by people they thought they could trust, while out walking with them. Thus did the gruesome record continue, until 125 victims had been accounted for.

By the end of July, Cornelisz was beginning to think about the annihilation of the outlying group on High Island. He saw them as a major obstacle to taking over the expected rescue ship, especially if they were able to warn her crew. He had already tried to win over some of the group, first with a letter to the French soldiers there, and on later visits with promises of wine, clothing and future riches. At no time was he successful since the group leader, a soldier by the name of Wiebbe Hayes, had become fully aware of what had been happening back on Batavia's Graveyard over the last few weeks. The group, now numbering around 50, was armed and on the defensive. A premature skirmish led by Davidt van Zevanck had ended in failure. With September approaching, together with the likelihood of a rescue vessel, it was time to act in force.

On 1st of September, Cornelisz made one last effort at conciliation, offering wine and clothes to Hayes' group in exchange for their boat. Next day he returned to the High Island with gifts, and an armed party of his followers. Here he made a tactical mistake in leaving the larger part of his men on an off-lying islet while he took only five to parley with Wiebbe Hayes—a mistake which probably cost him his ambitions. Treachery was suspected and their exchanges were short. Futile attempts were made to bribe some of the soldiers with Hayes to change sides when an attack was launched. Cornelisz' group was attacked and held instead, though one man escaped in their skiff. When those on the islet then showed signs of preparing a counter-attack, Cornelisz' accomplices, his principal councillors, were instantly killed while Cornelisz himself was taken captive.

The attackers withdrew. In Cornelisz' absence one Wouter Loos was elected as their temporary leader, who immediately adopted all the trappings of Cornelisz' leadership, including the occupation of his tent and the comforts of Lucretia Jansz. It was over two weeks before another attack was made on Wiebbe Hayes' group with the intention of rescuing Cornelisz and putting his captors to the sword. The delay was a fatal one.

As the assault was launched, the yacht *Sardam* carrying Commandeur Pelsaert and a rescue crew appeared. This was the vessel Pelsaert had boarded on reaching Java, and on which he completed his journey to Batavia. Within a week, Governor-General Jan Coen had had the yacht prepared for sea, and ordered its master to return to the Abrolhos to pick up the survivors and whatever could be salvaged.

On seeing the *Sardam*, Wiebbe Hayes and three others pull away in their boat to warn Pelsaert of the mutiny and its later consequences, reaching the yacht only minutes ahead of the pursuing mutineers. The mutineers also approach the yacht, displaying arms which confirm Hayes' hurried story. Faced with the threat of *Sardam*'s guns, the mutineers put down their weapons and are ordered aboard where they are arrested and tied. Hayes brings Cornelisz off High Island for imprisonment on the yacht and next day Pelsaert sails over to Batavia's Graveyard with a party of armed men, where the rest of the mutineers quickly surrender. The killing is over. The comment from one mutineer, 'Now there is a noose around our necks', would prove to be grimly prophetic.

Appalled by the shocking barbarity of Jeronimus Cornelisz and his men, the Commandeur wasted no time in holding inquiries into their behaviour, in council with officers from the *Sardam*. While these were being arranged, salvage work was also planned amongst the remains of the *Batavia*. By then, little of the wreck was to be seen above the water. The winter storms that beat upon Australia's western shores had broken the vessel apart and scattered pieces in disarray throughout the shallows. Planking and other wreckage was strewn around the islands and islets. Cannon were lying exposed on the reef where they had been jettisoned during the vain attempt to refloat the ship. There was little prospect of recovering much of her cargo, but the remains of the *Batavia* still contained the 12 money chests, the property of the VOC, for which the Commandeur was responsible. There was also a quantity of treasure to be located, including some valuable pieces of jewellery thought to have been owned by the artist Rubens. Pelsaert had no intention of leaving the Abrolhos without them.

The *Sardam* had arrived at the Abrolhos on 17th of September 1629. Pelsaert spent the next two months at the wreck site while he conducted his examinations of the mutineers, and supervised progress on salvage work whenever sea conditions allowed. Some of the mutineers openly confessed their part in the murders, while others were subject to torture, or the threat of torture, to extract their confessions. As a means of establishing the truth, torture was a permissible and occasionally necessary means under existing Dutch law, which Pelsaert was scrupulous in upholding.

The method used was a simple water torture, involving the pouring of water into a cloth bag tied around the neck and head of the accused. The only way a victim could avoid being drowned was by drinking the water until his body became distended almost to bursting point. Usually the threat was enough. Cornelisz gave in quickly in recounting his misdeeds, but would afterwards retract his statements, claiming coercion by his dead councillors. So closely did the Commandeur read the requirements of the law for a voluntary confession that such retractions caused him genuine concern for some time with regard to the Undermerchant's possible innocence.

Cornelisz' procrastinations were of little use in the end. On 28th of September, he and seven of his murderous accomplices were condemned to death by Pelsaert and his prosecuting Council. The sentences were death by hanging, preceded by the cutting off of the right hand of four of the offenders, and both hands in the case of Jeronimus Cornelisz. The executions were to be put into effect on Seals Island on the first day of October. Further judgements were handed down to others of Cornelisz' band while salvage work continued, to be implemented on their return to Batavia. Weather conditions on the reef caused a day's postponement of the murderers' executions, but on 2nd of October all but one of the sentences were duly carried out at the gallows. At the request of his disappointed followers, Cornelisz was hanged first so they could be sure he would not escape their collective fate. Jan Pelgrom, the youngest at 18, pleaded for his life and so was spared, only to be marooned on the mainland later in company with Wouter Loos.

Pelsaert succeeded in having 11 of the 12 treasure chests raised from the wreck, the last being left trapped under a cannon and anchor, and thus immovable. Unfortunately, the salvage effort cost the lives of the *Sardam*'s master and a boat crew when their craft was lost in a storm— a sad postscript to an unlucky voyage. The *Sardam* finally left the islands to return to Batavia on 15th of November 1629. On their way north, Commandeur Pelsaert abandoned the two mutineers whose lives had been spared on the mainland, with instructions to meet with the 'Southland' inhabitants, learn their language and discover what resources might profit the VOC. If they survived, they could leave the Southland on another visiting ship if that was still their wish.

Sardam reached Batavia on 5th of December, 1629. The remaining prisoners were handed over to the Dutch justices for confirmation of Pelsaert's findings. Some had already pleaded for trial by the ship's Council on 30th of November and had been punished by keel-hauling, dropping from the yard, and flogging before the mast. Other punishments awaited, however. Five more were hanged on 31st of January 1630, and one was broken on the wheel. The remainder were flogged, exiled in chains, and/or made to wear halters as a sign of their crimes, while all forfeited their pay for periods up to 18 months. Shortly after Commandeur Pelsaert left Batavia on his rescue mission, Jan Evertsz was hanged for his part in the assault on Lucretia Jansz. What became of Ariaen Jacobsz, the instigator of the whole bizarre episode, is unrecorded, and neither is it known how five other captives were punished.

Lucretia Jansz herself survived her ordeals and remarried in Batavia within a year of her rescue, though she remained childless thereafter. Some time around 1636 she and her soldier husband returned to Holland. The hero of the resistance, Wiebbe Hayes, was promoted to Standard-Bearer with greatly increased wages for his loyalty and steadfastness, with similar rewards to others amongst his supporters. There were no such rewards for Commandeur Pelsaert, however, despite all he did to bring rescue and justice to the castaways. Already in ill-health, he died in Batavia in September 1630, less than a year after his departure from the fateful Abrolhos.

The wreck of the *Batavia* lay beneath the waters off Western Australia for over 300 years. When research into the wreck's location began in the 1950s, there was much confusion as to which group of reefs represented the ship's last resting place. It was historian Henrietta Drake-Brockman who finally suggested the Morning Reef in the Wallabi Group as the place to search, rather than the more southerly Pelsart Group, where wreckage of a Dutch vessel had been found in 1840. Her choice was proved to be correct when cray fisherman Dave Johnson discovered one of *Batavia*'s anchors while setting pots in 1961, a discovery which was later confirmed by two of Johnson's diver friends in June 1963.

While some serious work was done that year by local divers to recover artefacts from the wreck—which helped to identify that it was indeed the *Batavia*—the wreck's discovery soon began to attract the unwelcome attention of treasure seekers and looters. The same thing was happening on the wreck of the *De Vergulde Draeck*, another Dutch East Indiaman which had been discovered about 100 kilometres north of Perth only a month or two before the *Batavia*. In December 1964, therefore, the first protective legislation was enacted in recognition of the historical importance of these wrecks, which was gradually extended to cover all wrecks in

Australian waters deemed to be 'historic', or over 75 years old.

Formal excavations by the Western Australian Maritime Museum were carried out on the *Batavia* site and nearby islands between 1973 and 1976, with many others visits since. Over the years the wreck has yielded a rich collection of artefacts, as well as part of the port side of the ship itself. The finds have included 128 prefabricated sandstone blocks for a portico once destined to grace the VOC fort at Batavia; a number of cannon; iron shot, silverware, coins and ceramics; a whole array of domestic items; and of course a large number of ship's fittings and equipment, including some of her navigation instruments. Human remains and relics have also been found at the camp sites of the murderers, their victims and their opponents, which have been the subject of recent studies.

Many of these artefacts are now on display in the Western Australian Maritime Museum, including a reconstruction of part of the ship that was raised for conservation, and a portico built from the sandstone blocks. More artefacts can also be seen in the Geraldton Regional Museum.

A replica of the *Batavia* has recently been built at Lelystad, Holland, using manuals of contemporary Dutch shipbuilders and archive material from the VOC. The replica is a full-scale reconstruction and one of a number of sailing ship re-creations which have been completed recently, including the *Duyfken*, the *Endeavour*, the *Enterprize* and the *Norfolk* here in Australia. The Dutch vessel is expected to visit Australia in 2000 as part of the new millennium celebrations.

Chapter 2

DE VERGULDE DRAECK
1656

Relics recovered from the *De Vergulde Draeck*.

'The survivors appear to have arrived ashore relatively unscathed. Wet, bedraggled, shocked and afraid, they nevertheless faced an uncertain future so far from civilisation, unless help could be obtained from their original destination, Batavia, still over 2,000 miles away.'

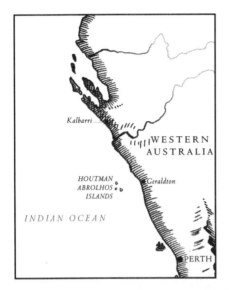

One of the few certain facts about the wrecking of the Dutch merchantman *De Vergulde Draeck* (Gilt Dragon) in May 1656, some 70 miles north of present-day Perth, is that of the 193 people aboard, 75 survived the loss of the ship to reach the Australian mainland as a cohesive group. This much was conveyed by seven of their number to the authorities in Batavia, the trading capital of the *Vereenigde Oost-Indische Compagnie* (VOC) in the Dutch East Indies, 40 days after departing the wreck site in one of the ship's boats in search of help for their fellows. Though several rescue craft were sent out, the remaining 68 survivors were never seen again. They had disappeared into the vastness of Australia, seemingly without trace.

The final fateful voyage of the *Vergulde Draeck* began on 4th of October 1655, when she sailed from the North Sea island of Texel, Holland, bound for the Cape of Good Hope and Batavia. This voyage was only her second in fact, for she was a new ship. Her maiden voyage was one completed a few weeks previously from the Netherlands to the East Indies and back. On her second and last voyage she was commanded by skipper Pieter Albertsz, with a complement of 193, including a small number of passengers, and a cargo of mixed merchandise valued at 106 400 florins. In addition she carried eight chests of treasure in coin worth a further 78 600 florins.

Though many ships suffered greatly from storm effects, outbreaks of disease, and the hazards of sail handling on extended passages around the world, the *Vergulde Draeck* apparently made good time to the Cape, and in relatively good condition. On the journey south down the Atlantic she lost two men overboard, but the health of those remaining appeared to be sound, while their ship was in good repair. Rather than staying for almost a month at the colony on Table Bay as was usual, to offload sick crewmen and cargoes for the Cape, and to take on fresh provisions and replacement crew while at the same time cleaning the ship, on this occasion the *Vergulde Draeck* left the Cape on 12th March 1656 after a stay of only three days. The voyage had the makings of a record in those days of bulky, beamy sailing craft had she reached her destination as planned. However, she never did ...

On leaving Africa behind she sailed south to pick up the westerly winds of the Brouwer Route which would drive her speedily east towards the distant and little-known coasts of the Southland. Unfortunately, sometime during the 28th of April 1656, the *Vergulde Draeck* was driven onto a reef off Ledge Point, Western Australia, near Cape Leschenault, where she quickly became a total wreck. It seems likely that the mishap occurred at night, perhaps during a storm or on another occasion of reduced visibility, for the coast would have been seen and avoided otherwise. The journal of one Jan Van Riebeeck stated that the impact was so violent, the ship being under full sail with a following wind, that she immediately burst open and sank. Many would have thus been drowned below decks before they had a chance to save themselves.

The facts and reasons surrounding the actual wrecking of the *Vergulde Draeck* are not fully known. Since Van Riebeeck's journal indicates that the ship broke apart immediately she struck the reef—despite her strength as an almost new vessel—the 'following wind' may have been a rising gale which the skipper failed to read quickly enough to either shorten sail or close up the ship. Alternatively, they may have been overtaken by a sudden squall, especially one descending on them at night. In such circumstances, if skipper Albertsz had not been wholly sure of his position—a quite understandable dilemma at the time—coupled with the proximity of hidden reefs, a sequence of unfortunate coincidences might well have combined into a gale-driven disaster. The coast of Western Australia absorbs much of the Indian Ocean's surging energy over short distances in relatively shallow waters. Caught on the entrapping rocks and in the grip of tempestuous inshore seas, there would have been little chance of saving anything of the ship before she was pounded to pieces.

Whatever the cause and time of her sinking, 75 castaways managed to reach the nearby mainland having successfully launched two of the ship's boats, while up to 116 others perished in the wreck. The survivors appear to have arrived ashore relatively unscathed. Wet, bedraggled, shocked and afraid, they nevertheless faced an uncertain future so far from civilisation, unless help could be obtained from their original destination, Batavia, still over 2000 miles away. Their predicament was compounded by the fact that there had been little time to collect spare clothing, or to grab food enough for their numbers before being forced to abandon the stricken ship. The wreck had occurred some way from the coast and only a few barrels of provisions would eventually drift ashore in their vicinity. Finding an adequate supply of water would also pose particular problems. It was essential, therefore, that a reliable boat-crew be sent out as soon as possible to force the passage to Batavia in order to aid the salvation of the other survivors.

The understeersman and six others of the crew were selected for the journey, for which they prepared the *schuyt*, the smaller of the two boats saved. Pieter Albertsz elected to stay with the remaining survivors for the purpose of maintaining order and discipline, since the memory of the wreck of the *Batavia* and details of its shocking aftermath were still vivid in the minds of all the VOC's commanders, even a quarter-century after its occurrence. As the schuyt left on its rescue mission nine days later, the last its crew saw of the other castaways, now numbering 68, were those engaged in digging the larger boat out of the sand where it had lain since an earlier capsize. It was said at this point that moves were afoot amongst those left behind to go some way inland in search of food and water.

The crew of the schuyt reached Batavia on 7th of June 1656, forty days after they had left the scene of the late wreck. In a short time, again no doubt spurred by the events surrounding the ill-starred *Batavia*, two vessels fortuitously in port were hurriedly prepared for the journey back to Cape Leschenault. These were the flute *Witte Valck* (White Falcon), and the yacht *Goede Hoop* (Good Hope). Together they made the passage by the middle of July, but they failed to find any of the castaways, even though their shelters were discovered 'knocked down and torn to pieces', without any signs of life.

How thorough the search was remains open to doubt. The *Witte Valck* was never able to approach the land on account of high seas (it was now the middle of the southern winter), while a boat from the *Goede Hoop* was lost with its eight-man crew in making landings which found no further trace of the *Vergulde Draeck* survivors. It was sent out to find three of the searchers who had become lost in thick scrub. Their boat got into difficulties and was later seen wrecked on the strand. All eleven were then given up as lost. If any had survived, they too would join the total number of Dutchmen lost on this part of the coast. Meanwhile, those in the rescue craft were themselves at risk in navigating a lee shore in the conditions which prevailed during their stay. Strong north-westerlies blew unabated, gales were common, storms were not unexpected and the seas were constantly rough. Every attempt to land through the high surf was fraught with danger.

Before long both ships were forced to leave the coast and return to Batavia. Parted in one of the seasonal storms, the *Witte Valck* arrived in mid-September, while the *Goede Hoop* took a month longer. The stories they told were in direct conflict. The *Witte Valck* had reported seeing men and portions of the wreck even though her crew had not landed, while the *Goede Hoop* told of seeing nothing. The result was an unsatisfactory and inconclusive undertaking—and up to 80 men might still be enduring a tenuous existence in the Southland's wilds. Consequently, another vessel, the flyboat *Vinck*, was requested to visit the wreck site on her way from Cape Town to Batavia the following winter. Finding conditions no better than those of the earlier searches she, too, was unable to make landings and so lodged a further negative report on her return to Batavia despite a careful scrutiny of the intervening coast.

The possibility that a number of men may have survived continued to trouble some in authority in Batavia, though most were of the opinion that they must by now have perished in the wilderness, if they had not been murdered. To be absolutely sure, a final search was to be mounted in the more congenial conditions of summer, using two galliots, the *Waeckende Boey* and the *Emeloort*, which were dispatched on New Year's Day, 1658, more than 18 months since the *Vergulde Draeck* came to grief. On this occasion the signs appeared more promising with the sighting of wreckage along the coastline, observations of numerous fires ashore and the rediscovery of the survivors' abandoned camp. Cannon were fired regularly to attract the attention of any surviving Dutchmen and search parties were put ashore at various parts of the coast, though all to no avail. Before departing the scene to return to Batavia, which they did at the end of March, they too would leave some of their number behind to swell the ranks of lost seamen.

The search parties that had been landed from the *Waeckende Boey* were led by the Uppersteersman Abraham Leeman, an Englishman. On 22nd of March, threatened by the prospect of a storm, Leeman and a group of 13 of his men had returned to the ship only to be ordered ashore again by her skipper, Samuel Volkersen. The threatening storm broke later that day, forcing the *Waeckende Boey* to stand out to sea, where she remained while the storm raged for the best part of a week. After six days the weather had moderated enough for the ship to return to the coast where, on sighting a fire that night, they let off a cannon which seemed to be quickly acknowledged from the shore. It appeared that the two groups were about to be reunited.

For some reason the shore party made no attempt to come away, and as the galliot had lost its other boat, there was no way skipper Volkersen's crew could effect a landing. Next day there appeared to be no sign of the group who had kept a vigil on the beach. Since the wind was beginning to rise again with the promise of more bad weather, the captain wasted little time in deciding that the group they had found were either Aborigines, or that his own men were now lost and their boat wrecked, so they sailed away without further ado. It was an action that defies belief.

One wonders what kind of man Volkersen was, what time in the morning he made his decision, what state of relations existed between himself and Leeman, and what further effort he made to let the men ashore know he had returned and was ready to sail. He apparently neglected to fire off another cannon, to wake what may have been a weary crew who were certainly left stranded without food or shelter for nearly a week. As it was, the fires had indeed been those of Leeman and his men—and they would no doubt have gathered later on the beach with a growing realisation that they truly had been abandoned.

No one was ever to know what became of the 68 people from the *Vergulde Draeck*, for whom Leeman's party and others had searched for several weeks. But now Leeman himself was virtually a castaway along with the 13 men he was responsible for. The reason why those ashore had not sought to regain the *Waeckende Boey* on the day she returned to collect them was that their own boat had been damaged and its rudder lost, and they had fully expected another of the galliot's boats to be sent off to pick them up. Skipper Volkersen had decided otherwise, and now they were left to their own devices with a disabled craft and little hope of any other means of rescue. They would therefore have to try to reach Batavia themselves.

Fortunately their boat was not so badly damaged that it could not be repaired. Using what materials were to hand, Leeman had the boat patched with seal skins while others fashioned a makeshift rudder from wreckage cast up from the *Vergulde Draeck*. The seals they had skinned were cut up as the only food available but they were harder pressed to carry enough water for their needs without suitable containers. Sealskins may well have been used for this purpose also. It promised to be a thirsty passage, but there was no alternative . . .

The 14 men set sail a day or two after the *Waeckende Boey* had left. They were lucky in that the weather they encountered was not severe enough to upset their crudely-repaired boat, yet was bad enough to bring occasional rain to supplement their water supply. They were lucky also that the winds were in their favour, and they made the passage to the southern coast of Java in little more than four weeks. Even so, three of their number died of thirst before the sea journey ended.

So desperate was their situation on reaching Java that seven of the men swam ashore to look for water, but alarmingly failed to return. What happened to them also remains a mystery. In attempting to land through heavy surf the following day, the other four narrowly escaped being drowned when their boat capsized and was wrecked on the beach. Though they had reached land after only four weeks, arriving on Java on 28th of April 1658, it took Leeman and his three remaining companions another five months to cross the island to Batavia, where they arrived weak and exhausted on 23rd of September.

———

There has been much conjecture on the ultimate fate of the survivors from the *Vergulde Draeck*, on whose behalf such efforts and sacrifices were made. While the remaining 68 from the merchantman were never found, no fewer than 18 others were lost from search parties put ashore by the rescue ships *Goede Hoop* and *Waeckende Boey*, to add to their number. If any of these people did somehow survive, especially in the longer term, they would soon have been obliged to meet and treat with regional Aboriginal groups in order to co-exist amicably at first, to sustain their survival, then later perhaps to intermarry. If that was so, it may be said that these men represent the earliest Europeans to settle on the Australian continent, albeit unwittingly, along with the two mutineers who were marooned on the mainland by Francisco Pelsaert after the *Batavia* incidents of 1629.

Was their survival likely? Much is contained in Gerritsen's book (*And their Ghosts may be Heard*) to suggest that some at least did survive. He suggests that by a remote chance (aided no doubt by the Aborigines' 'bush telegraph'), they may even have joined up eventually with the two *Batavia* mutineers who had been abandoned on the coast less than 200 miles to the north. Gerritsen also suggests that there may even have been another independent group of *Vergulde Draeck* survivors who drifted ashore elsewhere on debris or makeshift rafts.

A number of archaeological-type finds in the vicinity of Cape Leschenault and nearby Lancelin have fuelled this speculation, as does an analysis of local anomalies and apparent Dutch overtones in certain Aboriginal languages and dialects in the vicinity of Geraldton, and the headwaters of the Irwin River to the east. Both seem to point to the survivors' movements up and away from the coast over distances up to 200 miles: certainly enough to bring them into contact with the mutineers if they were still alive. Whether the linguistic influences were those of the travelling *Vergulde Draeck* survivors or some other Dutch group from the earlier *Batavia* or the later *Zeewyk*, we may never know. The artefacts that were found were more tangible, however, and their locations and finders are precisely known. They established a pattern which not only suggested a direction in which the survivors may have travelled, but which also led to the rediscovery of the wreck itself.

It was said by the men who set the rescue effort in train that the group they left behind was intent on moving into the interior at the time they sailed from the wreck site. Some of the 68 remaining survivors were excavating the capsized boat from the sand at the time of the schuyt crew's departure. Eighteen months later when the *Emeloort* and the *Waeckende Boey* made their searches, two wooden structures of planks set deeply in the sand were discovered, one opposite the wreck site and the other much further south. Since the *Vergulde Draeck* people had no reason to turn south, speculation has it that the southern structure may have been built by the men who went missing from an earlier search by the *Goede Hoop*. Whatever their origins or meaning, they served to indicate that someone had gone to considerable lengths to erect some kind of marker on the shore which displayed no Aboriginal associations.

Then in 1846, the first real evidence of a wreck's existence came in the form of an incense urn shaped like a ship's anchor, entwined by a dragon (a gilt dragon?), and topped by a bird with outstretched wings. It had been found by an Aboriginal shepherd some 20 miles south of Lancelin in the vicinity of Cape Leschenault. At this time, however, no actual wreck was suspected.

The next find was made around 1890, when two kangaroo hunters discovered a mast some 40 feet in length buried in a sandhill some 30 miles north from where the incense urn had been found, somewhat north of Lancelin. Found near the mast were a number of other large domestic items, one of which was a large iron pot which crumbled into rust when handled. The mast, complete with five iron hoops and six metres of heavy chain, was rediscovered *in situ* in 1956. It was this item which later gave rise to the conjectural second survivor group from the *Vergulde Draeck*.

Some 40 years later, two finds in close proximity began to suggest a specific source for what was being found. In 1931, two boys were playing in sand hills north of the Moore River estuary (again in the vicinity of the wreck site), when they came across a number of coins dating between 1618 and 1655, including several of the legendary 'pieces of eight' (Spanish *reales*). The find excited local interest, which was later intensified by the discovery of several bones by one of the boys amongst rocks in the same area. The bones were old and disintegrated when touched, but enough remained for them to be identified as parts of a human skeleton of considerable age. More coins were found by other children in the same general area in 1938.

Clearly, to anyone pondering these finds, there had to be a source of some kind in the near neighbourhood. Around that time stories were beginning to circulate about the wreck of a ship that had been found below cliffs much further north near Shark Bay, which had also yielded old coins and other curios. This would eventually be identified as the *Zuytdorp*, wrecked in 1712, though not found until 1964. For the time being, however, there wasn't enough information on which to begin searching for a wreck or some other treasure trove along the stretch of coast between Lancelin and the Moore River estuary—if that was where the source was.

As it happened there was no wreck on this stretch of coast. The reef that tore the bottom out of the *Vergulde Draeck* is located some three miles off-shore. The actual wreck site was not discovered until April 1963, and then quite by accident. A party of divers was spear-fishing from a boat along the reef when one of their number, teenager Graeme Henderson (now the Director of the Western Australian Maritime

Museum), spotted piles of bricks and elephant tusks littering the sea floor seven metres below. Not only did the discovery change his life, he had also found the first of four early Dutch shipwrecks that were thought to lie somewhere off the Western Australian coast, and which would go some way towards changing contemporary views of Australia's history.

This find began a stampede by others to exploit such wrecks. Two more were to be found—the *Batavia* and the *Zuytdorp*—within a few months. One of the original spear-fishing party, diver Alan Robinson, was quick off the mark in reporting the *Vergulde Draeck* whereabouts to the authorities, though he omitted the name of the true finder. Thereafter he was to claim the wreck and its contents for himself, even challenging the right of the Government to deny the 'rights' of the finder. He was to die in jail several years later, still making claims in connection with the *Vergulde Draeck*, yet he was only the first of many who would see the wreck as a source of easy pickings, belonging to no one and therefore 'up for grabs'.

The controversy surrounding Robinson's claims led to the enactment of the Commonwealth *Historic Shipwrecks Act* 1976 for the protection of similar wrecks. It was later extended to cover all shipwrecks in Australian waters over 75 years old. Between its discovery and the ensuing legislation, however, the *Vergulde Draeck* wreck was subject to looting and vandalism on many occasions, with the loss of much important historic material. Research had revealed that the ship was carrying large quantities of coin which in all likelihood had gone to the bottom with her. There was no evidence that the treasure had been raised by the survivors, who still had a boat at their disposal, nor by any of the subsequent rescue vessels. For many, the prospect of finding such riches was too tempting to resist.

Because of the plundering of the wreck site, the *Vergulde Draeck* was the first major shipwreck to be excavated by the Western Australian Maritime Museum. Work commenced in 1972 and continued for several seasons. Though nothing remained of the ship's structure, large quantities of artefacts were recovered which helped to demonstrate the trading activities of the VOC. Quantities of lead, ivory, amber and coral beads were brought up from the base of the submarine cliff which was the Dutch ship's last resting place, as well as hundreds of small clay building bricks which were probably being taken out to the Indies as ballast. The frowning face on the many 'Beardman' or Bellarmine jugs found on site has since come to symbolise the nature of the material recovered by maritime archaeologists in Western Australia.

The *Vergulde Draeck*'s treasure was also found and recovered. Nearly 20 000 coins were brought to the surface during the course of excavations, almost all of them being Spanish *reales* or 'pieces of eight', akin to those found on the nearby coast in the 1930s. Only a few Dutch coins were found since these were significantly less important and acceptable for trading purposes than the Spanish *reales*, much as the US dollar is a preferred currency in international trading today. The coins were struck between the years 1590 and 1654, with most being minted between 1651 and 1653. An analysis by coin experts showed that the majority of them were actually of Mexican or other South American origin and not particularly well-minted.

These coins were essential silver bullion nonetheless, and representative of that used in Dutch trade, which at the time covered an area stretching from Arabia to Japan. The spice trade had been one of the first attractions to European traders. By fair means or foul, the Dutch rapidly built a monopoly in the East Indies, or the 'Spice Islands' as they were often known, to supply the wealthy citizens of Britain and Europe with much sought-after pepper, cinnamon, nutmeg and cloves which rendered certain foodstuffs more palatable. Silver was the preferred medium of exchange since Europe had little else to offer the Asian markets of the day. A large part of it came from the Spanish colonies in the Americas, or it was sought in Japan. Over time, the silver was also used to purchase tea, silk and porcelain from China, tin and coffee from the Indies, or textiles, raw silk and dyes from India for which the *reales* had to be re-minted as rupees.

But the *Vergulde Draeck* carried one consignment that never reached its destination. Instead it lay on the sea floor on the eastern side of the Indian Ocean for more than 300 years, never to fulfil its intended purpose. Samples of the coins can be seen today at the Maritime Museum of Western Australia with many other artefacts recovered from the wreck of the *Vergulde Draeck*—as well as those from the three other Dutch craft which foundered off our western shores.

Chapter 3

ZUYTDORP

1712

The wreck site of the *Zuytdorp*.

'Zuytdorp *lost 112 of her crew of 286 to scurvy and other causes, while* Belvliet *lost 60 from 164 … horrendous figures when average casualties might only number three or four on this, the first leg of the outward passage.'*

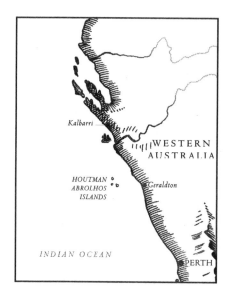

Should you ever wish to pick up local stories in remote parts of Australia, have a chat with the oldest inhabitants. To get to know more, do it over a beer or two. Do this over a few evenings, and before long an amazing tale could start to unfold. This may have been something of the experience of Phillip Playford, a geologist with West Australian Petroleum Pty. Ltd, when he met Tom Pepper, an overseer on Tamala Station south of Denham Sound, Western Australia, in June 1954.

Though not the oldest inhabitant, Tom Pepper was certainly one of the most knowledgeable. While out trapping dingoes one day in April 1927, Tom discovered the remains of the *Zuytdorp*, a Dutch East Indiaman lost in 1712. At the time of his discovery, of course, Tom had no idea of the type or the name of the ship from which the remains came. Even when he told Phillip Playford of his find over 27 years later, the wreckage was still as anonymous as the day he first saw it.

That the remains were part of a very old wooden wreck was clear. However, at that time Tamala was a long way from anywhere, and the coast on which he found the remains was one of the most remote in Australia. The wreck itself lay near the foot of steep rugged cliffs, and access was a hot, hard slog for miles through the bush where water was almost non-existent. And who, then, would have been interested in a distant pile of wreckage anyway, even though there were some interesting looking bits and pieces amongst the beams, broken spars and other heavy timbers? Though he made light of his find, it was not long before Tom, then one of the stockmen, had told others on the station of the mystery wreck he had seen on the coast. As a result, he and his friends made a number of visits to the wreck site over the next 10 years or so, as opportunities arose.

To mark such trips, the visitors invariably picked up a few relics as mementos, or as curios which might decorate a mantelpiece or find a spot behind a bar. Sometimes they might even fetch a bob or two! Many artefacts were removed in this way, so that when rumours of an ancient wreck eventually reached the wider world of Geraldton and Perth, they were strong enough to interest the media.

In 1939, the *Sunday Times* newspaper organised an expedition to view the Tamala site, only to find that conditions in the bush rapidly stifled participants' enthusiasm. Thirst, the heat, flies and dense tea-tree scrub all combined to dissuade the city dwellers from their destination. Little was achieved on that occasion, and interest in the wreck quickly waned when, later that year, larger happenings in the outside world began to claim their attention.

During the years following the end of the Second World War, Phillip Playford was probably the first person to show more than a passing interest in the Tamala wreck. While Tamala's isolation was less than it had been, Tom Pepper was still around, and he was more than willing to pass information of his find to the young geologist, who fast became an avid listener. So fascinating was the older man's story, backed up by some of the relics he had kept, that before very long the geologist had made the round trip of 90 miles over rough bush tracks in just one day, and found enough relics in the 20 minutes he spent at the site to know that a serious expedition would be justified. In 1954, therefore, the media once again gave its support to an exploratory expedition, but while a number of artefacts were recovered, the sea was always too rough for diving. The wreck's identity therefore remained an elusive secret for another four years.

By 1958 Playford's own research, which he undertook in conjunction with archivists in Holland, had produced enough evidence to suggest that the Tamala wreck was most likely that of the *Zuytdorp*, a ship of the Dutch East India Company that was lost on a voyage between the Cape of Good Hope and their base in Batavia in 1712. Furthermore, should that prove to be so, preserved company records indicated that the wreck was likely to yield a substantial treasure if it could be found and retrieved. Another expedition was therefore organised which spent three weeks at the site in April 1958—but again the seas were too rough to permit diving. In the time spent in the area, however, searches about the cliffs, gullies and surrounding bush revealed signs that a number of people had survived the wreck, reached the shore and there established a camp. So was the ship really the *Zuytdorp*? And if so, where was the treasure, and what happened to the survivors?

Playford's research began soon after he became interested in the wreck and its possible origins. Having examined coins in Tom Pepper's possession which bore the name 'Zeeland', the date '1711', and the distinctive mark of the Middelberg Mint, from information available in Western Australia he was soon able to establish that the ship was indeed likely to be the *Zuytdorp*, using the coins as a key. The information on hand referred to a number of VOC ships which had been lost on the high seas, and contained details of their origins, ownership, crew numbers, cargoes and destinations.

The *Zuytdorp* was owned by the VOC Chamber of Zeeland, the largest of a number of formerly independent companies which had merged in 1602 to form the Dutch United East India Company or *Vereenigde Oost-Indische Compagnie*. Built in 1701, she had already made two passages to the East Indies, of four and three years' duration respectively, before being posted missing on her third voyage. On this particular voyage the company records show that her master was one Marinus Wysvliet. They go on to confirm that amongst many other items, her cargo contained a large part, if not all, of the entire Middelberg minting of *dubbele stuivers* and *schellingen* for 1711, valued at 100 000 guilders. All of this currency had originally been destined for transfer by the VOC in Batavia to Ceylon. Instead, it was these particular coins that finally confirmed the Tamala wreck as the *Zuytdorp*, around 250 years later.

The information also showed that a considerable sum of other types of coinage had been carried by the *Zuytdorp*—including gold *ducatons* and pieces-of-eight in the form of *pilaren* and *mexicanen*—so that the final sum of specie on board would have totalled approximately 250 000 guilders, along with a number of gold and silver bars. A treasure ship indeed. However, despite all the wealth she carried, the *Zuytdorp*'s third voyage was not a pleasant or promising one. *Zuytdorp* had left Vlissingen on the 27th of July 1711 in company with another Chamber of Zeeland ship, the *Belvliet*. Normal passage times between Holland and the Cape of Good Hope usually lasted between three and five months but on this occasion, for reasons which are not clear, the two ships took almost seven months. Records from the Cape indicate that on arrival there, many from both crews had either died or deserted, or were too ill to sail further. The *Zuytdorp* lost 112 of her crew of 286 to scurvy and other causes, while *Belvliet* lost 60 from 164, in both cases over a third of each complement—horrendous figures when average casualties might only number three or four on this, the first leg of the outward passage.

Having landed the sick, nearly half of each crew had to be replaced at the Cape before their respective voyages could continue. Though the *Belvliet* reached Batavia after 10 weeks, having departed Cape Town 17 days behind *Zuytdorp*, what befell the *Zuytdorp* during this time can only be guessed at. As noted earlier, the wreck site lay remote and inaccessible on what has been described as one of the most inhospitable parts of the Western Australian coast. The cliffs along there stretch over

250 kilometres in both directions and in places reach heights of 250 metres. In fair visibility the cliffs should have been seen for miles. It is thus difficult to believe that the crew would have remained unaware of their peril until too late. It is much more likely that the ship was carried in a wild rush into the unseen cliffs, either at night or during a storm, or possibly both.

After leaving the Cape on 22nd of April 1712 in company with the *Kockenge*, which arrived in Batavia on 4th of July, the *Zuytdorp* might well have encountered an early winter storm sometime in June which drove her headlong to destruction. Sailing ships in such conditions could often do little but run before the wind. A crew's fear and anxiety on a wild rainy night can then be readily imagined, given that somewhere ahead of their careering ship stretched an unseen coast, perilous by repute. Their fear would have been sharpened by their total inability to exert control of any kind. Men would surely have prayed as never before. How many would have survived the drama of the ensuing wreck is hard to tell, though some clearly did, as demonstrated by the mute relics found at their campsites.

Curiously, no graves or burial sites have been located in the vicinity. Perhaps few survived, and those that did were unable to cope with the many bodies that were washed ashore, or alternatively the sea may have taken the dead and left little to bury. Either way, human remains have never been found. However, it seems that a considerable number did reach the shore, and in good health and heart. Relics from their camp suggest that for a time at least they set about salvaging cargo, including nine heavy breech-blocks from their cannon, though not the cannon themselves, and equally heavy rolls of lead which they shifted up to their cliff-top camp. Why they expended such effort in view of the plight they faced, regardless of their numbers, is beyond imagination, but the implication here is that access to the cargo, and thus from wreck to shore, was relatively easy and that there was energy to spare amongst the survivors to move some large quantities of non-essentials up cliffs 100 or so feet high!

That the survivors moved inland in search of water is certain, as indicated by Playford's own discovery of barrel remains in a gully about 1.5 miles from the cliff-top campsite. That they seem to have moved north sometime later is apparent from old Dutch coins discovered in the vicinity of Shark Bay. Playford himself postulated two possibilities for the fate of survivors—either they stayed near the coast in the hope of sighting a ship and eventually died there, or they salvaged a boat or built one from the wreck timbers, and perished in an attempt to sail to Batavia.

What kind of archaeological relics remain in place to support either theory? A long-term stay at or near the coast would probably have yielded a much larger number of artefacts from what would clearly have been a permanent base. These would have included shelters and burial sites, as well as more widely scattered artefacts and signs of wider explorations if the number of survivors was in any way substantial, or their stay protracted. And if they could spend energy on salvaging such items as breech-blocks and lead rolls, they would surely have already secured enough supplies in the form of food, clothing, tools and utensils, tent materials, and so on. This would then require appropriate storage areas, with dumps for domestic refuse close by. Likewise, if a boat of any size was built, some signs would surely remain in the form of tools, scrap, supports or launching points, again with some form of long-term camp—but none have been found in either instance. The salvaging of one or more ship's boats for a journey north to the Dutch colony in the Indies remains a fair prospect, of course, though one unlikely to be proven since no such vessel(s) ever arrived in Batavia to tell the *Zuytdorp*'s tale.

The evidence of the Shark Bay coins, coupled with observations by Daisy Bates in 1938, may suggest a third possibility instead—that the castaways were found and taken in by local Aborigines, with whom they eventually intermarried. While some of the earliest encounters with Aborigines were undeniably hostile, involving incidents usually sparked by European outrages, many other encounters were friendly and occasionally life-saving. Sooner or later, the *Zuytdorp* castaways would have no doubt come upon Aboriginal bands, even if they never ventured far from the wreck site. Their camp fires would almost certainly have alerted members of either the Nanda or the Mulgana tribes to unheralded intruders, near whose territories the *Zuytdorp* was wrecked.

As a further alternative on this theme, some of the survivors may have progressed as far north as Raffles Bay in their determination to return to civilisation. They may even have remained in that vicinity to establish the colony of 'Hollanders' supposedly found by a certain Lieutenant Nixon in the course of an expedition to north-west Australia in the early part of the 19th century. This story first appeared in England, in the *Leeds Mercury*, on the 25th of January 1834.

According to extracts from Lieutenant Nixon's journal, the two-month long expedition came upon a place that was 'different from the rest of the landscape', and 'laid out as if it were in plantations, with straight rows of trees'. One of the settlers they encountered was said to speak a kind of broken Dutch, which Nixon was able to understand, who told him that the 80 men and 10 women of their settlement were descended from the survivors of a Dutch shipwreck which happened more than 100 years earlier. Though the report excited considerable interest in the Netherlands and raised the question of offering help and materials, nothing further seems to have been heard of this mysterious group. Satellite imagery and modern archaeological techniques should be capable of identifying the signs of such a remote settlement in the Australian outback if it ever existed, but such a discovery has yet to be made.

Regardless of such a possibility and in the absence of more convincing proof, the most telling 'evidence' of the fate of the *Zuytdorp* castaways seems to lie in Daisy Bates' 1938 publication, *Passing of the Aborigines*. She recognised that certain Aboriginal groups in the Gascoyne and Murchison River areas around Kalbarri, Shark Bay and Carnarvon once exhibited some quite marked European features, particularly the facial characteristics, the stocky build and fair curly hair typical of the Dutch. Other people have reported similar observations. Unfortunately, the original inhabitants of these areas were never subject to anthropological studies, and regrettably they are said to be almost extinct today. If their ancestors *did* meet up with Dutch seamen though, there were at least two possibilities of this happening: first in the survivors from the *Batavia*, wrecked in 1629, or those from the *Zuytdorp* in 1712. Two men, Wouter Loos and Jan Pelgrom de Bye, were marooned near the Murchison or Hutt Rivers by Commandeur Pelsaert as a penalty for lesser crimes they committed during the *Batavia* incident. How many castaways the Aborigines may have encountered from the *Zuytdorp* is unknown.

Evidence from another independent source, however, gives credence to the possibility of some form of long-term contact. A rare metabolic disorder, *Porphyria variegata*, amongst surviving Aborigines in the area, offers genetic evidence which appears to suggest an early association with outsiders. This disease was known to exist amongst Dutch settlers at the Cape of Good Hope in 1688, and so might well have been transmitted by one or more men from the Cape who went aboard *Zuytdorp* as part of the replacement crew obtained there. As both of the earlier survivors from the *Batavia* were from Holland, it is unlikely that they were carriers, assuming they survived long after their arrival. The genetic problem therefore seems more likely to have originated in men from the *Zuytdorp*, though a firm link has never been established. Similarly, another rare disorder amongst Western Australia's Aborigines, the Ellis-van Creveld Syndrome which features polydactylism, or the possession of extra fingers and toes, also has genetic links with the Dutch.

In his book *And Their Ghosts May Be Heard*, Rupert Gerritsen presents strong, albeit conjectural arguments for Dutch–Aboriginal liaison and intermarriage, particularly with the Nanda people. This is based on genetic and linguistic evidence, and some marked influences on yam culture, the building of shelters, and circumcision rites. Furthermore, his assertions include the possibility that such developments could derive from contacts with more than one group of stranded seamen. The *Vergulde Draeck* and the *Zeewyk* crews were perhaps but two of these. At least three other Dutch vessels of this period (*Ridderschap van Holland*, *Fortuyn* and *Aagtekerke*) may also have come to grief along this stretch of coast in circumstances similar to those of the *Zuytdorp*. Any of their crews might equally have contributed to these genetic and cultural phenomena as carriers if they succeeded in reaching the mainland.

While none of the early expeditions to the Tamala wreck site were able to find and dive on the actual wreck, a considerable amount of work was done on the site of the cliff-top camp to give some indication of the survivors' plight. Tom Pepper had already noted the quantity of timber present, including the decorative figure of a woman that was suggestive of a ship's figurehead. He found the broken remains of green glass bottles, coins, rolls of lead and several large brass objects which were later identified as the breech-blocks of cannon, together with dress items and several measuring instruments.

The expeditions of 1954 and 1958 uncovered more relics of this nature, including more instruments, more broken bottles, parts of muskets, fragments of clay smoking pipes, and the metalwork from barrels, chests, and the ship itself. Many more coins were found, apparently having been cast up from the sea bed, as were a number of broken writing slates and two large keys. Evidence was also found of large fires that had been lit at the foot of the cliff and on the cliff top, perhaps in a vain attempt to attract the attention of other ships turning north on the Brouwer route at this point. The 'figurehead' was identified as a decorative piece from the stern gallery of the ship, while melted brass fittings from chests found amongst the long-cold ashes suggested a startled rush to build as big a fire as possible with anything combustible in order to signal a passing ship.

It was not until 1964 that the wreck was located and successfully dived. As had been imagined, the wreck lay in the surf zone just off the shelf at the base of the cliff, immediately below the cliff-top camp site. Water depths were quite shallow, with a minimum of 1.5 metres. The first dives, always in potentially hazardous conditions, were undertaken by private individuals from Geraldton led by local diver Tom Brady, who quickly noted the presence of two anchors, several cannon, quantities of lead ingots and piles of ballast stones. The Western Australian Museum was informed, with whom they worked on later dives. It took three years of perilous work, however, before the vessel's stern could be closely examined, at which point the fate of the ship's treasure became clear. What was described as 'a carpet of coins several square metres in extent' lay before the divers—at which point it might truly be said that maritime archaeology in this country was born.

News of the finds from the *Zuytdorp* spread quickly. Very soon it became most apparent that unless something was done to protect the wreck, it would fast become another target for treasure seekers and looters. Only remoteness and treacherous sea conditions kept such people temporarily at bay, but modern equipment was making safe diving available to many, and a dauntless few were quite prepared to take on the risks involved to secure the wealth that was there for the picking.

The first shipwreck legislation was enacted in the 1964 amendments to the *Museum Act* 1959 (WA), to extend legal protection to the *Zuytdorp* and five other sites in Western Australian waters. A team of professional divers was subsequently established at the Western Australian

Museum to work not only on the *Zuytdorp*, which required some urgent prescriptive diving to recover all the visible coin and other attractive items likely to be lost to looters, but also to work on other wrecks that had been recently discovered, namely those of the *Trial*, the *Batavia* and the *Vergulde Draeck*.

Work on the *Zuytdorp* has never been easy. Huge swells breaking in the shallows where the wreck lies are always a threat to divers on such an exposed, high energy coast. Two flying foxes built to carry divers directly from the cliff top, over the breakers and into the sea by means of a cage were apparently destroyed by the elements. An airstrip cleared nearby was a hazard in itself, while the watch-keeper's caravan was deliberately burned by persons unknown, along with a quantity of diving gear and some of the Museum's early records. As a result of the dangers and difficulties associated with the *Zuytdorp* site and some changed priorities regarding two other recently discovered wrecks, work on the *Zuytdorp* was suspended from 1981 to 1985, although pressure was maintained for it to continue.

Work recommenced in 1986, but in a different regime than five years earlier. A series of research dives had given a greater appreciation of the dynamics of sand drift and scour wrought by the seasonal cycle, and the rapid day-to-day changes that were possible. A wider strategy was developed to encompass work on the land sites, as well as that underwater. Detailed maps and supporting material were prepared for each of the terrestrial sites, while a comprehensive site plan was completed for the wreck itself, though neither was without a considerable degree of difficulty. On the downside, many more people were now 'dropping in' on the *Zuytdorp* in faster, more reliable boats. It became clear that some were looters who had continued to remove historic items despite the 'protection' of the Commonwealth's 1976 *Historic Shipwrecks Act*. A positive move, therefore, in order to know what relics were held in private hands, was the declaration of the Australia-wide amnesty of 1993 which sought to record, but not reclaim, all items which had been salvaged from wrecks in the years preceding that were over 75 years old.

Fortunately, the availability of faster boats also favoured the maritime archaeologists. This meant that they were now able to reach the site more swiftly when conditions were at their best, particularly as they were able to operate from Kalbarri only two hours away by sea. The Museum teams have been progressively augmented by various specialists, who now constitute the staff of the Western Australian Maritime Museum in Fremantle. This institution has rapidly become the principal focus, indeed a Centre of Excellence, for the pursuit of maritime archaeology studies both in Australia and overseas.

Research and excavations on the *Zuytdorp* have continued steadily over a number of seasons, and are not yet complete. All work associated with the wreck is carried out under the guidelines behind some well-defined aims for the project, which themselves reflect the objectives and resolutions of ANCODS, the Agreement between Australia and the Netherlands Concerning Old Dutch Shipwrecks. Since its discovery a wide variety of artefacts from the wreck has been brought to the surface for conservation, interpretation and eventual display, in conjunction with material recovered from the land sites, and for correlation with material from similar wrecks. All such items are now lodged either in the Maritime Museum in Fremantle, or its counterpart in the Geraldton Regional Museum.

Chapter 4

ZEEWYK

1727

Relics recovered from the Dutch ship, *Zeewyk*.

'Discipline then broke down progressively as the sailors plundered the liquor stores and broke open the treasure chests, and wild scenes followed while they celebrated their new-found wealth in drunken fantasies.'

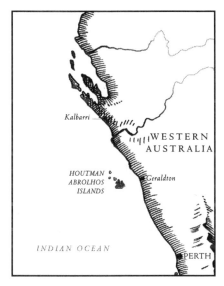

Some 75 kilometres off the coast of Western Australia, about the latitude of Geraldton, lie the Houtman Abrolhos, a relatively insignificant cluster of the Indian Ocean's islands and reefs—except for one thing. In the days of sail, long before Australia was first colonised, they were a trap for unsuspecting merchant ships bound from the tip of South Africa to the East Indies. But why were such ships trapped there of all places, so far from a more direct route? And whose were these ships? What is the meaning of 'Houtman Abrolhos', and what do they represent? The answers to such questions have perhaps had the most significant influence on the growth and development of maritime archaeology in Australia.

Houtman Abrolhos, or the Abrolhos Islands or Houtman's Rocks as they are sometimes known, consist of three island subgroups with deep channels between. To the north lie the Wallabi Group, divided from the central Easter Group by the Middle Channel. To the south, beyond the Zeewyk Channel, is the Pelsart Group, mistakenly named in the belief that this was where the *Batavia* was wrecked in 1629, after the ship's commander Francisco Pelsaert. Abrolhos is said to come from a contraction of the Portuguese *abri* (open) and *olhos* (eyes), meaning 'watch out' or 'beware', a reminder that danger lay amongst these scattered shoals and islets. Abrolho also means 'a thorny barrier'. They were named in 1619 by Frederik de Houtman, commander of the Dutch ship *Dordrecht* as a warning to others, but they nevertheless claimed the *Batavia* 10 years later, just as they would claim the *Zeewyk* a century after that. There is a strong possibility that they may have caught one or two other vessels as well—the *Fortuyn* and the *Aagtek-erke*, for instance—but this is running ahead of the story.

All of these were Dutch ships using the southern Brouwer Route from the Cape to the Indies, as was required of them by their parent VOC, to make faster passages on the prevailing westerlies. However, should a vessel's captain go too far east when calculating his longitude, a very inexact science at this time, he risked being wrecked on the unknown coast of Southland, or carried onto its off-lying reefs. History records that several did, some being able to extricate themselves after no more than a fright and a light grounding, while others were held fast forever, so providing the basis for the development of maritime archaeology in this country over little more than the last 30 years. Because of the ships that were lost there, the Houtman Abrolhos have become a major focus of archaeological studies, which may yet yield future discoveries of wrecks that are known, but are still to be located.

The Dutch ship *Zeewyk* was one of the earliest wrecks to show traces of its presence in this area. Though no wreck was visible at the time, during survey work in 1840 the crew of HMS *Beagle*, which eight years earlier had carried Charles Darwin on his voyage to fame, found signs of a survivors' campsite on one of the islands in the southern Pelsart Group. They gave it the name of Gun Island after finding a brass swivel cannon there, which they took back to England. During the 1890s, guano miners on Gun Island found bottles, pots and other relics which further suggested the proximity of a wreck. A number of visits by vessels of the Royal Australian Navy in the 1950s were marked by the finding and recovery of three other cannon from the reefs fringing Gun Island, two of which were lodged with the Western Australian Museum.

These finds led on to media-sponsored expeditions in the 1960s to discover the wreck itself. Meanwhile, there was also the prospect of a second wreck in this area, since it was known that in 1727 the *Zeewyk's* own survivors had found beams and timbers from a prior wreck amongst the reefs and islets of the Pelsart Group. This second prospect seemed to be confirmed in similar sightings reported by Commander Stokes of HMS *Beagle* on the long island, which he had then named Pelsart Island in the belief that the earlier wreck was that of the ill-fated *Batavia* . . .

Zeewyk was a new vessel of the Zeeland Chamber of the VOC when she left on her maiden voyage to Batavia, Dutch East Indies, in November 1726. She was the first command of her skipper, Jan Steyns, who had been a late replacement for one Jan Bogaard who had been too sick to sail. Aboard on leaving Vlissingen was a crew of 208, a cargo of building materials for the Indies, and the rich sum of 315 836 guilders securely stowed away in 10 chests. Steyns proved to be somewhat foolhardy in his new command, for after leaving the Cape on 21st of April 1727, he was determined to visit Eendracht Land, an area north of present-day Geraldton, Western Australia, for reasons unknown, before going on to Batavia. This was contrary to strict instructions from the VOC and, it transpired, also against the advice of his steersman to avoid going too close to the uncharted southland coast.

In the darkness of evening on the 9th of June 1727, *Zeewyk* crashed heavily onto Half Moon Reef on the western edge of the Pelsart Group, with an impact so great as to dislodge the rudder, snap off the mainmast which then fell overboard, and hole the ship so badly that her maiden voyage very soon became her last. Breakers had been sighted at least half an hour before she struck, but they were thought merely to be moonlight reflecting from the sea, until it was too late. Chaos reigned, and for a while Jan Steyns was lambasted by his angry crew over their predicament and his loss of the ship. Discipline then broke down progressively as the sailors plundered the liquor stores and broke open the treasure chests, and wild scenes followed while they celebrated their new-found wealth in drunken fantasies.

Sea conditions were such that at least 10 men were drowned in the first attempts to launch a boat. Only after a week of heavy swells and breaking waves was a boat launched successfully to reach one of several islands and atolls lying close by. In the interim a tentative discipline was restored with the aid of a ship's council of officers and common hands, though insubordination and abuse continued to be the officers' lot. Fortunately the wreck held together well, enabling some of the more aggressive survivors to resist leaving it for over four months. The others were ferried to what later became known as Gun Island, where their main camp was established and where they were to live for the next 10 months.

More than half the crew perished in the wreck and its aftermath. Fewer than 100 were moved ashore, during which time a start was made to salvage as much as possible from the wreck to meet their immediate needs, before the wreck began to fall apart. The small number who had refused to leave the wreck were intent on prolonging the supply of free grog for as long as possible. Meanwhile the island on which the others found themselves was rocky and low-lying, a mere 800 by 350 metres with narrow beaches and only sparse vegetation, but it offered one important life-saving commodity at that time—fresh water.

The survivors were thus able to sort themselves out, remove many items of food and shelter from their stricken ship, and also to collect all the treasure chests together in anticipation of eventual rescue. It soon became clear that the ship was not likely to break up quickly, so hard and fast was *Zeewyk* aground on the reef, though it was equally clear that she could never be floated off either. Some kind of rescue mission was therefore imperative, a demand which was angrily reinforced by a drunken party of petty officers and common hands who threatened mutiny in the face of what they saw as Jan Steyns' and his officers' incompetence. As part of their demand, 11 of the fittest survivors had been nominated to accompany the First Mate, Pieter Langeweg, in the longboat to bring help from Batavia.

Steyns and his officers could only capitulate, since such a venture was essential anyway. All necessary preparations were made over the next month after which they set out, on 10th of July, with the aim of replicating the feat of *Batavia*'s commander, Francisco Pelsaert, in bringing a rescue craft back from the Indies. After more than three months had passed, however, it became very apparent that no such rescue ship would come. The longboat had been apparently lost in a winter storm with all those aboard, for it had never arrived at Batavia. The *Zeewyk*'s remaining crew were once again thrown upon their own resources.

Fortunately these were plentiful in the circumstances, with large quantities of all types of material having been saved from the wreck while the longboat crew were away. As well as victuals from the ship's stores and cargo, the availability of fish, seal meat and fresh water had kept the castaways in good health, so that no one died during their stay on Gun Island apart from the trauma victims of the first few days. There was more than enough material from both the cargo and the wreck to fabricate another craft in which to escape the islands, as well as appropriate skills amongst the seamen with which to build it. A decision was therefore made to start the construction of a stout sloop capable of carrying all the castaways on to Batavia.

The keel of what became known as the *Sloepie* was laid down five months after the day of the wreck, on 7th of November. A few days later the sternpost was fixed in place, and the stern of the boat started in earnest. Material for the fore part of the sloop was taken from that of the *Zeewyk*, while *Zeewyk*'s spare mainmast and the stump of her mizzen were used to support two square-rigged sails. Local mangrove timber was used in part for ribs and knees, with others fashioned from *Zeewyk*'s oak. For her planking and decking the carpenters used baltic pine and more oak from the wreck. All essential fittings for rigging and running gear came from the *Zeewyk*, as did their anchors, cable, navigation equipment and the ship's bell. To protect the treasure chests they would be carrying from any risk of piracy in the Indies, the sloop mounted two light bronze swivel guns for close-quarter work. The whole of her design finally resembled a beamy, 60-foot North Sea fishing craft so typical of contemporary Dutch shipbuilders, with which so many of the crew were familiar. For a while at least, the affectionately-named *Sloepie* was to unite the men in their bid to reach the Indies.

The boat that was assembled on this obscure Australian island took four months to build. She was launched as the *Sloepie* on 28th of February, 1728 and so became the first vessel ever built in Australia. The significance of this would probably have been lost on its builders, even had they been aware of it. Instead they toasted their efforts with three barrels of the wine they had salvaged from the disintegrating *Zeewyk*, and set about preparing their new craft for departure at the end of the cyclone season. In order to ensure that they would not be caught again within the complex of reefs, for the *Sloepie* was a large boat with a laden draft of six feet, a safe passage was charted through the shallows by the Second Mate, Adriaen van der Graeff. This was also the man who kept a journal of the *Zeewyk* story for the eventual benefit of posterity. On 26th of March the *Sloepie* was finally ready. With appropriate provisions and three tons of treasure already placed aboard, on that date she embarked the last of 88 officers, seamen and soldiers and in the early morning set sail for Batavia. The remains of 120 others were left behind in scattered graves amongst the dunes, including those of two boys who had been marooned on separate coral cays, without food or water, after being found guilty of the 'stupid sin' of sodomy.

The long journey north lasted another month, during which time six men had died from the rigours of the passage. *Zeewyk*'s survivors arrived in Batavia Roads in the late afternoon of 30th of April, 1728, eighteen months after they had left Holland. For skipper Jan Steyns it was a small triumph, having delivered so many of his fellows from the island wastes off a distant Southland. His original folly in losing his ship had not been forgotten by the surviving crew, however, and before long he was called to stand trial before Batavia's High Court of Justice, charged with causing the *Zeewyk* disaster as a consequence of approaching the Southland against the orders of the VOC.

It was found also that in explaining the wreck and his subsequent conduct, he had deliberately falsified the ship's records and his own report to appear in better light in the inquiry he anticipated. He had in fact had notes smuggled ashore ahead of his arrival, pleading helplessness from scurvy while being held captive by his mutinous crew. The truth was otherwise. He was duly prosecuted, as a result of which he lost his position and salary with the Honourable Company, forfeiting all his property and wealth to the Gentlemen XVII Directors of the VOC. As a further humiliation he was sentenced to be exhibited at a place of public execution wearing a board labelled 'Falsifier', and thereafter was banned for life from all territories under the VOC's jurisdiction. He was to be spared only the humiliation of exposure with the board after a subsequent appeal.

———

From about the mid-19th century following the rediscovery of the survivors' camp, many objects were recovered from the site of the *Zeewyk* disaster, first by naval visitors, later by guano diggers, and most recently by archaeologists from the Western Australian Museum, the parent of the Western Australian Maritime Museum in Fremantle. As well as the first cannon (the origins of which were clear from the familiar VOC mark of the Dutch East India Company), in 1840 the men from HMS *Beagle* found harness brasses, some large glass bottles, clay pipes, and two coins dated 1707 and 1720 which helped to confirm the identity of the site. As a mark of confidence in their discoveries they named the Zeewyk Channel after the wreck, but at the same time were unknowingly mistaken in their naming of the Pelsart Group. The Colonial Schooner *Champion* was active in the area between 1840 and 1848, investigating reports by others of finds amongst the Abrolhos' islands and atolls. And in 1953, the reefs of Gun Island yielded three other cannon from the shallows, during visits by HMAS *Mildura* and HMAS *Fremantle* of the Royal Australian Navy.

Towards the end of the 19th century the Pelsart islands were being surveyed for their guano deposits, the extraction of which went on to obliterate most signs of their earlier occupation by Dutch sailors. By good fortune, however, in removing the thick deposits of phosphate-rich bird droppings down to the bedrock, one of the directors of the phosphate company Broadhurst & McNeil, Mr Florance Broadhurst, took a personal interest in the archaeological finds from the former campsites and nearby graves. Not only did he collect and catalogue all the finds that came from the diggings, he also traced earlier relics held by private individuals, as well as those found by the original surveyors of the island which were then placed in the Perth Museum.

By the end of the century the guano deposits had been largely cleared. Further extraction would become progressively uneconomic, but by then Mr Broadhurst had accumulated a magnificent collection of *Zeewyk* artefacts, most of which he donated to the Western Australian Museum. His generosity masked an underlying frustration, however, which was never satisfactorily resolved. His enthusiasm for maritime history and its associated discoveries had led him to obtain a copy in Dutch of *Ongeluckige Voyagie van t' Schip Batavia*, the story of the *Batavia* tragedy written by Jan Jansz in 1647, which he then had translated locally. He was clearly hoping that his collective zeal would eventually turn up items from the wreck of the *Batavia*, especially since he believed the Pelsart Group, according to Commander Stokes of the *Beagle*, was where it would be found. Such a coup might have sustained his interest for many a year. Alas for him though, the *Batavia* would not be found for another 70-odd years, and then at a site on the Wallabi Group some 50 kilometres to the north. This discovery crowned the years of painstaking research by the historian Henrietta Drake-Brockman, author of the maritime classic, *Voyage to Disaster*.

The wreck of the *Zeewyk* would also not be found for much the same length of time, and when it was found, it was purely by accident. An expedition in 1963 led by Hugh Edwards—journalist, diver, and later author of *The Wreck on the Half-Moon Reef* which tells the *Zeewyk* story in full—had found cannon, cannon balls, ship's timbers, and glass and metal indicators, but this was not the actual wreck. The first sign of the proximity of the elusive wreck came in March 1966 when he literally stumbled upon it by way of an elephant's tusk, of all things, while spear-fishing with friends on a reef they had already explored many times before. Such is chance! Hugh Edwards was subsequently instrumental in leading maritime archaeologists on expeditions to the reef and its island cluster. In March 1968 he finally came upon the remains of the *Zeewyk* itself as a scatter of cannon, anchors, and conglomerates of coral-encrusted cargo items.

Zeewyk was the last of the four Dutch shipwrecks to be found in the waters off Western Australia. Like the other three, she was subject to surveys, excavations and other research by staff of the Western Australian Museum to assess her own particular story, her place in Dutch and Australian history, and her archaeological potential. Formal surveys were conducted underwater and on the land sites in 1972 and 1974, with annual expeditions by the Western Australian Museum to excavate, record and recover items from the wreck and its associated encampments between 1976 and 1979.

Through each successive season a whole array of artefacts was systematically removed and catalogued, which represented something of the life and substance both of the crew of a Dutch East Indiaman of the times, and of the lifestyle and trading activities of the gentlemen officers of the VOC. Building materials, glass and ceramic bottles, jugs and jars, clothing adornments, containers and cooking utensils, cutlery, crockery and other domestic items, fishing gear, furniture fittings, ship's fittings, personal items, smoking items and drinking vessels, tools, weapons and heavy armaments—all are durable remains which suggest in some detail the practicalities of shipboard life and the richness of life in the Dutch colony, while telling nothing of the hardships of either. Many of these relics can be seen and pondered over in the Western Australian Maritime Museum in Fremantle today, though the stories they carry of the people who made and used them remain forever untold.

And what of the mystery wreckage noted by the *Zeewyk*'s crew and others, consisting of heavy timbers and a ship's figurehead, with an assortment of other fittings found later? What stories might unfold here could that ship's whereabouts be discovered? Those of the four wrecks found so far on the fringes of Western Australia tell their own stories by way of dusty archives and crusted fragments from the past, as well as stimulating the kind of speculation and conjecture that forges connections with other aspects of our early history. It is such a web of disparate parts that often adds to the fuller fabric of our nationhood, while identifying contributions from unexpected quarters. There is apparently a fifth ship lying somewhere amongst the reefs and shallows of the Abrolhos, though searches by specialists from the Western Australian Maritime Museum have so far not brought it to light.

In all probability the wreck was the *Aagtekerke*, a vessel lost like the *Zeewyk* on her maiden voyage to the Indies in 1726, though two other ships thought to have been wrecked in these waters might be other possibilities. In 1727 the men from the *Zeewyk* who discovered the remains reported finding both relatively fresh timbers and fittings, which they assumed came from their own shipwreck, as well as other apparently much older remains. So here there is a puzzle: one additional shipwreck, or two? Given the amount of archaeological and treasure-seeking attention devoted to these islands in the last half century, it would be hard to believe that two wrecks remain to be found within the bounds of Houtman's Abrolhos, though they do cover an area of more than 1800 square miles, or almost 4800 square kilometres in extent. In the absence of more concrete evidence or chance finds, however, we can only speculate on what has come to us in records from the past—which was precisely how wrecks as diverse as the *Batavia* and the *Titanic* came to be discovered.

The freshness of the items found in 1727 may suggest that the wreckage came from the *Aagtekerke*, a new vessel that was lost in 1726. Under the command of Jan Uitenboom, she left Holland in May 1725 with a crew of 212 and a cargo which included a consignment of bullion and specie valued at 200 000 guilders. She reached Cape Town early in January 1726, sailing later that month for Batavia—and oblivion. In October that year she was officially considered lost, but only after *Zeewyk*'s own survivors had reached Batavia in *Sloepie* was any thought given to the possibility that the *Aagtekerke* might have been wrecked on the infamous Abrolhos Islands. Another wreck prospect about this time could have been the *Fortuyn*, also lost on her maiden voyage, this time in 1724. Having sailed from the Cape in convoy with three other Dutch ships, she had still not arrived in Batavia when the *'s Graveland*, arriving two weeks after the others, reported sighting the wreckage of a Dutch ship off the Cocos Islands, a group far to the north of the Abrolhos, but still en route to the East Indies capital, Batavia.

When the implications of much older timbers amongst the finds are considered, the loss of the *Ridderschap van Holland* in 1694 demands most attention as being the most likely identity behind the unknown wreck. When fears were felt for the safety of the ship after it was seven months overdue in Batavia, three search ships under the command of Willem de Vlamingh were dispatched to retrace the *Ridderschap van Holland*'s route from the Cape, including a passage along the coast of Western Australia, but to no avail. In time, a number of conflicting reports were heard that the lost ship had either been wrecked, or captured by pirates, both in the vicinity of Madagascar.

For the moment, the truth about the fate of any of these vessels remains intriguingly unknown. That old wreckage and other signs of shipwrecks were found by the survivors of the *Zeewyk* cannot be denied, but what was the ship and where is she now? Searches for a fifth Dutch shipwreck off the Western Australian coast have so far produced nothing. Neither has anything been found on the mainland or offshore islands that cannot be ascribed to the wrecks already found. Consideration of the evidence by Graeme Henderson of the Western Australian Maritime Museum has thrown no light on the prospect of a fifth wreck amongst the Abrolhos, instead suggesting that the wreckage could have drifted to the islands from a wreck site anywhere in the Indian Ocean. But undoubtedly there *was* wreckage . . .

Wasn't it Alexander Pope, writing at the time of these shipwrecks, who penned in *An Essay on Man* the well-known phrase, 'Hope springs eternal'? Perhaps one day, by another lucky chance, someone looking amongst the Abrolhos reefs or searching the long coasts either side of Geraldton might happen upon that one, all-important clue.

Chapter 5

HMS *PANDORA*
1791

The *Pandora*.

'Captain Edwards was one of the first to leave the sinking ship. In the ensuing mayhem the shackled prisoners were forgotten by all but two of the crew.'

Though the impact of contemporary events was not immediate, the story which was to highlight the later career of His Majesty's Ship *Pandora* actually began on the 28th of April 1789. At this time she lay 'in ordinary' up the River Medway, above the Chatham Royal Naval Dockyard in England. This is to say, she had been placed in reserve to await her next call to duty, after taking part in the American War of Independence for which she was built. In this state she had been stripped of her masts, sails, guns and rigging, while her upper deck was covered over to protect her from the elements. Meanwhile, far away, on the other side of the globe, a drama was unfolding which would seal the fate of all those immediately involved, and eventually that of the men who, 18 months later, would ultimately sail forth on HMS *Pandora's* last voyage. But this anticipates the story ...

By the last decade of the 18th century, the fortunes of HMS *Pandora* and HMS *Bounty* would become inextricably entwined. Each was one of the smaller ships of the Royal Navy, lesser lights serving as the work-horses of the fleet, in sharp contrast to the majestic first rate battleships that were making history for Britain about this time. Both ships would have fitted well into the First Fleet which came to Australia in 1788. As a 24-gun 6th-rate frigate, HMS *Pandora* was similar to the First Fleet's flagship, the 6th-rate HMS *Sirius*. The smaller HMS *Bounty*, a converted merchantman, was similar to the First Fleet's tender, HMS *Supply*. Destiny had other plans for the two vessels, however. While *Pandora* continued to languish up a Kentish backwater, the *Bounty* had sailed on a special commission to carry breadfruit plants from Tahiti in the Pacific to the islands of the Caribbean where they would be a cheap form of sustenance for slaves working on the plantations there. It was a voyage which gave rise to perhaps the most enduring sea story of all time.

The events behind the infamous mutiny on the *Bounty* are well-known, having long been the stuff of film and fiction. HMS *Bounty* was commanded by William Bligh, a 33-year-old naval lieutenant who had served on Captain Cook's *Resolution* during the great explorer's final circumnavigation between 1776 and 1780. Though Bligh seems to have been much maligned by Hollywood in terms of his reputed harshness and brutality in flogging his crew, history has found that his actions were no worse than Captain Cook's in this regard, particularly in light of the universal severity of naval discipline then. The *Bounty*'s voyage was long and arduous, however, 30 days having been spent in trying to pass through Cape Horn's stormy Magellan Straits alone before Bligh turned round and headed east towards Tahiti instead. They were trying times.

The attractions of the tropical Society Islands, and especially of the Tahitian women, must have seemed like paradise to the *Bounty*'s crew after the trials of their 10-month journey to get there. To ensure the viability of the plants they had come to collect, Bligh was forced to spend five months amongst the islands, while his crew made the most of the Tahitians' welcome. Owing to his high moral standards, Bligh is said to have been the only man aboard the *Bounty* who did not take a Tahitian consort. Having loaded more than 1000 breadfruit plants, however, on 4th of April, 1789, the ship finally departed for the West Indies, manned by a resentful crew driven by a tyrannical captain.

Three weeks later, at dawn off the Tongan island of Tofua, Bligh was rudely awakened by the master's mate, Fletcher Christian, and others of the crew who had overpowered the *Bounty*'s officers and taken charge of the ship. When Bligh refused the mutineers' demands to turn back to

Tahiti, he was set adrift in the ship's longboat with provisions and 18 loyal supporters and left to his own devices. Christian and the rest, including some reluctant crew-members, ostensibly sailed away to the Tahitian idyll and their grieving ladies, while Bligh made the most of his lot and turned his overloaded craft towards the nearest islands.

The voyage in the open boat eventually carried William Bligh and his men more than 3600 miles to the Portuguese island of Timor, via the Torres Strait. He had lost only one man on the 41-day journey, stoned to death by angry natives on the first island they had tried to land on. In time, his unparalleled success would be hailed as a remarkable feat of navigation, seamanship and endurance. Meanwhile, Bligh had himself and his followers taken from Timor to Batavia in the Dutch East Indies, thence on to England aboard a Dutch ship. His dispatch to the Admiralty caused consternation amongst the Lords Commissioners, who demanded appropriate justice and retribution. At this juncture, HMS *Pandora* was re-commissioned and fitted out for passage to the South Seas to seek out and capture the *Bounty* mutineers.

If the mutineers were disgruntled over their treatment at the hands of Lieutenant Bligh, as they would eventually claim, they would come to see him in a different and kindlier light after their encounter with Captain Edward Edwards, master of His Majesty's Frigate *Pandora*. Captain Edwards' instructions were to '... proceed to the south seas in order to endeavour to recover the *Bounty* and to bring in confinement to England Fletcher Christian and his mutineers or as many of them have survived and you may be able to apprehend.' He therefore lost no time in readying his ship for Tahiti, where he fully expected to find Christian and his fellow hedonists settled once more in their tropical heaven.

The *Pandora* departed Portsmouth late in 1790 and arrived at Matavia Bay on 23rd of March, 1791, after a fast passage, but Captain Edwards was able to find only 14 of the original 25 mutineers. Two had died on the islands whereas Fletcher Christian, fully aware that he might soon be pursued by a relentless Royal Navy, had taken the other mutineers, their Polynesian consorts and a few Tahitian men, and sailed off into the South Pacific where they effectively disappeared.

Having taken aboard the 14 captives from Tahiti, Captain Edwards dealt with them with a natural cold contempt. With his own experiences of mutinous crewmen, he was unyielding in his attitude towards them and little concerned for their well-being and comfort. A wooden cell had been constructed on *Pandora*'s quarterdeck measuring 11 × 18 feet (3.3 × 5.5m), with only a single scuttle, 20 inches (50cm) square, for air and access. In this the captives were manacled by leg irons to a central beam, and there left to suffer in their own filth on verminous bedding, through tropical heat and torrential downpours with only minimal food and water. The cell was called 'Pandora's box', but in this case it was truly devoid of hope.

Captain Edwards had been ordered to return the mutineers to England for trial, but he had no intentions of wasting stores or ship-space on them in the process. Though his wish was to bring every one of the mutineers to justice, subsequent searching amongst the islands to the north and west failed to turn up any sign of Fletcher Christian or the stolen ship. Both had vanished into the vastness of the South Pacific and were by then on distant Pitcairn Island, a tiny speck more than a thousand miles south-east of Tahiti, where the *Bounty* had been burned. Aware of his greater duty, Captain Edwards therefore made sail for England, which they were to reach via James Cook's Endeavour Strait at the tip of Cape York, then on through the broader Torres Strait.

In following this route, *Pandora* had to run the gauntlet of the Great Barrier Reef off north-eastern Australia, a perilous passage full of shoals, coral cays and uncharted reefs ever ready to trap a stranger. Late in the afternoon of 28th of August, 1791, Captain Edwards dispatched a yawl to find a way through the coral and into the open water that lay beyond. George Hamilton, the ship's surgeon, described the events that followed:

> At five in the afternoon a signal was made from the boat, that a passage through the reef was discovered for the ship; but wishing to be well informed in so intricate a business, and the day being far spent, we waited the boat's coming on board, made a signal to expedite her, and afterwards repeated it. Night closing fast upon us, and considering our former misfortunes of losing the tender and the jolly boat, rendered it necessary, both for the preservation of the boat, and the success of the voyage, to endeavour, by every possible means, to get hold of her.
>
> False fires were burnt, and muskets fired from the ship, and answered by the boat reciprocally; and as the flashes from their muskets were distinctly seen by us, she was reasonably soon expected on board. We now sounded, but had no bottom with a 110 fathom line, till past seven o'clock, when we got ground in 50 fathom.
>
> The boat was now seen close under the stern; we were at the same time lying to, to prevent the ship fore-reaching. Immediately on sounding this last time, the topsails were filled; but before the tacks were hauled on board, and the sails trimmed, she struck on a reef of rocks, and at that instant the boat got on board. Every possible effort was attempted to get her off by the sails; but that failing, they were furled, and the boats hoisted out with a view to carry out an anchor. Before that was accomplished, the carpenter reported she had made 18 inches of water in fifteen minutes; and in a quarter of an hour more, she had nine feet of water in the hold. (Hamilton, G. 1793/1998.)

In darkness, in unknown waters and with a rising wind, the *Pandora* and her crew were in desperate straits. All hands were called to the pumps and to bale where they could, while some of the prisoners were released to help in the crisis. To add to the emergency the gusting wind grew rapidly to a full gale, and the storm that developed drove the ship bodily across the reef, crash by crash in a welter of flying spray. By 10 o'clock they were able to drop an anchor in deeper water at 15 fathoms. There, guns were manoeuvred overboard while others prepared a spare sail in an attempt to fother the leak, but it was not long before the pumps began to fail, other plans to save the ship were abandoned, and most of those aboard were put to frantic bailing to keep up with the inrush of the sea. Fearing the ship would sink, the other prisoners had broken out of their bonds, but Captain Edwards harshly ordered their re-attachment. To further restrain the desperate men in their cell handcuffs were applied, and despite the ship's predicament, armed sentries were also spared to watch over the captives.

The battle to save the ship continued without let all through the storm-lashed night. During those dark hours the *Pandora* took on a list which sent loosened guns careering across the decks, killing one man while another died beneath a falling spar. By daybreak the stricken frigate was settling fast. Realising then that all was lost, the officers ordered everything buoyant to be cut loose to provide floats with which to save lives. All the boats bar one had already been sent clear to avoid their loss. The heel of the ship increased steadily, reaching a point where water began to pour in through the larboard gun ports, though many of the crew still struggled manfully at the pumps in a last vain effort to check the slant of her masts against the raging sea.

The *Pandora* was doomed, nevertheless. As her bow dipped towards the leaping crests and curling waves began to break across her decks, those aboard began to save themselves as best they could. Captain Edwards was one of the first to leave the sinking ship. In the ensuing mayhem the shackled prisoners were forgotten by all but two of the crew. At the risk of his own life the bosun's mate climbed upon the wooden cell and threw the scuttle clear, while the master-at-arms dropped in the keys before saving himself.

Imagine then the frenzy amongst the mutineers as the ship heeled her last. The scrabble for the sliding keys as water surged into their accursed prison, the swirl of flotsam about their chests, and the tumble of spars and parting rigging which threatened to entomb all as *Pandora* began to slide beneath the waves—all to the groans of straining timbers, the crash of shifting cannon and tumbling barrels, the anguished cries of drowning men, and the mighty roar of the triumphant sea. Panic indeed, and every man for himself as the drive for survival trampled former mates underfoot, clutching hands sought to push or pull obstructing bodies away or through the only narrow exit, and then the gasping, bubbling struggle to reach the surface of the overwhelming tide before that final oblivion. It is something of a wonder that 10 of the 14 managed to escape, though a few may still have been free to assist with the overnight baling. At roll call next day, four of the prisoners were found to have gone down with the ship, along with 31 of her unfortunate crew. There were 99 survivors.

For a day or so the survivors gathered what they could from the wreckage, and collected it together on an island nearby. There was pitifully little. Food and water were in short supply since there had been no time to gather enough to fill the needs of a hundred hungry men. And they were far away from any other form of help or sustenance. Rationing would be severe. Fortunately they had managed to save four of the ship's boats and it was at this time that Captain Edwards came into his own as a true naval officer. Discipline was established, and a plan devised to head west from the cays towards Timor, as William Bligh had done. Parties were divided between each of the four boats, and appropriate rations allocated as far as they would go.

Through all these preparations Edwards' attitude towards the mutineers remained unchanged and he was not softened by their naked plight.

He would only spare them enough to get them back to England alive, and beneath a merciless sun the luckless 10 had to bury themselves in the sand to minimise sunburn and dehydration. Even so, their pale skin peeled away in shreds, and they spent the rest of their time in the boats in cruel discomfort.

Captain Edwards' voyage from the wreck site began on 31st of August, and carried the *Pandora*'s survivors to Timor just 11 days later. From there they reached Batavia, all without losing a man. At the Dutch port they obtained passage aboard a Dutch vessel bound for Europe, but on reaching South Africa were able to transfer to a British ship for the last leg to England, which they reached on 18th of June, 1792. His mission complete, the 10 captives were handed over into naval custody to await trial for mutiny—an offence which carried the death penalty.

At the subsequent court martial four of the ten were acquitted as being reluctant participants in the mutiny. Of the original 25 who had sailed away in the *Bounty* after abandoning her master and his followers to their fate, 13 had gone unwillingly with Fletcher Christian and his men as people who were essential to the continued running of the ship—carpenters, the armourer, the cook, a sail-maker and a navigator, for instance. The remaining six were sentenced to death, three of whom were duly hanged from the yardarm in the prevailing naval tradition, while the other three were pardoned.

Christian himself, and those who sailed to Pitcairn Island with him after leaving 12 of their associates on Tahiti (two of whom were killed on the islands prior to the arrival of HMS *Pandora*), all escaped British justice only to suffer a form of natural justice at the hands of their Tahitian *confrères*. Pitcairn remained a secure haven for the mutiny's ringleaders until the island was rediscovered on 14th of May, 1809 by the American whaler *Topaz*. Her master, Captain Folger, landed there to find 'natives' who spoke English. Their leader, an Englishman called

Alexander Smith who was also known as John Adams, proved to be the only survivor of the *Bounty* mutineers after the others had been killed in a revolt by the Tahitians over their treatment. A British frigate called in at the island some 30 years later and found Adams still living as head of an island population of 40. However, the changes in attitude to naval justice during this time had been such that Adams was not taken back to England for trial, but allowed to remain on the island to spend the rest of his days in peace.

As an end to the saga, there was still to be one final irony concerning the main purpose of the *Bounty* voyage and the lesser objective intended for the *Pandora*'s—the collection and delivery of the humble breadfruit. To celebrate their triumph, the mutineers had thrown all those stowed aboard the *Bounty* into the sea. Captain Edwards had therefore collected more breadfruit from Tahiti, but these were also lost. Undaunted by his recent experiences, in 1792 Lieutenant Bligh again went off on yet another breadfruit expedition, this time to be fulfilled—but as the breadfruit proved to be an unappetising alternative to the bread it was supposed to resemble when roasted, it was entirely rejected by the slaves on West Indies' plantations.

HMS *Pandora* sank in 17 fathoms of water on the Great Barrier Reef, approximately 110 miles south-east of Cape York. She was the first recorded shipwreck off this part of Australia. The site of her loss became known as the Pandora Entrance, and there she lay for 187 years until she was rediscovered in 1977. The first serious attempt to locate the *Pandora* had taken place seven years earlier, but without success. Deep-water searches are often costly and time-consuming even within the confined waters of the Great Barrier Reef, and are not to be undertaken lightly. To finally pinpoint the wreck location, it took a considerable amount of research amongst British naval archives, the combined efforts of two well-equipped diving teams, and the cooperation of the Royal Australian Air Force (RAAF) using a Neptune aircraft equipped with a magnetometer and other sophisticated sensing gear.

Despite the intense rivalry between the two search teams, headed by marine scientist Steven Bomm and dive celebrity Ben Cropp, their joint research had narrowed down the likely wreck sites to an area less than 2 kilometres in diameter. There were some nail-biting moments on 15th of November, 1977, therefore, as each team watched the RAAF Neptune checking out first one prospective site, and then another, from their respective vessels. Then success, as smoke flares fell from the aircraft, and both boats dashed in to drop marker buoys and divers to confirm the RAAF's equipment readings. There on the sea floor was the certain outline of an old shipwreck, one measuring about 40×10 metres, with the encrusted remains of two cannon immediately visible close by the arching fluke of a large Admiralty pattern anchor. The *Pandora* had been found!

After various 'firsts' had been claimed—'first to see', 'first to lay hands on', 'first to recover artefacts to aid identification'—telegrams were sent to notify the Minister for Home Affairs of the discovery. Within 48 hours the *Pandora* had been declared a protected historic shipwreck under the 1976 *Historic Shipwrecks Act*, in legislation that was especially extended to cover Queensland waters. A reward of $10 000 was subsequently awarded to the two team leaders under the same Act, in recognition of their successful venture.

HMS *Pandora* is perhaps the most important shipwreck known today on the east coast of Australia. Her remains embody historical, archaeological and social values of international significance. As well as representing the sequel to the mutiny on the *Bounty*, in her own right she offers a picture of life aboard one of the lesser elements of the Royal Navy towards the end of the 18th century, while also being a mute testimony to South Sea explorations around the time when the colony at Port Jackson was only three or four years old. The wreck is both exciting and evocative—but also a tempting target for would-be fossickers and treasure seekers. Responsibility for securing, recovering and conserving the *Pandora*'s remains is therefore vested in the Queensland Museum, whose Maritime Archaeology Department engages in regular expeditions to the wreck site for these purposes, in association with the Australian Maritime Museum and the Western Australian Maritime Museum.

The wreck had been found 30 metres deep on an almost level bed of coral sand, lying roughly NNW by SSE, bow downwards to the north with a list to starboard. The remains were so ordered as to suggest a gentle bottoming and later disintegration, with no disturbance as a result of local turbulence. The first expedition, in 1979, was to confirm that the shipwreck was indeed that of the *Pandora*, and to assess its archaeological significance and the prospects for future excavations. These were judged to be potentially highly revealing, since much of the hull appeared to be buried beneath the sand. A second expedition in 1983 established a survey grid across the site to assist in plotting the position of various parts of the wreck, and all artefacts found in association. A large number of maritime archaeologists from all over Australia participated in this first 5-week season, since underwater activities at those depths were limited to a mere two 18–20 minute dives each per day, weather permitting. Before the close of the season, however, the first artefacts had been raised, including one of the *Pandora*'s cannons, a 6-pounder measuring 2.7 metres in length and weighing over a ton.

Survey work and excavations have continued since over a series of all-too-brief seasons. On such an exposed site, where wind, waves and currents often surge in conflict amongst the coral outcrops, the extent of activities is largely determined by weather and sea conditions. The work in any case is painstakingly slow and laborious, but even so, a wide variety of artefacts has been found. As well as the larger cannon, anchors, the ship's oven, metal rudder fittings and copper sheathing, many smaller items such as glassware, stone jars, buttons, personal items, the contents of Surgeon Hamilton's apothecary and even his silver fob watch, have also been collected. Human remains, too, have come to light, both as grim reminders of the tragedy as a whole, and of the incarcerated souls chained and drowned within *Pandora*'s Box.

Each item recovered must be carefully raised, bagged, tagged and securely stored as the first conservation essentials. Only one or two small sections of the wreck are treated at any one time. Then to preserve the wreck itself, all the sand that is removed must be replaced at the end of each season. The *Pandora* was a relatively large ship, and it appears that much of her still remains beneath the sands. Both excavation and conservation take time, and so it seems there are many seasons of careful work ahead yet before all of *Pandora*'s secrets are known. Whether the hull itself will be raised eventually remains to be seen. Such a project would inevitably require a multi-million dollar undertaking likely to involve years of planning, unknown problems in deep and exposed waters, and, as England's *Mary Rose* project would testify, more years still for its total preservation.

The 1999 expedition was 39 members strong, and research continues on the assemblage of material recovered so far, on work that ranges as broadly as: DNA extraction from human bones; the contents and purpose of substances in surgeon George Hamilton's pharmacy; the process of disintegration of shipwrecks; the reflections of social status to be found in the belongings of officers and crewmen; and an analysis of Polynesian fish hooks and lures that were taken aboard *Pandora* as souvenirs.

Chapter 6

CATARAQUI
1845

The *Cataraqui*.

*'The collision threw many of those lying miserably below out of their
bunks and into a state of panic ... In the darkness pandemonium
reigned as women screamed, families cried out for each other, and the
men shouted ...'*

Great Britain in the early decades of the 19th century was a land of sharp economic contrasts and deep social inequalities. On the one hand were the wealthy industrialists, the successful cotton kings and coal, wool and railway barons, the prosperous merchants and bankers, and the hereditary landowners, all of whom supported the growth of new technology, improved efficiency and higher profits in their enterprises. This was a reflection of developments sparked by the on-going industrial revolution, the commercial trends which stemmed from the recent Continental wars, and the burgeoning trade drive associated with the spread of Britain's empire.

On the other hand there were many in poverty as a result of land enclosures and large-scale industrialisation, the rising cost of living and poor wages. Many smallholders and farm tenants had been evicted following extensive land consolidation and the introduction of new farming methods. Large numbers of process workers in the once widespread rural cottage industries were made redundant by the introduction of factories and new machinery. Industries shifting in response to energy and raw material sources and transport connections abandoned age-old skills in people they no longer needed. Economic imbalances were rife.

For those losing their livelihood in the countryside, Britain's growing towns and cities became a focus of hope. Rural dwellers began to move away in large numbers expecting to find work there, or in new industries elsewhere. Itinerant jobbers desperately sought employment wherever they could find it, often in competition with the urban unemployed, child labourers, the hungry and the destitute. The age-old Poor Laws had failed to remedy the lot of such people. Work-houses soon became poor-houses, institutions of last resort. The jails were full of those driven to petty crime in order to survive.

The families of the lower classes at this time were frequently large, and their incomes correspondingly small—assuming suitable work was available. Better water and drainage services were helping to improve general health and reduce infant mortality, which brought increasing population pressures without commensurate growth in employment opportunities, or at least in employment where it was most needed. Britain was prospering, riding the wave of entrepreneurial success in commerce, manufacturing and expanded trade, but at the cost of much social dislocation.

Little wonder then, that when chances arose to leave such misery and venture off to the colonies abroad, many were willing to go. The alternatives were stark: leave, face the perils of the journey and hope for better luck elsewhere, or stay and starve. The situation in Ireland was becoming especially critical. A total of 367 of these so-called 'able-bodied poor' and their families thus embarked on the emigrant ship *Cataraqui* in Liverpool on 19th of April, 1845, to sail the following day for Port Phillip, Australia. They had nothing to lose and everything to gain in a new country on the other side of the world. With them went a crew of 44.

The escape from penury and the attractions of a new home were not the only factors which persuaded migrants such as these to risk all on a chance of betterment. Their passages were free. Those aboard the *Cataraqui* were the last of a larger group of 'Statute Adults' being carried under the bounty system whereby ship owners contracted with the then New South Wales Government to take selected migrants to Australia, with a bounty to be paid per head on arrival. Furthermore, efforts were also made to persuade extended kin to travel together for mutual support and encouragement. It was a system which enabled the Poor Law

Commissioners and regional Poor Law Unions to use family connections to rid themselves of whole and often large extended families this way, their only cost being the provision of suitable clothing (from work-house supplies) and fares to ports of embarkation. Others received help from the church and various charities.

Some two-thirds of the *Cataraqui*'s passengers therefore came from quite localised parts of England, in particular a dozen or so closely-connected villages within a 15-mile circle between Bedford and Cambridge, and nine villages in a similar area to the east of Oxford. Smaller numbers came from villages near Lincoln, Nottingham and Leicester, but the bulk of the remainder were from various parts of Ireland. Without exception, all were of one class.

While the English passengers were mainly couples or young family groups, many with at least seven children, more of the Irish were couples or single people, 26 being single girls. Over a third of the migrants were aged between 15 and 30, and only 10 were aged 40-plus. Children aged 14 and under numbered 171. Given the excitement of the voyage, the freedom from the constraints of society and the promises of the new land, the *Cataraqui*'s first trip to Australia was very likely a jolly one, at least in its early stages. Everyone was eagerly looking forward to a bright new life.

The first half of the trip, the six-week 6000-mile passage to Cape Town, passed uneventfully while the different groups adjusted to ship-board life. During the first week or two the food would have been fresh and adequate, perhaps better than most were used to. The weather remained warm and fine, allowing them time on deck with opportunities to get to know each other, away from the cramped accommodation below. The children no doubt played noisily together under the watchful eyes of the master, Captain Christopher Finlay and the Surgeon-Superintendent, Dr Carpenter, while the ever-segregated young singles sought stronger acquaintance wherever possible. The evenings would have been filled with supervised songs and dancing until lights-out, or the weather determined otherwise.

The weather apparently continued fair even after the *Cataraqui* rounded the southern tip of Africa about the beginning of July, and entered the Indian Ocean. As she pressed southwards to meet the speeding winds of the latitudes known as the Roaring Forties, however, all of this changed. Being winter in these southerly climes, it became progressively colder. The winds blew more strongly with occasional gales and hail storms, while rain squalls increased in both frequency and intensity. Gone were the sunny days and balmy evenings of the Atlantic summer and the heat of the tropics. Where once the passengers could relax on deck, or feel cooling breezes blowing through the ship, now they were confined below with companionways and hatches closed up and battened down, and skylights and scuttles fully secured. The weather worsened halfway across the Indian Ocean, the sole benefit being faster sailing as the ship pitched and rolled incessantly, to the discomfort of all aboard.

The last two weeks of the voyage became a nightmare of suffering during which six of the infants died. The motion of the ship brought nausea, misery and fear. Crashing seas found their way below where water ran in cascades amongst loose possessions. It leaked through the decking, found its way over hatch coamings, and poured in through broken skylights to drench the suffering migrants and their bedding and spare clothing equally. At the worst times when the ship shuddered convulsively and her list seemed such that she must surely capsize, panic would set in amongst the women and children, and not a few of the men who feared for themselves and their families. In the dark confines of the storm-tossed ship conditions then became indescribable, a bedlam. Nevertheless, the crew went about their work stoically, the ship was stoutly built and only five years old. Despite their experiences the migrants' unhappy ordeal was no worse than any other at sea about this particular time.

On a particularly wild, storm-wracked night in early August, on her approach to Bass Strait and Melbourne, the laden ship had struggled to a standstill through heavy rain and high seas. Visibility was near zero in the blackness of the southern waters, especially so at a time of year when fog, clouds, rain and spray obscured moon and stars, and everything else. Somewhere in the murk to port, Cape Otway marked the entrance to Bass Strait, while off to starboard, equally unseen, the bulk of King Island sprawled across the path of any vessel rash enough to attempt a passage in such conditions. Because Captain Finlay was unsure of his position, he had prudently heaved-to as darkness fell, letting the ship ride with helm lashed a-lee under much-shortened sail, her head to wind. There were as yet no welcoming lighthouses on the unseen coast, either to give assurance of its proximity or to warn of the hazards of the Strait, and any other lights might well have been non-existent.

As she lay hove-to in the darkness, hurricane-strength winds and violent waves tossed the ship helplessly to and fro in a frenzy of the elements. Due to the weather of the last four days, Captain Finlay had been without sights of sun or stars to help plot *Cataraqui*'s whereabouts on the Southern Ocean. Dead reckoning, based on nothing more than estimates of the distance travelled from the last known position under the influence of winds and currents—now in ferocious conflict—placed him at latitude 39°10' South, longitude 142°20' East, or approximately 60 or 70 miles from the western entrance of Bass Strait. If he was right, daylight on the morrow should see them pass to the north of King Island. Meanwhile, his overnight caution was fully justified with the safety of more than 400 souls in his keeping.

Around 3.00am on 4th of August, to make up lost time, he ordered sufficient sail set (three close-reefed topsails and a reefed foresail) in order to enter Bass Strait in better light soon after dawn. It was his second fatal mistake, the first being his earlier dead reckoning estimate which had placed him 60 miles north of his true position directly opposite the notorious King Island. An hour and a half later, in conditions little better than those experienced overnight and still in total darkness, Captain Finlay's ship drove hard up onto King Island's rugged south-western reefs. As the island's latest victim, the *Cataraqui* was also about to become what would always remain as the worst disaster in Australia's maritime history.

The rending impact as the ship struck the reef flung the helmsman away from the wheel and jolted the rest of the crew into instant action to save the ship. They had no doubts as to what had happened. The collision threw many of those lying miserably below out of their bunks and into a state of panic and utter confusion, their worst fears realised. In the darkness pandemonium reigned as women screamed, families cried out for each other, and the men shouted for answers or assistance in their plight. Then came a second shock as the ship struck again, careering over another reef to crash then into a third, where she finally stopped and canted over.

Almost immediately the following seas took over in raging torrents, sweeping the *Cataraqui* from end to end, bent on final destruction. The crew turned to help passengers struggling up from below against the surging waves and the blast of the storm. People fell and were swept aside in the confusion on deck, crying out in their distress while Captain Finlay and his officers tried to assess the state of the ship. Very soon it became clear that the ship could not be saved and from amongst the desperate crowd on deck Captain Finlay mustered enough seamen to begin cutting away the masts to stabilise her remains, and to give those on board something to cling to. Already the pounding seas had swept people away, but nothing could be done to save anyone until daylight.

Many drowned within the ship after the stairs to the deck collapsed, trapping them below.

The sight which people saw at daybreak was one of bleak desolation—land only a little way ahead of the wreck, which was now breaking up from the stern, but the intervening distance filled with sharp serried rocks around which the angry sea boiled and crashed. Mountainous waves continued to sweep their flimsy refuge, plucking away a child here, a crew-member there with every surge, all to the accompaniment of wails, tears and abject prayers. The cold wind and icy wetness of the winter day, the stark forlornness of the blustering storm, were also taking a toll. The weaker folk, especially the younger children, soon succumbed to shock and exposure, remaining lifeless on the bosoms of their parents, or slowly releasing their hold on life to be swept away in turn.

The list to port grew progressively worse as the hull of the stricken ship canted further over. Perches became perilous and holds gave way, the streaming deck pitching more people into the threatening sea. Boats fell away from their chocks or were stove in under the weight and thrust of water on deck. Attempts to launch the last boat failed with its crew slipping, cursing and drowning by degrees beneath the deluge, finally to be capsized and lost in the relentless surf. Brave attempts to reach land by swimming or clutching at flotsam ended on the jagged reef where many were rendered senseless, and then engulfed. Efforts to float a line beyond the rocky barrier were thwarted by thick bands of kelp. No one reached the nearby shore alive throughout that dreadful day, while the number clinging to the *Cataraqui's* remains steadily diminished.

The first person to land on the broken beach did so more dead than alive, nearly 24 hours after the first strike. Mercifully, the darkness cloaked a sea of battered and dismembered bodies which was all that remained of many once-hopeful migrants, lost within sight of their promised land. With the coming of daylight once more, children could be seen floating palely in the heaving waters, the battered bodies of their parents mounding the beach. Bodies of crewmen seemed to cling doggedly to rocks even in death, while everywhere it seemed lay the near-naked corpses of so many young men and women, extinguished in their prime. Wreckage from the ship was beginning to litter the rocky shoreline for miles in either direction.

From a vessel bearing 367 people to new lives in Australia, together with her crew of 44, only 9 survived. All but one were crew. Over 400 had died. Those who had managed to stay alive throughout the horrendous calamity had clung grimly to the bow as the ship steadily disintegrated, and floated or were flung ashore when this also finally collapsed. Forty others with them were less fortunate, and they too died from the combined effects of grief, shock and exposure, in the still raging sea, or on the waiting reef. The one surviving passenger was Solomon Brown, the first man ashore, who had boarded in Liverpool with his wife Hanna and four children. All had perished, along with nearly 50 other families.

The survivors lay cold and stunned, spray-drenched and wind-swept for some time while they took in the enormity of the disaster. The nine came slowly together at daybreak, appalled that so many had been lost. The scene on the beaches of intermingled bodies, flotsam, parts of the cargo and personal effects told of their worst nightmares. As they stood together surveying the desolation, nothing they could say gave adequate description to the horror and mutilation all around. Though others had been alive that morning, including the captain and his second mate, there were now no signs of life around the shattered wreck. They had little idea initially of where they were, though Guthery, the Chief Mate, felt they were on King Island. Their refuge appeared low-lying and treeless, and as bleak as the weather. They had neither food nor water—but they would have to survive there for the next six weeks.

Though they were cast up on what was clearly a deserted shore, and in all likelihood a remote island, the nine survivors had not long to wait before being discovered. Thinking they may have been stranded some-where on the mainland, the main fear of the castaways was attack by hostile inhabitants, against whom they would have been powerless. It was with some relief, therefore, when the solitary figure they saw approaching on the day following their salvation turned out to be a white man, and a Scotsman to boot. He was able to confirm that they were not on the mainland, that there was no fear of native attack on the largely uninhabited King Island, but rescue might be some time coming since visiting vessels were rare. His name was David Howie, a former convict, and he was on the island to collect seal and kangaroo skins.

Howie's presence undoubtedly saved the lives of the castaways on this shelterless strand, and eventually helped to carry news of the *Cataraqui* tragedy together with her survivors to the worried authorities in Mel-bourne. The *Cataraqui* had been listed as overdue, but her fate or whereabouts were not known at the time the survivors arrived at Port Phillip. Howie's own inkling of something greatly amiss on the island coast came with the sighting of wreckage drifting in the vicinity of Yellow Rock River where the Scot and his party were at work, some 35 miles north of the wreck site. Suspecting the worst in view of the foul weather of the last few days, and being very aware of the island's record as a trap for Strait shipping, Howie immediately divided his party to scour round the coast in both directions. Though they were uncertain of when the wreck occurred, it seemed likely that any survivors would be faring badly in the winter storms without help or shelter.

The survivors were fortunate in being found by David Howie within a day or so of leaving the wreck, for they were indeed in a poor state. However, he was able to leave them the food he had brought, make up a fire and build them a rough shelter before returning to his own camp for more supplies, which he and his party then hauled across country to the site of the *Cataraqui* wreck. In case a visiting ship called at the Yellow

Rock camp, Howie penned a note with details of the wreck and attached it to the door of the hut. It was a precaution that might have brought an early rescue had it been noted by the men of the barque *Governor Gawler*, which very soon sought shelter from a rising storm under the lee of New Year's Island, across from the Yellow Rock River. Though entranced by their anchorage and spending time ashore on New Year's Island, Captain Underwood did not visit Yellow Rock camp across the water. After 12 days he sailed away to Portland with no more knowledge of the *Cataraqui* disaster than when he arrived.

More propitious was the visit of the cutter *Midge* a fortnight later, whose skipper did call at the deserted camp and found Howie's note. Immediately he sailed south to find the wreck site and the survivors, despite the dangers his small craft might face in the shape of seasonal storms and off-shore reefs. At the place where the *Cataraqui* came to grief, the reefs were at their worst—high and craggy, and difficult to approach. Rescuing the survivors took no less than three days, the anchored vessel at all times exposed to the risk of further gales. Fortunately the weather held. On the 9th of September, 1845, the *Midge* departed King Island with the *Cataraqui*'s nine survivors and arrived in Melbourne early in the morning five days later.

The news of the survivors' rescue and the story they had to tell shocked Melbourne. Fears for the *Cataraqui*'s safety were growing since the ship was well overdue. She had been expected in Port Phillip during the second week of August, and vessels leaving Liverpool after the emigrant ship were arriving without having sighted her. The emigrants aboard the *Cataraqui* were eagerly awaited to help solve the growing problem of farm labour shortages, but this gave way to increasing anxiety as the days passed without news. On the Saturday morning the survivors arrived, their news was too late for the normal press. The loss of over 400 lives was a major tragedy, for which hurried copy was compiled. Horror and disbelief followed the somewhat distorted early accounts, but the plain fact remained—a large ship had been lost with almost its entire complement, and at a point where lighthouses had long been advocated, but had not been built. There would be a calling to account for this, and for the loss of the ship itself . . .

The need for strategically-placed lighthouses along Australia's wild southern coast had long been debated in the New South Wales Parliament, then responsible for the Port Phillip District, without result. During the inevitable public meetings which followed in the wake of the tragedy, many demands and resolutions were made to press the Government for urgent action on essential lights, and an end to purposeless debate and procrastination. Some of these same meetings sought to point the finger of blame at Captain Finlay for gross mismanagement and poor seamanship, at the ship's builders for shoddy workmanship, or at the owners for having greater interest in pursuing substantial insurance claims. The statements were both emotional and premature in the absence of fact or firm evidence.

In time, the official reports on the *Cataraqui* tragedy would attach no blame to either Captain Finlay or his Chief Mate Guthery. Each of them had been selected for their roles, and both were well-experienced and highly regarded. Nor was there any question concerning the seaworthiness of the ship. As required by Britain's Colonial Land and Emigration Commissioners and Lloyds maritime underwriters, the *Cataraqui* had been thoroughly examined in a Liverpool dry-dock before taking on her role as an emigrant ship, and was found to be entirely sound and appropriately fitted out.

As a result of the wreck of the *Cataraqui*, moves towards the establishment of lighthouses on prominent capes and island bluffs progressed a little faster, though their construction invariably took considerable time. By the end of 1846 preparations were well advanced for the building of lights at Cape Howe, Gabo Island, and on the Kent Group in Bass Strait. The light for King Island's Cape Wickham took rather longer, however, and did not operate until three years after the *Cataraqui* was lost. Even then it was not especially effective as later wrecks were to demonstrate, and so a larger and higher one was completed at the Cape in 1861.

While others sought to analyse the causes of the disaster and take the Government to task on its neglected responsibilities, there remained the grisly consideration of what to do about the 400 victims on King Island who had not been given proper burial. Before the survivors were taken aboard the *Midge*, only a few burials had been possible, there being only one spade on the entire island. In any case, the task of drawing together the 400 dead, or their dismembered remains, was far beyond the capacities of the few who had themselves been near-victims. For them it was all too recent, and too disturbing. Even so, it concerned Superintendent La Trobe that so many of the dead still lay unburied on the distant barren shore, to the point where he proposed to send an interment party over to King Island as soon as the seasonal weather improved. He was also concerned to have a suitable monument placed at the site of the tragedy.

His proposal was not long aired before David Howie entered the picture once more, willing to take on the task of burial for an agreed sum. Though there was some hesitation over Howie's convict past in giving him the job, few others were as willing. Two weeks after delivering the few survivors into Melbourne, David Howie sailed again for King Island on the cutter *Mary Jane*, in company with Alexander Sutherland who had gained salvage rights to the wreck, and two or three others. Howie's instructions were to assemble as many of the human remains as possible to bury them in one place, at the same time keeping appropriate records of the number of bodies found, and the graves into which they were placed. For his trouble, Howie was to receive the sum of £50.

David Howie returned to Melbourne three months later, having completed his task. He and his men had dug five graves near the wreck site, the largest being 16 feet × 12 feet × 12 feet deep into which they had put the remains of 206 victims, the smallest being 7 feet × 6 feet × 5 feet deep to contain those of 10 victims. Other graves were dug at isolated spots to bury smaller numbers. In all, they were able to lay to rest 342 of those who died with the *Cataraqui*. A monument was put in place three years later but time, neglect, and the raw elements saw its eventual destruction. In 1956 another memorial tablet was put in place, but by then the locations of the graves had become overgrown and lost. It was not until the 150th anniversary of the wreck in 1995 that efforts were made to relocate and clear the graves, which are marked now as a significant part of our early maritime heritage.

An aspect of melancholy pervades this wind-swept site, which on occasions is said to be something tangible, enhanced perhaps by a grey sky and a greyer sea on the approach of yet another winter or out-of-season storm. Maybe the spirits of the dead still linger. Little remains of the *Cataraqui* herself, the wild seas having scattered her traces far and wide along the coast, but over the years many small items have been found amongst the rocks and reefs at low tide. In 1975 a group of divers recovered two cannon and an anchor from the ship, along with a collection of cutlery and a range of ship's fittings. Most of these items can be seen today in the King Island Museum in Currie.

Chapter 7

DUNBAR & CATHERINE ADAMSON

1857

The *Dunbar*.

'The first cascades of seawater followed the thunder of contact with submerged rocks . . . Passengers drowned in the rising frenzy and the struggle to survive, which was short-lived for most in the Stygian blackness of their flooding tomb.'

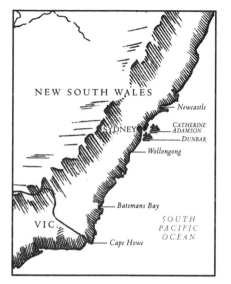

It was indeed 'a dark and stormy night' around midnight of Thursday, 20th of August, 1857, out to sea off Sydney Heads—a foul night of shifting cloud, swirling fog and teeming rain above heaving seas, all in the thick of a howling north-easterly gale. It was a primordial night, spawned in the blackness of the elements, plucked from the beginnings of time.

Mighty waves rolled in through the darkness under pressure from the driving winds to dash themselves to pieces at the foot of unseen cliffs. Columns of spray were flung high in the air to join the descending torrent, while their broken bases recoiled from the bastion of the hidden land to hurl forward again in a timeless repetition. The seas boiled in confusion as the backwash from streaming rock walls surged amongst the advancing rollers—leaping, swirling, seething in spume-streaked turmoil. And into this rode the migrant clipper *Dunbar*, skippered by Captain James Green, groping slowly, blindly towards the land and the promise of safety, yet holding off for fear of the unknown—the hazards of night and a perilous storm.

Somewhere ahead lay her sought-after haven and the solitary light which guarded a narrow entrance through the craggy coastal barricade. The single beam of the South Head's Macquarie Light had swept the seas and pierced the blackness for nearly 40 years, beckoning ships to the shelter of Sydney's inner harbour. Ships had often welcomed this friendly beacon on the far side of the world, near the end of long passages from Europe and America, particularly when winter's bitter winds screeched through the rigging and wild seas broke across the decks in the age-old struggle between men and the world's oceans. Never was the light more gladly seen than on this night, as it first pierced the gloom on the port bow, giving both a welcome and a warning that a haven was close, but so were the rocks and reefs of the narrow Heads.

Only a few hours earlier, just on dusk, the *Dunbar*'s eager passengers and crew caught their first glimpse of the Sydney coastline through the intermittent rain off Botany Bay. This landfall promised home and security for some of the old colonists the following morning, and the beginning of a new life in a young country for the rest. Almost three months ago their ship had left the busy port of Plymouth, England, at the start of her second voyage to Australia. For the migrants this was the start of an adventure—an apprehensive leap into the unknown in a new land—while the others on board who were now returning home told of their own success and prosperity. All were excited by the prospect of arriving in Sydney the next day.

Their only other sightings of Australia had been at King Island in Bass Strait a few days earlier, and the turn of the coast around Cape Howe onto their last leg to Sydney. The stories they had heard of shipwrecks in Bass Strait and its threatening winds and weather at this time of the year had caused a stir amongst the more nervous of the passengers. However, they had then been jovially assured by Captain Green that he had threaded this particular needle many times before, and that the gap between the mainland and the island was at least 50 miles wide. It had been a relief, nevertheless, to learn one morning that they had passed safely through the Strait during the night on the breast of a stiff south-westerly. The way was now clear, with only a dozen miles to go before they gained entry to Sydney's beautiful landlocked harbour.

But that was before the gale—a winter's gale at that. This was not just a brisk blow that was good for the constitution, but one that Captain Green knew to be a 'black nor'easter' in local parlance, and likely to get worse before it got better. The wind had changed direction and picked up soon after dark. Heavy rain squalls were already sweeping the pitching deck. Now they faced a winter storm on a lee shore, seeking guidance from a light they badly needed but could barely see. There it was again, flashing through the murk every 90 seconds—when it was visible—a mile or so south of the mile-wide passage he was aiming for.

Sydney Heads—no 50-mile gap this one, like the 'Eye of the Needle' as they called Bass Strait after world-circling voyages, nor even like the two-and-a-half miles of the notorious Rip, the turbulent channel at the mouth of Victoria's Port Phillip Bay. With little latitude for error, Captain Green would need a perfect bull's-eye to hit his narrow target this particular night. Thank God for his experience and knowledge of previous visits, and the chance to visualise what the charts didn't show, and what he couldn't see anyway. Where *was* that light?

The Captain peered anxiously through the dark of midnight, spray slashing his face, bouncing off his oilskins, stinging his eyes. The hunched shapes of the two men straining at the nearby wheel were barely discernible through the slanting rain and beating wind. As one lookout was no longer safe, more eyes would be needed for'ard soon if the ship was to pass through the Heads and anchor in sheltered waters tonight. The *Dunbar* heaved and plunged through the mounting waves, rolling against the shrouded sky in a motion which told of shallowing waters beginning to absorb the energies of the huge Pacific swells. The rigging screamed anew in a violent gust which sent waves flying high over the starboard quarter to crash heavily across the deck.

Conditions were clearly deteriorating, and the prospect posed a fresh dilemma for the clipper's master. Should he still try to enter the harbour tonight before the weather closed in completely, or stand off until daylight tomorrow or the day after and subject his passengers to the miseries of seasickness so close to sanctuary? It was hard to know just how long the gale would last or how bad it might become, but this certainly wasn't the place to be at the wrong time, that much he knew. His distance from the lee shore was only a best estimate based on his last sighting, his compass heading, and glimpses of the intermittent light. As the gale was blowing strongly shoreward, the *Dunbar* would doubtless be making leeway he was unable to measure. On such a night as this, any miscalculation could spell disaster.

The light flashed again dimly through the sheeting rain, beckoning, telling him he was still on track and so making the decision for him. He would make the run in.

———————

Sydney was comfortably battened down that night as rain slashed the streets and gusting winds rattled the roofs and gables of the town. No one ventured forth on nights like this, though one or two people did have a need to stay awake and alert, especially those on duty at the coastal stations. The keeper of the Macquarie Light went to check the working of his lamp a number of times to ensure its continuity as the weather blasted around its exposed housing. On one occasion the duty personnel of the nearby signal station saw lights dimly out to sea through the cliff-top murk. The wife of one, James Graham, was later reported to have awakened from a bad dream in which she saw a large vessel in difficulties at the nearby Heads, but dismissed it as a manifestation of the noises made by the wind and the rain.

But in the seas below, Mrs Graham's dream was beginning to turn into a reality. Having made his decision to attempt a transit of the Heads, Captain Green had called for more sail and sent James Spence and John Pascoe, the second and third mates, forward to the forecastle to warn of breakers that might herald danger ahead. Captain Green himself had seen the Macquarie Light again, much closer on the port bow and so knew that by bearing away to starboard a mile or so he could begin his run through the Heads to safety. He had to be certain of not over-running the entrance in clearing South Head, however, and therefore he needed to know the position of North Head if it could be seen.

Then with chilling suddenness came a lookout's cry of, '*Breakers ahead!*' Captain Green instantly snapped out orders to haul the ship to starboard, away from the looming danger. What was it? In his mind the breakers no doubt signified the proximity of a reef, possibly that known as the Sow and Pigs, if they were passing too close to South Head, pushed by the wind in reduced visibility. But then the cliff top light flashed its warning once again—from immediately above their swaying masts! They were hopelessly out of position, with little seaway beneath the menacing cliffs. Desperately the crew tried to wear the ship round and away from danger, but the *Dunbar* continued to wallow sluggishly with no momentum and insufficient sail to take a grip on the wind and draw away against the press of the waves. A blue distress rocket was let off which soared high over the cliffs, though it brought no acknowledgement from above.

The wind shrieked loudly as the thunder of the ocean swells echoed from the rearing ramparts. For a few tense moments the crew worked desperately to stave off the inevitable disaster, while bewildered passengers began to emerge from below in response to the commotion on deck. Their screams and cries added to the din of distress, faintly heard above the booming waves and the unending shriek of the wind-whipped rigging. With the realisation of their nightmare situation came a surging sea which caught the stricken *Dunbar* on the beam, lifting her high against the rock face before dumping her with a resounding crash against the base of the cliff. The shock of the mighty collision jarred everyone to the deck, dislodging the topmasts, yards and supporting rigging from their mountings to be thrown down amongst the frantic gathering below. The dark night was filled with terror as the doomed vessel rolled heavily, broadside on into the next rushing sea, tearing away the lifeboats, crushing some people and hurling others to watery oblivion.

Down below, panic quickly took the place of sickening fear as the ship was first thrown aside, then lifted and dashed bodily against the unyielding rock. The few dim lights allowed in the accommodation areas were quickly extinguished, after which people fought, screamed and tripped in the dark amongst the tangle of personal belongings and other struggling bodies to get to the canting decks. Their horror was magnified by the first cascades of seawater which followed the thunder of contact with submerged rocks at the foot of the cliff, and which jetted ever more strongly with each fateful pounding of the splintering timbers. Passengers drowned in the rising frenzy and the struggle to survive, which was short-lived for most in the Stygian blackness of their flooding tomb.

Waves swamped across the ship and down companionways to meet the waters rising from below as she rose and fell in the grip of the breakers, seemingly struggling in death throes that were punctuated time and again with the grating crash of battering rocks. The surging seas swept the decks clear of everything except the drowning few caught in tangles of rigging and broken woodwork. Only a few minutes after the first smashing impact, the ship started to break up as the heavy masts came down, levering apart their supporting timbers and splintering the buckling deck beneath their weight. The shattered strakes then burst asunder as heavy cargo items tumbled forth, admitting the thrust of the seas which very quickly began tearing the remainder of the *Dunbar* to pieces. Barrels, crates and ragged spars were swept or thrown like so many rampant missiles against ancient rock and youthful bodies alike, battering, tearing, impaling, mutilating. And all the while, amidst the ceaseless roar of waves and weather, the Macquarie Light above the wreck maintained its impassionate 90-second swing casting brief illumination over the dread tableau below.

The next day the gale-force winds had abated little. Soon after daylight, men from the Watsons Bay Pilot Station were up on the cliffs to scan the seas beyond for any ships that might need a pilot after riding out the overnight storm. The men from the Signal Station were up early too, still puzzled by Mrs Graham's strange dream and keen to investigate the source of the lights they had seen the previous night. The sight that met their eyes at the foot of the cliff came as a cold shock. The wreckage of what had obviously been a large ship was swirling and turning in the rough seas below, with massive timbers and pieces of cargo being washed back and forth amongst the boiling waters. Worse still, there were bodies to be seen here and there, battered beyond recognition. Sydney was about to wake up to news of a major maritime disaster.

More than 120 people died in the wreck of the *Dunbar*—most of the 63 passengers in the chaos below decks and all but one of the 58 crew in the maelstrom of the sea. Only one man survived the tragedy, a young Irish seaman by the name of James Johnson, but even he lay exposed for nearly two days on a hidden ledge, a prey to the wild elements before he was spotted and recovered, barely alive. In the meantime, Signal Master James Graham had sent a hurried note to Sydney to alert the city authorities of the wreck. This was shortly confirmed when the masters of two coastal steamers, *Nora Creiner* and *Grafton*, reported entering the Heads in the early morning, the former having seen the *Dunbar* out at sea, the latter having passed through a wide debris field. Wreckage was also being washed up along the coast. This was soon followed by reports of the first shockingly battered bodies drifting ashore within the Harbour.

Still there were no clues as to the identity of the vessel. By mid-morning it had become clear that the ship was a large one, from the type and quantity of wreckage seen below the cliffs, from the items of cargo swirling amongst the broken seas, and from the mutilated bodies of women, children and animals. The nakedness of some of the bodies told of a night-time disaster, a victim of the storm. A count of those visible but still unreachable indicated the possibility of it being an immigrant vessel, with many more dead than could be seen. News of the wreck quickly spread through the nearby city, bringing forth hordes of sightseers and many people anxious to know the name of the ship and the fate of any relatives who may have been aboard. Boats were turned out to try to find some means of establishing the ship's identity. A reward was posted for anyone finding anything that might provide a name.

For a while there were fears that the vessel may have been the migrant ship *Vocalist*, which brought tears of grief amongst bystanders who were expecting friends or relatives aboard that particular ship. Late in the day, however, a comparison of certain pieces of cargo against invoices of what local traders were expecting from overseas was beginning to suggest that the ship was the *Dunbar*, then the pride of Britain's Duncan Dunbar Line. This was confirmed before nightfall by the discovery of a mailbag and some ship's stores bearing the name of the lost ship.

Many items from the wreck were already being brought in to aid the task of identifying both the ship and its passengers and crew. With moderating weather, the following day was therefore given over to the tasks of recovering as many of the bodies as could be found on the rocks and beaches beyond the Heads, and preparing those already brought ashore for identification and burial. For the first task the steamer *Black Swan* was chartered to act as mother ship to various search boats and the Water Police, but the scene on the quayside that Saturday morning resembled a near riot from people demanding to be carried to the scene of the wreck. Some claimed to have had connections with those on board the *Dunbar* and had a right to be there, while others attended through morbid curiosity. Force had to be used to restrain the over-eager, while the sight of many coffins being loaded aboard the steamer brought renewed anguish amongst those who had genuinely lost loved ones. The second task of identification was not easy as the bodies of those recovered so far were badly torn, bruised, or dismembered.

The extent of the disaster shocked the people of Sydney, all the more so because it had occurred virtually on their doorstep, almost within sight of the town. The one small consolation was the recovery of the crewman, James Johnson, who had been spotted on a ledge below the cliffs by a sightseer seeking a better view. Saturday had brought an excursion-like atmosphere to the wreck site, with many more people curious to visit the area around The Gap than on the previous day. The scene was no better as the men in the search boats went about their gruesome task of collecting the corpses and other human remains that could still be seen from the cliffs. For Johnson though, this may have been his salvation.

He had seen the crowds collecting on the cliffs and was waving feebly to attract attention. His position was such, however, that for a while he could not be reached, nor was he able to help himself. Long ropes were eventually brought out from Sydney, and a young man named Antonie Wollier volunteered to go down the rope to retrieve the survivor. A derrick had been erected on the cliffs, but it took the daring youngster two attempts to overcome his own fears and master the cliff face before Johnson could be reached and hauled to safety. Wollier himself was cheered roundly by the crowd, and reluctantly accepted an on-the-spot subscription pressed on him by the Mayor of Sydney, then an onlooker in the assembly.

In the immediate aftermath of the wreck many questions were put in the New South Wales Parliament, first in regard to the recovery and salvage processes, then seeking to determine how such a tragedy could have happened, and soon querying the adequacy of lights at the Heads, an issue that had been raised several times before without resolution. While this was going on the City Coroner had begun the process of formal identification, but only a dozen or so of the victims could be recognised. Many in attendance were deeply disturbed by the condition of the bodies. Meanwhile, out at the wreck site the looters and scavengers were secretly at work, stealing away with items of cargo and valuable fittings until a police guard was mounted to deter the thefts.

The question of lights was pursued by the *Sydney Morning Herald* on 24th of August, which echoed witnesses to a recent commission on coastal lights in saying that the entrance to Sydney Heads was not only poorly lit, but that the existing light, whilst efficient, was also potentially misleading. In hindsight, it was thought to have misled the late Captain Green despite his knowledge of the landlocked port. The newspaper pressed for urgent consideration of a light for the North Head, while the need for one there was reinforced during the subsequent Coroner's inquest, which also noted the need for improvements to the pilot service.

Later newspapers were full of editorial opinion and letters suggesting ways and means of preventing similar tragedies. In Parliament, the issues of a new lighthouse at North Head and improvements to the pilot service were again taken up. But while the debate continued, a Bill which might have addressed these concerns was defeated, and soon afterwards the defeat of the Government put the entire question of port safety on hold. Sydney had mourned the loss of the *Dunbar*, large crowds had gathered to pay their respects along the route of the victims' funeral cortege to Camperdown cemetery, the need for improved facilities at the harbour entrance was widely acknowledged but nothing had been done in time to avert a second major disaster at Sydney Heads only nine weeks later.

———

The *Catherine Adamson* was an Aberdeen Line clipper only half the size of the *Dunbar*, but being of a similar age and operating on the same routes she had quickly established a reputation as one of the fastest ships afloat, delivering mail between England and Australia in 68 days compared with the *Dunbar*'s performance of 81. In the latter half of 1857, the

Catherine Adamson had left England seven weeks after the *Dunbar*, also bound for Sydney, arriving off the Heads on the night of Friday, 23rd of October, with no knowledge of what had happened to the larger ship. Once again it was blowing up a gale, this time from the west, though conditions were nowhere near as bad as that fateful night in August—yet.

Captain Stuart, a part-owner in the *Catherine Adamson*, duly hove-to off the Heads around 9.00pm, and fired a blue light as a signal to those ashore that he required a pilot. The Signal Station acknowledged his request and notified Captain John Hawkes, who had recently assisted in the search for *Dunbar* survivors, that a ship awaited his services in negotiating the harbour entrance. Before long the pilot cutter emerged between the Heads, but by the time John Hawkes had climbed aboard the clipper, conditions had changed for the worse with a strengthening westerly wind and a rising swell, and a certainty in the pilot's mind that weather showing these signs was more than likely to deteriorate overnight. If confirmation of his thoughts was needed, the sky had taken on a mass of dark threatening cloud which soon obscured the moon. Captain Hawkes displayed no concern, however, as he took over the ship from her master, who went below to complete his log. Before long rain squalls began to beat across the ship. Soon it would be better to be snug within the harbour rather than riding out a storm beyond.

John Hawkes had a good record as a pilot, and so Captain Stuart had no qualms about entrusting the ship to him despite the shifting conditions. If anyone could handle a ship off Sydney, whatever the conditions, it would have to be one of the regular pilots. Hawkes quickly had the necessary sails set to get under way, and turned the clipper's head as near the wind as it would go. The westerly was blowing strongly into their faces, and it would therefore require some precise tacking to pass through the Heads and gain a safe anchorage inside.

They had passed safely into the harbour by these means, and were about to tack again to reach the shelter of Camp Cove, just inside the South Head, when things began to go wrong. First they were struck by a vicious south-westerly rain squall which cut visibility in the narrow waterway between Middle and South Head. To avoid the near-shore reefs, Captain Hawkes changed his mind about the Camp Cove anchorage and turned instead for the greater shelter of Spring Cove in North Harbour. As the squall passed and the wind eased more sail was ordered to help maintain way, but no sooner had this been set than another squall ripped across the ship, blowing the foresail to pieces. The beating winds made it impossible to set the mainsail, and with little steerage way the ship began to drift rapidly downwind in heavy rain and near total darkness towards the rocks of the inner North Head.

At this point Captain Stuart re-emerged from below, alarmed by the struggles on deck and the odd feel of his ship. He had been reluctant to interfere with the command of the pilot, but what he saw on reaching the deck appalled him, for already he could distinguish the paleness of breakers downwind, towards which they were drifting, almost without control, at an alarming rate. Immediately he demanded that the ship be turned towards the open sea rather than seeking what might be dubious anchorages in such conditions. This unfortunately provoked a stubborn response from the harried pilot, who refused to listen and just as bluntly told the master he was fully intent on reaching Spring Cove. A furious argument then ensued, during which little progress was made despite continuous tacking to stay away from rocky shores and hidden reefs. As a compromise, satisfying neither party, the argument was ended when Hawkes ordered both anchors down and all sail handed in, in the shadow of the cliffs known as Old Man's Hat.

As holding ground the selection was a poor one, as was evident around midnight when the wind swung to the south, blowing as strongly as ever. The anchors dragged, the clipper swung stern-on to the rocks, and her keel began to bump ominously. Captain Stuart, fearing for the safety of everyone aboard the ship, fired off blue distress rockets, which were answered soon after by the paddle steamer *Williams*, entering from Newcastle. Captain Creer of the *Williams* saw at once the danger threatening the *Catherine Adamson*, and bellowed out his willingness to tow the clipper out of danger. This immediately gave rise to another heated argument aboard the threatened ship, Captain Stuart being willing to accept any form of assistance to save his vessel, the pilot dismissing the ability of the steamer to perform the task and demanding the assistance of a tug from Sydney instead. On this occasion Captain Stuart prevailed, backed by Captain Creer's bluff retort that he had more power available on hand than any steam tug around the harbour.

Two efforts to get a line aboard the steamer failed, but the *Williams* could approach no closer without endangering her own safety. The *Catherine Adamson* was drifting very close to the cliffs by now, and time was clearly running out. In desperation, two boats were launched to reach the steamer, for reasons not entirely clear. Captain Stuart stated that he wished to parley further with the master of the *Williams*, but he still took with him half the ship's complement, including four passengers. Others later claimed that he had abandoned his charges, particularly after the boats were swamped in the heaving seas, and the *Williams'* crew had pulled everyone aboard and sailed over to the Watsons Bay Pilot Station to secure more assistance.

The delay was a fatal one. When help arrived early next morning it came too late. During the night the *Catherine Adamson* had swung broadside to the rocks, and beaten by both winds from the south and seas surging through the Heads, had been battered to pieces at the foot of the cliff. The ship had broken apart, scattering wreckage far and wide across the harbour, repeating the scenes of nine weeks earlier when the *Dunbar* had come to grief in similar circumstances. Everyone who had remained overnight aboard the clipper, 21 in all including the pilot and four passengers, was lost. Only the bodies of John Hawkes and four seamen were found—the other 16 had disappeared.

Again the cargo attracted looters and scavengers, particularly this time as news soon spread that the *Catherine Adamson* had been carrying large quantities of liquor that were destined for the goldfields, including 10 000 gallons of rum, 4500 gallons of wine, over 4000 gallons of brandy and 2000 gallons of gin. It was a booty few could ignore, and people descended *en masse* to grab what they could, where they could, before the police arrived on the scene. This they did in strength, apprehending many of the weekend opportunists, but the incidents showed sharply the darker side of human nature even where disasters occur. This exploitation was not an isolated outbreak, as the aftermath of other mishaps in later years would prove.

A total of 142 people lost their lives in the wrecks of the clippers *Dunbar* and *Catherine Adamson*. Their causes were due mainly to the prevailing weather, which was bad in both cases, compounded by an indistinct, inadequate and confusing light on the one hand, and shortcomings in the qualities of the pilot service on the other. No blame was attached to the late Captain Green or his crew for the loss of the *Dunbar*, who were felt to have done all they could in the circumstances to avert disaster. Neither was Captain Stuart blamed for the loss of the *Catherine Adamson*, despite the charges of desertion. Captain Creer had backed her master's story at the inquest, which laid the blame squarely on errors of judgement by the late pilot, John Hawkes.

Fifty years after the wrecks, that of the *Dunbar* was subject to further plundering, though at the time it was regarded as salvage, and in the spirit of the day was quite legitimate. The wreck was rediscovered in 1907 by men from the nearby pilot station, who had noted the presence of large anchors near the wreck site after prolonged searching. When divers went down in 1910, two of the anchors were recovered, one of which weighed 4 tons, but immediately there were doubters who felt that they were not necessarily those of the *Dunbar*. Others were equally convinced that they were. Over the years various other artefacts were recovered, but the worst depredations came with the advent of scuba-diving in the post-war years, and the ready proximity of the wreck to Sydney divers.

The *Dunbar* has thus been one of the most heavily exploited wrecks in Australia, and it is said that more relics now lie in back-yard sheds around Sydney, than still adorn the seafloor off South Head. Fortunately some of these relics have been well-preserved, like the ship's bell hanging in St John's Church, Darlinghurst, and a large bible used in the same church that was held privately for many years. Today the artefacts are steadily being catalogued where they can be identified with certainty. The wreck itself, like that of the *Catherine Adamson*, has been declared a historic shipwreck under the State and Commonwealth legislation.

Chapter 8

SS *ADMELLA*
1859

The *Admella*.

'The stunned watchers cowered in fear and disbelief as the centre part of
their ship then collapsed noisily in a tangle of masts, rigging and hissing
machinery ... some of the passengers and crew were already gone ...
all within a mere 15 minutes!'

I t was a racehorse that first led to the sinking of the SS *Admella* in August 1859. The drama that subsequently unfolded became one of courage and endurance on the part of the few survivors, suspense and frustration for their many well-wishers and beach-side onlookers, and tenacity and triumph for their eventual rescuers.

The *Admella*, one of the earliest screw steamers serving Australia's south coast, was only two years old when she was lost. The name 'Admella' was an acronym based on the first letters of the main ports she was intended to serve: AD for ADelaide; MEL for MELbourne; and LA for LAunceston. Built in Glasgow, Scotland, she was a graceful, well-appointed vessel of 500 tons, and had been brought out to Australia under sail. A refit in Port Adelaide had her prepared for her first voyage under steam, but the passage between Adelaide and Melbourne in the winter of 1859 would also prove to be her last. Eighty-nine people would die with her.

Friday, 5th of August, 1859, was cold and grey when the SS *Admella* departed Port Adelaide on her first trip to Melbourne, under the command of Captain Hugh McEwan. She carried 81 passengers in both saloon (first class) and steerage, together with a crew of 28. At Semaphore she was to pick up three more passengers and another seaman, to bring the total number aboard to 113. Her cargo consisted of a range of general merchandise, a consignment of flour for Victoria's goldfields, over 100 tons of copper ingots and pig-lead, and seven horses, four of which were destined to take part in the up-coming racing season in Melbourne.

All was well throughout the morning in the calm waters of Gulf

St Vincent. Passengers strolled the decks and chatted together at the rails as time and the South Australian coastline slipped by. On leaving the shelter of Kangaroo Island, however, by way of the Backstairs Passage, they sailed into the first heavy swells of the Southern Ocean, which soon led to an uncomfortable roll for everyone aboard. Particularly uncomfortable were the seven horses being transported in stalls set up on the open deck. They were unused to such motion and became anxious and fretful in not being able to either counter or cope with it. One horse in particular, the champion flat-racer 'Jupiter', became so agitated by the late afternoon that it lost its footing on the shifting deck and fell down on its back inside the stalls. The incident was to be the start of all their later troubles.

To right the horse, Captain McEwan slowed the ship and turned her head into the swell to provide more stability for those trying to calm the animal and put it back on all four legs. Then a sling was rigged to give it additional support, after which the *Admella* turned once more to the south and continued on to Melbourne. The process took over an hour, during which the *Admella* drifted some way from her earlier course and position. That night, as the nauseating pitch and roll persisted, heavy fog descended, though in the master's view they were safely some 16 miles off-shore, and would round Cape Northumberland, South Australia's southernmost point, sometime before dawn. It was not to be.

Shortly before 5.00am the *Admella* ran onto a hidden reef. The shock was barely perceptible to most of the sleeping passengers, but the ship travelled forward a further distance on the back of each swell until she came to rest, with a tilt to port, on what were later recognised as Carpenters Rocks, an off-shore reef some 20 miles WSW of Mt Gambier, and 17 miles before reaching Cape Northumberland. When she failed to answer the helm, their predicament became clear. They would not be able to shift from the reef without assistance, and meanwhile the high seas around the stranded ship began to break on deck as her immobile bulk started to interfere with their passage.

The engines were stopped, and after hurried consultations Captain McEwan ordered the boats to be prepared for launching while the stewards went round the cabins, rousing their occupants and urging them to dress and hurry up on deck. They found the *Admella* aground and canting alarmingly to the left. All were astounded and more than a few grew afraid about what was happening. It was still dark, the fog still hung in dank clouds, and all around them the seas were beating high across the stranded ship and the reef. And they were a long way from either Adelaide or Melbourne.

Suddenly, with little warning, the ship gave a lurch and the tall funnel toppled and fell, crashing onto one of the lifeboats being readied for the sea. Its momentum seemed to be followed through with a creak and a groan as the ship heeled further—then split across with a resounding squeal of rupturing metal, her beams giving way under the uneven strain of perching on the reef. The *Admella*'s unsupported bows then continued to split away further as they and the midships section separated into deeper water.

The stunned watchers cowered in fear and disbelief as the centre part of their ship then collapsed noisily in a tangle of masts, rigging and hissing machinery. When their screams and hysteria subsided they were horrified to realise that their once solid, well-appointed vessel had somehow broken up beneath them, that only the bow and stern now gave sanctuary from the threatening waves. Some of the passengers and crew were already gone, lost to the sea in the sweep of the falling funnel—all within a mere 15 minutes! What seemed like a nightmare was a cold, wet and precarious reality.

Dawn revealed two pathetic groups clinging forlornly to the remaining fore and after parts of their stricken ship. All were cold and wet and decidedly unsure of their fate. On the canted bow could be seen a large group with many of the women and children huddling fearfully together, the tilting remains offering few holds for those who were desperately depending on them. Some of the men had climbed into the rigging of the foremast for more secure perches, but no one knew how long that section of the ship would last before it either collapsed further or slipped into deeper water. Before long the mast swayed and sagged, then fell with a crash, throwing aside some of those clinging to it while trapping others as it subsided beneath the turbulent waters.

Only two or three managed to reach the safety of the poop, including Captain McEwan. This part of the wreck seemed to be more securely wedged on the reef, no doubt held in place by the massive weight of copper and lead in the cargo stowed aft. But the people here were just as exposed as those across the water, and there was no way either party could move over the void that had once been the *Admella*'s steamy heart. Dismay was soon added to everyone's discomfort as the fog cleared sufficiently to reveal a desolate coast little more than a mile away, the intervening distance being filled with a leaping sea that seemed certain to engulf any boat they tried to launch.

But what about the boats? One had certainly been smashed by the falling funnel, and another was found to have been stove in against the mast during an abortive launch attempt in the darkness. The one remaining boat still hung awkwardly in its davits on the after end of the poop, but fouled its falls, hanging down by the bow, when the captain and others sought to lower it. The enthusiasm of one of the passengers then put paid to any hope the boat might have held of some people gaining the shore when he cut through the binding falls. The ropes parted, pitching the upended craft bow first into the breaking seas where it overturned and drifted rapidly away. It was a cruel disappointment.

Their spirits were low, chill winds cut through the wet clothing of adults and children alike, and a number were already showing signs of creeping exposure, lying palely mute and shivering. Yet this was only the first day. The captain mustered a few rockets from somewhere within the wreck which he hoped might alert the keepers of the lighthouse on distant Northumberland Cape, but because they were damp only one fired ineffectively. It was a bad, almost hopeless situation. Captain McEwan againt went down into the tumbling waters to catch a spar that had drifted free, which might help in the making of a raft, although he emerged cold and enfeebled from his efforts. Their one remaining hope, he said, was for some brave soul to face the rough and rising seas, hopefully to gain the land and fetch help.

Captain McEwan was loath to order men into the swirling waves at the risk of their lives, but several younger members of his crew responded to his selfless examples by volunteering to try to reach the shore. The first attempt was made by fireman Adam Purdon, who straddled a piece of wreckage and, half-swimming, half-paddling, pushed off through the perilous breakers. Half way there, with his strength waning, the currents caught him and swept him out to sea where he disappeared. Next to try was seaman Soren Holm, who sought first to retrieve the upturned stern boat by swimming out and attaching a line. Unfortunately a knot slipped or the line broke, and while trying to paddle the boat back to the wreck with a piece of timber, he too was swept away from the reef and lost.

Hopes were dwindling when a shout drew their attention to a steamer which emerged through the fog about two miles away. 'A ship! Here comes a ship!' Immediately spirits soared and people danced and called as far as their precarious holds would allow, while others rang the ship's bell wildly, willing those on the other vessel to see their plight and bring rescue. The other ship was the *Havilah*, a coastal steamer on one of her regular runs. However, if anyone aboard saw the wreck it may then have become indistinguishable from any number of coastal outcrops encircled by foam and spray. Whatever their reaction, the *Havilah* held her course and sailed on into the mists. The ocean seemed a wild, empty, despairing place afterwards, and many wept.

One more attempt was made to reach the mainland that day when Mr Johnson, the Swedish mate, volunteered to swim ashore wearing a life jacket. With everyone's hopes and best wishes he plunged into the sea and struck out strongly towards the beckoning surf line, only to vanish under the dumping combers, never to reappear. There was nothing that could be said for the loss of yet another brave man, so numbed were the watchers. As the day wore on the remaining survivors sat in listless silence, cold and hungry, drenched by flying spray and the higher waves, no longer daring to hope that help might come soon. Yet when the cry of, 'Lights, a steamer's lights!' broke the gloom of evening and the red, white and green lights of an approaching ship were seen, excitement soared once more with the thought that help was at hand, and their suffering would soon be ended.

Again such feelings were dashed. Despite the steamer coming so close that it seemed she might also run aground, they had no means of drawing her attention. The rockets found earlier in the day were as useless as before, there was nothing dry to burn nor lucifers to give a flame, and their parched throats were by now robbed of any ability to do more than croak. The ship sailed on unseeing, all hope receding with the fading of her lights. It was the end of the day, they had not been found, it was doubtful even that anyone was aware of their circumstances, and they were increasingly plagued now by hunger and thirst in addition to their cold, wet misery. How much more, or how much longer, could they endure?

Next morning it soon became clear that their numbers had diminished during the night. Cold, fatigue and hunger had taken their toll, especially amongst the children, who had slipped from the grasp of their weary parents and were no more. Others had been washed away as they slept. Grief also took its toll, absorbing sorely-needed resources to stay alive. People were slowly losing the will to live. A bright sunny day offered some relief, and the wind had subsided a little. The tossing waves, too, beat lower around their broken perches, but during the night another danger threatened, becoming increasingly more apparent as the bow section shifted unsteadily, weakened by the unending surge.

Amongst the passengers stranded on the unstable bow was one Captain Harris, an elderly mariner used to the ways of the sea and aware now of the precariousness of their position. With little prospect of outside assistance, the survivors were forced to rely on their own resources if they were to stay alive. Captain Harris now came to the fore. It was becoming essential to move people from the shaky bow across to the greater security of the stern section. Calling for a rope to act as a lifeline, he was to encourage his group, still numbering more than 20, to risk the turbulent crossing before the bow completed its threatened collapse. Captain McEwan tried several times to heave the line over the gap without success, until one of the seamen, John Leach, clambered over the tangle of spars to reach the end of the rope.

Three men succeeded immediately in hauling themselves across, but the women and children had no such strength. In desperation, one man strapped his two children to his body and started out along the line. Half way across, however, his strength gave out, his hands slipped from the wet rope and all three plunged screaming into the angry sea below. Two other men died the same way. In all, 15 people reached safety on the other side, but the remaining families chose to stay together to take their chances or to share their fate. Soon enough, fate triumphed as the bow section finally broke up, while those on the stern watched their final struggles in helpless despair.

The 70 or so survivors clinging to the tilted stern were no better off than those on the bow save for the stability of their part of the wreck. How long it might remain so was unknown. On the slanting perches people were still exposed to the elements, the penetrating cold and constant wetness steadily sapping their reserves. Little food and water had been available throughout the previous day, but once more Captain Harris knew these would be vital for anyone to survive the stranding and, just as important, if anyone was to attain the nearby land. He therefore took it on himself to search for food and refreshment from within the shattered wreck, as well as any blankets and extra clothing he might find.

With other members of the crew, he dived amongst the twisted wreckage and was able to reach the various compartments, searching submerged cupboards and lockers below for anything that might sustain life. Some dry clothing was found and given to those suffering the greatest exposure, though a quantity of meat, some cheese and a few bottles of porter and spirits were all that could be saved as food from the flood. It was barely enough, but parched throats and splitting lips discouraged many from consuming much.

After eating what was available, thought was given once more to somehow reaching the shore. Having lost the chance of alerting passing ships, it was the only way they could be certain of carrying news of the disaster and bringing rescue, so barren and dead was the coast across the way. Several of the crew assembled a raft from spars and floating timbers, fashioning its shape with the aid of a meat cleaver. Though it looked unwieldy, it was all they could contrive. Seamen Robert Knapman and James Leach volunteered to face the still vigorous waves as they were the fittest of the crew. It took them more than three hours of lusty paddling with makeshift planks to reach the line of breakers opposite, while those on the wreck prayed for their strength and safety. The raft was awkward and difficult to steer, but eventually it carried them through the surf and grounded on the sand beyond.

The survivors on the wreck cheered hoarsely, hugged and gave thanks for the men's deliverance. It was nearly dark when the pair had recovered strength enough to set out for the Cape Northumberland light. Captain McEwan had seen them on their way through his telescope. All that could be done now was wait through the night, sleep if possible, and conserve their strength for the morrow when help might come.

They spent a desperate night. The wind swung to the south, blowing progressively colder and whipping up the seas to such an extent that many sought shelter in the accessible cabins, as crowded and uncomfortable as this was, while the air outside grew thick with flying spray. Huge waves regularly swept the wreck as cold swells rose around the *Admella*'s remains, dislodging those still exposed on the stern, sweeping away others too weak to hold on further. Some became delirious, having resorted to drinking seawater to assuage their thirsts despite warnings from Captain McEwan that they should desist. Others lay comatose, seemingly bereft of life. It was thus a sorry group that emerged to greet the dawn on the third day, Monday, the 8th of August.

Throughout the day they waited in vain for signs of life on the beaches. But the two seamen had only reached their objective at seven o'clock that morning, and it took some time to send away to Mt Gambier and Portland with the news, and for the men to return with the lighthouse keeper to the wreck site. Before this, Ben Germain, the keeper of the light, had set out himself to carry the news to Mt Gambier, but on being thrown from his horse, had struggled back to pass the duty of warning the police and bringing a search party to a neighbouring settler. The distance there was nearly 20 miles, with 20 miles then from Mt Gambier out to the *Admella* wreck on Carpenters Rocks. Portland lay some 70 miles away on the other side of desolate Discovery Bay. Nightfall came again upon the survivors without promise of salvation.

From the wreck, the first signs that the two seamen had succeeded in their task was a gathering of people on the beach early next morning. It seemed the overnight prayers of the survivors had been answered, for some at least. The last remains of the bow section had disappeared, however, and with it the family of five who had elected to remain there. In the hope of an early rescue, the last of the food was consumed, for across on the beach they could see that a boat was being readied (it appeared to be the one that had drifted away from the wreck with seaman Holm three days ago) and an encouraging crowd was growing by the hour in the hope of seeing them safe.

In the interim, since the sea was still rough and the winter winds blew strongly, many continued to huddle below in the compartments still above water to conserve their strength in anticipation of rescue. It was then, without warning, that an internal bulkhead gave way under the incessant surge and thrust of the waves, drowning all within amidst struggles and screams, while those above felt the deck shudder and sag, and clung for dear life while the wreck settled once more. The hope of rescue gave way to a sickening fear of imminent death, for it was soon clear that there would be no attempt to put out in the boat in such conditions.

For the rest of that day and well into the next, the surviving party lapsed into apathy and uncaring dejection, no longer believing that relief would come in time to save them. In the afternoon, hardly daring to hope, they watched as another boat was brought onto the beach and launched by willing helpers, only to be swamped as it cleared the surf. The crew struggled ashore, weak and exhausted. As conditions grew worse no further efforts were made that day.

All the while though, the survivors were growing weaker and their numbers thinner, one dying quietly here, another snatched by the waves there. Nothing could be done to sustain them. They had been five days almost without food or water, existing in acute discomfort and thoroughly demoralised in the face of death. They seemed beyond hope. In a vain attempt to be rid of the wreck, steward John Hills donned a life jacket and plunged into the sea using driftwood as a float. He had not gone far to the shore, however, before he threw up his hands and disappeared. Watching in sickening horror, the others realised he had been taken by a shark. Even the sight of an approaching steamer, the SS *Corio*, did little to lift their spirits, but it offered some measure of assurance in anchoring off for the night, with the prospect of bringing aid if conditions improved next day.

Successive attempts were made to reach the wreck the following morning, the 11th of August, though without success. More efforts to launch boats from the shore ended in them being swamped in the wintry seas. Dismayed by the continuing hopelessness, Captain Harris rallied the remaining members of the crew to help build another raft, for which they lashed together a number of spars and on which they secured a platform made of cabin doors. Unfortunately it slipped from their grasp on launching, so debilitated were its builders, and floated away before anyone else could take hold. It nevertheless served to occupy the minds of those alert enough to care, and to divert them for a while from creeping despondency.

That afternoon the steamer *Corio* closed on the wreck as near as was safe, while one of her boats battled for nearly an hour before being forced to retreat to the beach without reaching the wreck. A bitter belief amongst the *Admella* group that the boat could not be re-launched from the beach proved to be distressingly correct when two further attempts to set out again were thwarted by the raging surf. Adding to their bitterness and sorrow, several more of their number died during the day despite the scant comforts and encouragement others tried to give. Some slipped quietly away, some died in delirium, another threw himself into the sea. Amongst them was old Captain Harris, whose efforts to bring encouragement and comfort to others had cost him dearly. He too slipped away in the early afternoon, having lost much of his spirit with the loss of his raft.

By Friday, 12th of August, a week since the *Admella* had left Port Adelaide, a large collection of craft had gathered at the scene of the wreck, but still no rescue had been effected. No boat had even reached the wreck. The crowd on the beach was becoming impatient with the weather, concern was deeply felt for the survivors on the wreck, whose numbers were unknown, but still the high seas which swept the *Admella's* remains prevented any successful launching of the assembled boats. The latest to arrive was the steamer *Ladybird* towing the Portland lifeboat, in company with the smaller steamer, *Ant*. The *Ladybird* was no stranger to disaster at sea, having survived a collision off Cape Otway two years earlier which sank her sister ship *Champion*.

On board the *Ladybird* was Captain James Fawthrop, Harbour Master at Portland, and skipper of the lifeboat which followed in the *Ladybird's* wake. Having assessed the state of the wreck, Captain Fawthrop wasted no time in putting out from the *Ladybird* despite the forbidding state of the seas. He and his crew had encountered worse. Even so, they were still to be thwarted in their early efforts when, having closed on the wreck, they were twice unable to land rocket lines across the heaving waves, followed by several unsuccessful attempts to heave a line over from closer in. But there was a limit to how close they could approach without endangering their craft on the lift and plunge of the surging swell. This quickly became apparent when several large rollers crashed over the wreck, picking up the lifeboat as though weightless, and submerging all in a welter of spray.

For a moment the lifeboat crew fought desperately for their lives, in danger of being thrown onto the wreck or smashed on the reef, and almost drowning where they clutched at their oars. Several oars were snapped off as the torrent raged around them. When the boat surfaced, however, she was still intact, though all but four of her oars were gone and her rudder was lost. Such was the skill and fortitude of the boatmen that they were still able to right their craft, haul away from the wreck through menacing breakers on four oars, and reach the *Ladybird* once more to recover. New oars were found for the lifeboat, and the crew was preparing to try again when conditions were deemed too dangerous and life-threatening. Though they waited for the rest of the day for conditions to improve, even approaching the wreck with another line, they were beaten away by the height of the surf around her and had to abandon further attempts. The thoughts and feelings of the remaining survivors are impossible to imagine.

On the next day, Saturday, one week since the *Admella* foundered, an all-out attempt was made to reach the wreck and bring off the poor souls still stranded there. Without food, water, shelter or dry clothing, and as exposed to the winter elements as they were, their situation would surely have gone beyond the point of desperation. For those still alive, only the Almighty held their fate, for they would not last much longer if the next rescue bid failed.

Early on Saturday morning, Ben Germain set out on his third attempt to reach the *Admella*, come hell or high water. Time was fast running out for those aboard. With luck and determination he was able to heave a line across, which was quickly seized and held long enough for three of the fittest survivors, Captain McEwan included, to scramble into his boat and be taken over to another craft standing off, while he went in again for more. This time he was less lucky, and succeeded in bringing away only one other person, but his efforts were enough to show that conditions would allow others to approach if it was done quickly.

Captain Fawthrop and the Portland lifeboat were already on their way. As Ben Germain's weary crew pulled aside, the lifeboat drew abreast of the wreck and succeeded in placing another stout line across. Though the lifeboat rose and fell alongside, and sometimes seemed in danger of fouling the scattered wreck, with shouts and encouragement the 19 remaining survivors were coaxed across the shifting gap to safety. Only one moment of drama occurred when Miss Bridget Ledwith, the only woman survivor, slipped and remained dangling over the water until the lifeboat was adroitly manoeuvred back into place to take her off. The rescue seemed complete. As soon as the survivors were taken aboard the *Ladybird*, the steamer set sail for Portland with the lifeboat in tow. Fate had one last throw at the rescuers, however, as Ben Germain took his boat back to the beach. He still had his last survivor with him as he attempted to ride the surf through to the beach. A heavy wave caught his craft and tipped everyone in it into the sea. The survivor drowned.

A total of 89 people died in the wreck of the *Admella*. It was one of this country's worst maritime tragedies, and the worst off South Australia. Not all the heroes of the incident were recognised or rewarded in the publicity and acclaim that followed the event, but the two most prominent, Ben Germain and James Fawthrop, received due reward for their bravery and were presented with both medals and monetary gifts from a number of bodies in acknowledgement of their roles in the rescue. No blame was attached to Captain McEwan or his officers for the wreck, since the principal cause was later deemed to be a strong inshore current—and, of course, the racehorse 'Jupiter'.

The *Admella* wreck site was rediscovered in 1957, almost 100 years after the disaster. Thereafter the wreck was frequently visited by skin divers and treasure hunters and much was removed. The cargo of copper was eventually recovered by a salvage syndicate, but then the Commonwealth stepped in as the Receiver of Wrecks. After no ownership claims had been validated over a period of 12 months, the copper was sold, though only a small proportion of the proceeds went to the syndicate.

The Federal Government took similar action in connection with a brass signal cannon recovered from the wreck in 1982. The finders went to considerable lengths to restore the cannon, including the building of a replica carriage, which was afterwards loaned out for exhibition. Requested for another exhibition in 1986, the cannon then became the subject of a protracted legal battle over ownership which the Federal Government, in conjunction with the South Australian Government, eventually won. A sum of $3500 was paid as a reward for the find. Little remains of the wreck today.

Chapter 9

MARIA
1872

The *Maria*.

'After two weeks of near ceaseless turmoils, land was sighted on 25th of February, 1872. It was a miracle they were still alive, but their troubles were far from over.'

The brig lay alongside the Sydney wharf with an abandoned air: old, worn, semi-derelict. Her paint was flaking, her rigging sagged, and her sails were patched and stained. At and below the waterline her hull showed a line of marine growth that waved gently with the shifting tide. The grime in her scuppers and ingraining her decks told of a former life as a collier. However, she appeared sound enough to the group of miners from the New Guinea Prospecting Association who stood on the wharf nearby. She was ideal for their purpose, and for a payment of £300 the price was right! After all, they agreed, she would only be needed for the one voyage across Torres Strait. Her name was *Maria*.

The year was 1871, and the first flush of gold discoveries in California (1849), Australia (1850s) and New Zealand (early 1860s) was past. The feverish pursuit of wealth which had followed had also largely petered out, save for the persistence of the stubborn or the optimists, and the Chinese who worked carefully over the old diggings for their lesser yields. This country's later discoveries would not be made for another decade or more, nor would Canada's Yukon beckon until close to the end of the century. Meanwhile a new generation of bored and restless young men yearned for their own El Dorado, so when rumours began circulating of gold finds in New Guinea, this generation pricked up its ears and asked, 'Where?'

It all began with a statement attributed to the naturalist, John MacGillivray, during the exploratory voyages of Captain Owen Stanley, commander of HMS *Rattlesnake*, which avowed 'that gold exists in the western and northern portions of New Guinea has long been known'. This was later enlarged upon by the Reverend John Dunmore Lang in an address to the Royal Society of New South Wales, when he offered the findings of John MacGillivray as proof positive, based on items of the local pottery which supposedly contained flakes of gold as evidence. The words of the good reverend quickly became accepted into conventional wisdom, at least amongst his gold-starved listeners, though the claim was later seen to be false.

In enthusiastic response, the New Guinea Prospecting Expedition was quickly formed. Soon afterwards, on the 2nd of December 1871, an announcement appeared in the *Sydney Morning Herald* which expounded on the 'rich deposits of alluvial gold' to be found in the big island to the north. Copies of the Expedition's prospectus were available to interested parties, it said, which further stated that it was 'satisfactorily proved that in the vicinity of Redscar Bay, and along the south-eastern coast of New Guinea, there exist very rich deposits of alluvial gold'. The Expedition offered places to willing young men and other 'volunteers' at a price of £10 per head. For this, subscribers would gain a place aboard a suitable ship bound for New Guinea where, by none-too-subtle implication, they would all become rich.

Alas for the gullible, and the easily-conned. Mark Twain once defined a gold mine as 'a hole in the ground owned by a liar'. True enough, the gold was there, but in 1871 it had not yet been found, nor was it in the places being touted as 'rich fields' in the Expedition's prospectus. The principal gold wealth of New Guinea lay on the north-eastern side of the Bowutu Mountains facing the island of New Britain, and would not be discovered for another 50 years. In 1871, New Guinea's 'gold mines' had not even reached the stage of being pools for wash-dirt let alone 'holes in the ground', but someone somewhere was already peddling rumours of major finds amongst the misty peaks and steaming jungles in the seldom-visited interior of New Guinea. For what purpose was never fully discovered.

Needless to say, where gold was to be had, there would be men to seek it. Such is gold fever. The formation and objectives of the New Guinea Prospecting Expedition were not long announced before its organisers were deluged by applications from people eager for places on the first ship. But first a ship had to be purchased, though its purchasers were none too fussy about the ship's condition, hence the *Maria*. Her gear was rotten, she leaked in many seams, and her accommodation was fetid, cramped and cockroach-infested. Her owner was a dubious character who had no qualms about leaving his unseaworthy craft in the hands of its passengers. There was no crew.

Even so, it was not long before 76 lucky applicants were selected to go on the Expedition's first venture. Amongst them, and no doubt why they were chosen, were many gentlemen deemed to be very well-connected in New South Wales by virtue of their birth and education. Not only would they add lustre to the undertaking in anticipation of future sailings, but their inherent wealth no doubt guaranteed the wherewithal to purchase the first ship. Though others of their class were inclined to regard the enterprise as ill-conceived and badly-equipped, and publicly said so, its 76 itinerants were keen to be gone regardless of any short-comings. A gold 'rush' is just that, and any delay could mean others might reach the gold before them.

The claims that the venture was ill-prepared—some said 'hare-brained'—were not without good cause. Apart from all the obvious deficiencies of their vessel, shortly before they sailed their departure was frustrated by an official ruling under the current *Navigation Act* that the *Maria* did not have sufficient life-boats aboard for the number of passengers she was to carry. The Expedition's organisers responded with a reading from the Act which had revealed that the life-boat require-ments applied only to the number of passengers aboard, without specific provision for the crew. By inviting all those who were intent on sailing with *Maria* to sign on as 'crew', therefore, two immediate problems were solved: the *Maria* could leave for New Guinea with a full passenger complement aboard, as well as having all the necessary hands to sail her.

The one essential item they didn't have at this time was a competent master to take the ship north, and to successfully navigate the reef-ridden waters of the Coral Sea and Torres Strait. The man from whom they bought the ship had taken off into the fleshpots of Sydney, no doubt glad to be rid of a liability and the likelihood that the ship would probably never reach New Guinea's shores. As a seaman he would have been fully aware of the threat posed by the north-west monsoon at that time of the year, a time also notorious for cyclones off Australia's northern coasts. He perhaps had the best of the bargain. Captain Gillespie, the master mariner engaged instead, soon resigned as Captain, pleading ill health, though no doubt unwilling to risk his life in such a vessel. At short notice, therefore, his responsibilities were taken up by the First Mate, one Thomas Stratman, who had quickly volunteered to take his place.

Seven weeks after the first notification had appeared in the Sydney newspaper, the Expedition was ready to sail. Apart from the 'well-connected gentlemen', the other volunteers were a motley collection of miners, adventurers and ne'er-do-wells from several different countries, with little in common save an ability to speak English, the arms they all carried, and their lust for gold. Before leaving, the company was addressed by the same Reverend Lang on whose words and opinions the expedition hung, and who wished them Godspeed with the sentiment that, had he been a younger man, he would gladly have sailed as their leader. Thus blessed, the *Maria* set out from Sydney on 25th of January, 1872, New

Guinea-bound. Only four of her complement had any claim to seafaring or ship-handling experience, while others felt some concern over the uncertain capabilities of Captain Stratman. Many ashore held stronger reservations about the enterprise as a whole.

———

One of the well-connected young men who sailed with the *Maria* that day was Lawrence Hargrave, who was to become known in his later years as one of Australia's leading aviation theorists, and to modern Australians as the face amongst the box-kites on one of our first $20 notes. At the time of the expedition, however, Hargrave was still a youth of 21, who broke his apprenticeship with a Sydney shipbuilding company to be part of the New Guinea Prospecting Expedition. His motives were vastly different from those of his shipmates, however, in that his main purpose for going to New Guinea was exploration rather than any pursuit of wealth. New Guinea at this time was one of the few places on earth that had not been explored, and young Hargrave had yearned for such an opportunity since his mid-teens. This venture was therefore to be his first encounter with the mist-shrouded island, though others were to follow with larger measures of success.

Lawrence Hargrave was born in London in 1850. When he was six, his lawyer father left England to establish a life in Australia, accompanied by his younger brother Edward, and his eldest son Ralph. Before long, Hargrave Senior had become a district court judge and New South Wales parliamentarian, and would soon rise to be the State's Solicitor-General, then Attorney-General, before taking his place as a Judge of the Supreme Court. At the age of 15, young Lawrence followed his father to the colony, becoming entranced on his outward voyage by ship-board life, and seafarers' stories of strange lands in remote parts of the world. New Guinea was one such land, to which he came enticingly close on his first voyage around Australia aboard the clipper *Ellesmere*, shortly after his arrival.

His late teens as a shipyard apprentice and engineering draughtsman did little to stifle his urge to explore, instead strengthening his desire on account of the boredom and routine. When the opportunity came to join the New Guinea Prospecting Expedition, therefore, he wasted no time in seeking paternal approval for the adventure ahead. On being accepted as a 'volunteer', he pitched eagerly into supply arrangements as a member of the Expedition's working committee, and took on the nominal role of sailmaker as part of the makeshift 'crew' to overcome Government concern regarding lifeboat provisions for passengers. Like the others he heard, but chose to ignore, warnings that the enterprise might prove a shaky one. New Guinea's gold and jungle wilderness exerted a stronger pull.

For the first couple of weeks the *Maria* ploughed north with blue skies and fair winds. They encountered nothing that the scratch crew couldn't handle, which perhaps built up a false sense of security amongst the would-be prospectors. By letter, Lawrence Hargrave was able to let his father know all was well, though some had complained about the food and accommodation. The consensus was accepting, however, and so the voyage progressed. As they entered the tropics, heavy rains found the gaps in the shrunken timbers of the deck, but still conditions were accepted as being no worse than on many other ships of the day, though coal dust tended to stain everything they possessed. Their equanimity was soon to change.

On the 12th of February 1872, the eighteenth day at sea—and rapidly-darkening clouds and a rising sea were the first signs of worse to come. Knowingly or otherwise, they had entered the cyclone belt at a time of year when high winds might develop with little warning, on a part of the coast that was strewn with reefs and islands ever likely to snare the unwary—or the foolish—in such adverse conditions. This was the region of the Great Barrier Reef, which runs as a chain of atolls, lagoons, islets and channels for 1260 miles, or over 2000 kilometres, off the coast of north Queensland. Had the crew been more experienced, or the master more knowledgeable, such warnings would have been heeded in time to reduce sail before the onslaught of a north-westerly gale. Instead the ship heeled heavily under the pressure of the wind before the first sails burst, after which the rigging howled above a deck awash beneath piling seas, while men cowered below in fear of the elements.

Nothing would persuade them to go on deck or climb aloft to furl the remaining sails, so the hapless *Maria* was left to her own devices, driven downwind as rotten canvas split asunder, the following seas threatening to overwhelm her straining bulk. Deck timbers quickly opened up their seams in the working of the ship, which at least galvanised those below into some kind of action to keep the *Maria* from foundering under the sweep and crash of the waves. The captain ordered hands to the pumps in a voice scarcely under his control, while the second mate had buckets broken out to help bale the ship. Years of accumulated coal dust found their way into the bilges, clogging the inlets of the pumps or reducing their flow. Little did the miners realise then that the only use to which the buckets would ever be put was to temporarily clear water from within the ship.

Gale-force winds and pounding seas harried the *Maria* for more than a week before the danger passed, and conditions eased enough to allow some review of their plight. The ship was near-devastated from the battering wrought by the storm. She lay heavily in the water with her sails in shreds. Her strained rigging threatened to collapse, parts of the bulwarks were missing, and the tiller had been lost to the seas. The men themselves were exhausted, bruised and bone-weary from hunger, sea-sickness and lack of sleep. Staying alive as the ship rolled and plunged had used the last reserves of many. Now they only wanted to go home.

To this end, a deputation approached the captain and asked that they be put ashore, their shares in the enterprise to be willingly forfeited.

Others demanded they should at least seek shelter to assess the damage and the ship's condition, and to recuperate a little from their ordeal. Captain Stratman was obviously as sick as the rest of them, however, and no way was it possible to get certainty or any sort of leadership from him as he struggled to come to terms with his inadequacies. Then the gales blew up once more, flailing the ship with spray and rain, and further driving the unfortunate captain into a state of helplessness. Lawrence Hargrave himself feared all would be lost if the raging winds continued. Lookouts were posted in the hope of finding a passage to calmer waters behind the Barrier Reef, or at least to warn of reefs or shoals onto which they might be cast.

After two weeks of near ceaseless turmoil, land was sighted on 25th of February, 1872. It was a miracle they were still alive, but their troubles were far from over. Sometime during that night Lawrence Hargrave awoke to a grinding sound from below, which was followed shortly by a stunning shock. The *Maria* had finally been caught on a reef. Lanterns in the darkness showed that the rudder had been unshipped, the sternpost was thrust up through the deck, while parts of the frail hull lay split and broken amongst the coral heads. Age and misfortune in the hands of incompetents had at last caught up with her: *Maria* was a wreck.

With the approach of dawn and a rising tide, the ship began to lift off the reef and drift towards deeper water. Water immediately began to pour in copiously through the broken hull planking. Even then, nothing had been decided on where they might be or what they could do to save themselves. Though the winds and seas had abated, land was far off, they were still at risk, and very soon the remains of their ship might begin to break up beneath them. Such was their state of indecision that when Captain Stratman proposed he should take six men and row north to Townsville to seek help, others readily agreed. Almost without further preparation, a boat was lowered, six men climbed aboard with the captain and rowed away—entirely in the wrong direction. Without the skills or sightings for effective navigation, the castaways were already well to the north of Townsville. Unbeknownst to them, they had grounded on Bramble Reef, some 30 miles off the Queensland coast opposite Hinchinbrook Island.

Only one man showed opposition to the captain's action, when Sonnichsen, the First Mate, took up a rifle and blazed away at the retreating surfboat, accusing Stratman of leaving the others for dead. By then it was too late. The rest of the survivors set about building a pair of rafts under the guidance of Second Mate Andrews, spurred on by the chance that the *Maria* might soon founder completely. The two remaining boats were also swung out while supplies of food were handed up from below, along with cases of spirits. A number of men rapidly became drunk in their desperation, while dismay over their plight rendered others useless as helpers. Then just as the rafts were being launched, the brig tilted without warning and lay over into deeper water, pitching some into the sea while others scrambled aboard the makeshift floats. At this point there were 15 men in the damaged whale boat, six or so in the sternboat, and a total of 25 aboard the rafts.

Confusion still abounded amongst the leaderless groups. The rafts began to drift away north, while those in the whaleboat set out to reach land. Hargrave and a number of others had climbed onto the mainmast, which was still above water, there to await the return of the captain with a rescue vessel. Though they had provisions and spare clothing to sustain them, their perch was sufficiently precarious for those in the sternboat to return and persuade some at least to come aboard, Hargrave included. For some reason, possibly the risk of overloading, half-a-dozen others declined. The sternboat group then pulled away westward and after rowing all day came ashore on an island beach at dusk.

Next day they were joined by the company in the whaleboat, which brought the number of survivors there to 28. The weather turned against them once more, however, confining them to the island for another three days. Because of their earlier navigational problems there was some disagreement as to where they were, Hargrave being adamant that they were on Magnetic Island, others that their landfall was Hinchinbrook. After three days of frugal living while the seas abated, the latter identity was confirmed as the correct one when they arrived at Cardwell on the mainland coast, badly sunburned and scarcely able to walk, six days after leaving the wreck.

Others from the stricken ship fared less well. Lawrence Hargrave went back to Bramble Reef aboard the steamer *Tinonee* in search of those left on the *Maria*'s rigging, but found only items of clothing there. There were no survivors, though they searched the area for three days. On his return to Cardwell, Hargrave left others to continue the search while he took passage to Sydney on the steamer *Boomerang*, little the worse from his experiences. His action subsequently brought him deserved criticism in having abandoned his fellows in the manner of Captain Stratman, since there were still some 50 people from the wreck not accounted for. As a member of the working committee, it was felt he held some responsibility for their safety and welfare. At this point, however, Hargrave's own association with the *Maria* ceased, for although 36 men died as a result of the wreck, no one was brought to account by the later inquiry.

Meanwhile the search for survivors continued, particularly by those who themselves had survived the wreck. Luckiest were those from one of the rafts, which touched land in the vicinity of Gladys Inlet. Its occupants struggled ashore and soon were met by friendly Aborigines who fed them and tended their wounds, then pointed the way to the nearest white settlement, by way of other friendly Aboriginal groups. A party of eight was thus eventually picked up near Cooper Point by the search ship HMS *Basilisk*, which was probing the coast north of Cardwell in the hunt for survivors.

The first news of a tragedy came from two of the men from Captain Stratman's boat, which had reached the coast some 10 miles north of Cardwell. Almost as soon as they had landed the boat's occupants had been attacked by hostile Aborigines who murdered the captain and two others after the remaining four, though wounded, had made their escape into thick scrub. The first two men had been speared, and they were starved, naked and near exhaustion having beaten their way south through heavy untracked bush. The remaining pair straggled into town a few days later, bearing the news that not only had their fellows been murdered, but they had been eaten as well.

Consternation and anger followed in the town when it was realised that cannibals were virtually camped on their doorstep. These fears were confirmed when a search for the other raft revealed that its occupants, too, had been murdered. In response, a police party was organised to apprehend or punish the murderers, in conjunction with the crew from a local vessel and a company of Aboriginal troopers. Innocent or guilty, the suspect tribe was located shortly afterwards and attacked before dawn. In the ensuing skirmish a number of the 'suspects' were shot down by the Aboriginal troopers, who were reported as showing 'unrestrained ferocity' in carrying out their task.

An investigation into the wreck of the *Maria* was conducted by one Lieutenant Gowlland soon after all the survivors were found, from which a report was submitted to the Attorney-General of New South Wales. Accounts of the wreck and its aftermath also appeared in various newspapers. The inquiry found Thomas Stratman entirely to blame for the loss of the *Maria*, and condemned him as incapable as a master, worthless as a navigator, and wholly irresponsible in abandoning his vessel and its passengers on the pretext of seeking assistance. The report went on to censure the leaving of those on the rafts to the mercy of the inclement weather (clearly the fault of the two ship's officers in the boats) instead of taking them in tow.

There was no mention of the fact that Lawrence Hargrave, as a member of the expedition's working group, had departed the scene before any other survivors had been found. Nevertheless, his conscience apparently troubled him enough to make his own reply through a letter to the *Sydney Morning Herald*, which stated that he and others in the boats had taken the most effective course of action, given the proximity of land. He claimed that it would have been impossible to tow laden rafts by laden boats the distance they had to cover, and that their intention instead had been to land most of their own people, then return to the rafts to take off the others. The alternative, he stated, would have involved an attempt to bring everyone aboard the boats in the first instance at the risk of swamping both craft, one of which was already damaged.

In light of the fact that few of the volunteers had been seamen themselves and with little leadership during the incident, Hargrave's response was probably right. That they were unable to return to the rafts on account of the weather seems to have been an unfortunate quirk of fate by which 36 men died.

Chapter 10

FIRE VICTIMS
1833–1894

The *Lightning*.

*'Nothing was more guaranteed to make even the most hardened sailor
blanch than that first alien whiff of smoke on the salt air, the telltale
escape of smoke wisps warning all was not well below, or the dread cry,
especially at night, of ''Fire! Fire aboard!!'' '*

Fire—a natural phenomenon once commonly described, like water, as a good servant, but a bad master. Never was this more true than in the world of 19th century mariners on ships in the latter days of sail and the early days of steam. Fire was especially dangerous while ships continued to be built of timber. Only when more ships came to be built of iron, and carried large capacity water tanks as well as steam-driven pumps to give more effective fire-fighting capacity, did the risks of ship-board fires diminish.

Securely contained and carefully husbanded, the fire in the galley had long provided welcome warmth and many a hot meal after long cold watches on the world-roving sailing ships. In fact, the galley stove was often the only source of heat available to the crew, so great was the fear of rampant fire on passages far from land. With the wider applications of mechanical power, fire became the means of producing energy to drive the engines of the early steam ships, to turn winches with which to lift cargoes and raise anchors, to pump out the bilges, and to be forever free of the often harsh demands of handling sails, all of which saved the energies of a crew.

Once out of control though, and in a place where it was not meant to be, nothing was more guaranteed to make even the most hardened sailor blanch than that first alien whiff of smoke on the salt air, the telltale escape of smoke wisps warning all was not well below, or the dread cry, especially at night, of 'Fire! Fire aboard!!' This would be immediately followed by the clangorous din of the ship's bell, and a thunder of pounding feet from the often abruptly roused crew. Any fire aboard ship—and always on sailing ships—was urgent indeed for it could very quickly become life-threatening, and all the more so should it happen at sea.

A quayside blaze was bad enough as it was likely to result in damage or loss of the ship, and a part if not the whole of a valuable cargo. There, however, was usually a place for her complement to muster or to escape the showering sparks. Her crew could then stand and fight the gusting flames by means of piped water and hoses, bucket chains, pumps on board, on the dock or on boats brought alongside, and perhaps with the aid of horse-drawn fire engines.

On busy wharves, a ship's owner or master might expect or be able to call on the assistance of crewmen from other ships moored nearby, if only to protect their own ships from the spreading flames. With the assistance of other craft, a burning vessel might also be towed clear of her neighbours to a point where she could be grounded or scuttled. In such cases carpenter gangs would then cut holes below the water line to settle a burning vessel, all the while cringing from the searing heat and the twisting, fiery tongues. Alternatively, all other options gone, she might finally be left to burn while her crew and passengers remained safely ashore. In extreme cases the local militia might be called out to sink a blazing wreck with cannon shots, or to scuttle it with mines or torpedoes.

Many fires aboard ships around Australia have occurred at night, and most usually at or lying off a busy port. Both Sydney and Melbourne recorded some spectacular fires as the 19th century progressed. At sea, on the other hand, fire was infinitely more menacing and the means of fighting it far more limited, usually reliant only on buckets and pumps, and the swiftness of the crew. If not quickly extinguished a fire at sea could not only threaten a ship and her cargo, but also the very lives of everyone on board. Imagine what lay behind the message found in a bottle on a beach in New Zealand in 1879, which stated starkly:

'*Strathnaver* on fire off Polly Beach, 29th of April 1875. W. Waller, Chief Officer.' The barque *Strathnaver* was never seen again after leaving Sydney on 27th of April, 1875.

The causes of shipboard fires in those days were numerous, ranging from hot coals spilling from an unguarded galley stove, through spontaneous combustion amongst flammable cargoes, to the deliberate burning of a vessel by its owner or the crew. Arson was especially suspect in a number of incidents involving ship fires between 1853 and 1861, when the ships *Protector, West Wind, Columbian, Catherine Sharer, Sovereign of the Seas III* and *Empress of the Sea* all succumbed to what appeared to be acts of incendiarism. Four of these incidents occurred in Port Phillip Bay and may have been caused by crews who were keen to leave for the Victorian goldfields, though this could not be proved.

Deliberate burning almost certainly brought about the destruction of the American ship *Columbian* off Williamstown, Victoria, on 26th of April, 1854, whose crew was found to have deserted on being called out at the start of the fire. By that time the gold deposits being discovered around Ballarat, Mt Alexandra and the Ovens were well-known. However, when fire destroyed the *Empress of the Sea* while she was preparing to depart her anchorage at Queenscliff, it was known that threats had been made by a number of the crew to stop her from ever putting to sea. The crew were said to be angered by the master's ruthless attitude towards them. She was burnt out near the Quarantine Station in December 1861. Afterwards, the ship was deemed to have been wilfully set alight, though by persons unknown.

As a fire risk, certain cargoes were always more prone to spontaneous combustion than others, particularly where they were loaded in large quantities or carried in bulk. Wool and coal, for instance, were likely to pose special problems, the former if it was damp and given to producing heat through the work of micro-organisms, the latter if it generated enough dust and exploded. Both might smoulder quietly for some time in the depths of their stowage before bursting into flame. The seat of the outbreak would then be difficult to detect. Cotton and copra were similarly prone, and if stowed adjacent to such items as tallow, timber, liquor or kerosene, would result in a spectacular blaze if ignited. Nothing was quite so dramatic amongst the crowded wharves of Sydney, Melbourne or Hobart, where many such fires occurred, as the sight of a blazing ship and the associated frenzy of activity wrought by the need to douse the flames before total disaster followed.

The worst risks of all were those inherent in carrying dangerous explosives aboard a ship, and the threat to anyone in her vicinity in the event of a mishap. Gunpowder and dynamite were always in high demand in the colony, particularly around mid-century for defence, and for mining and quarrying, road and railway building, and the clearing of forests and heavy bush. For many years such explosives were brought here from overseas by ship, stowed with other cargoes. The barrels of fine powder, for instance, would sometimes split and leak, leaving quantities of loose explosive around the holds during unloading. Just one spark or flame would then be enough to set off a major blast.

The *Ann Jamieson* was unloading cargo at the Kings Wharf, Sydney, on 30th of November, 1833, when such a disaster struck. She had first discharged a large quantity of gunpowder at the Neutral Bay storage depot before moving across to the city wharves to complete the unloading of her other consignments. It was later calculated that around 160 pounds of gunpowder had leaked from the barrels, which exploded without warning, killing six. A second explosion during the fire which followed the first blast totally destroyed the vessel. Similar fates befell the barques *Thomas* in Hobart and *Winchester* on Port Phillip Bay 20 years apart, when they caught fire at anchor while waiting to put out to sea. Explosives kept aboard completed their destruction, though there was no loss of life.

An unusually large number of ship fires occurred at night. A sample of 30 major fires aboard ships in Australian waters during the 19th century show 80 per cent as occurring during the hours of darkness, many of them after midnight and especially in the hours before dawn. The reasons for this are not clear. It may be that with fewer people about to detect the early warning signs of smell or smoke, fires gained a greater hold before their discovery, and so were correspondingly severe. Perhaps the act of securing the vessel and closing the hatches at night had a damping effect on materials capable of spontaneous combustion, so that when a companionway was opened or a hatch cover removed on detecting the first warning signs, the suppressed fire would flare up with the ingress of fresh air and quickly run out of control.

Night time was usually the time when people would have ceased work within a ship, perhaps leaving a forgotten lamp or candle alight, a cigar butt burning, or a galley stove insufficiently closed. This was certainly the time when anyone engaged in nefarious activities would have been least likely to be detected on a dark and near-deserted wharf. The following accounts contain all the elements identified earlier as contributing to the causes of some major ship fires, their attempted suppression, and the eventual fate of the vessels concerned.

———————

It was 1.00am on 26th of January, 1868, when watchmen aboard the Black Ball clipper *City of Melbourne* and the *Niagara* moored close by, noticed smoke issuing from the forepart of the *City of Melbourne* as she lay alongside Williamstown's Railway Pier, on Port Phillip Bay. She had on board over 3000 bales of wool as the bulk of her outward cargo, together with a quantity of hides and barrels of tallow. Though the cause of the subsequent outbreak was never determined, it was felt that it originated amongst the cargo of wool.

The alarm was raised immediately smoke was seen, which brought the ship's crew together to work the pumps, as well as the crew from the *Niagara* who came with extra hoses. Shortly they were joined by men from the nearby Government Dockyard, from HMVS *Victoria* and a number of other vessels, and by the Water Police. Together they poured immense quantities of water into the ship which did little to stifle the blaze amongst the packed bales. This soon caused a dangerous list which threatened not only the ship, but also the wharf itself and other vessels nearby.

With little effect from the firefighters, it was decided to cut the *City of Melbourne* loose to allow her to drift away from other trouble. When she was sufficiently clear of the wharves her anchors were dropped, and the fore- and mizzen-masts were cut away to help reduce the list caused by the tons of water she had taken on. While the ship continued to blaze over their heads, gangs of carpenters worked to cut holes at the waterline to try and scuttle the ship. The process was a slow one.

To speed things up and fully quell the flames, daylight saw the soldiers of the breakwater battery preparing to use their guns on the blazing wreck. A number of shots holed it sufficiently to sink the remains of the vessel in five fathoms of water, where it continued to burn until all was consumed. After the main mast fell, there was soon no surface indication that the *City of Melbourne* had ever been.

Her remains were raised in February 1868 and removed to a site on the Yarra River where they were converted into a substantial lighter of more than 1000 tons. In her new role thereafter she had a chequered career on the river and later on Corio Bay, belonging in part to the Ministry of Defence. In 1880, she was rammed by the steamer *Edina*, and over the next 10 years was grounded twice in different parts of Corio Bay before being moored as a landing stage for excursion steamers visiting the Point Henry Tea Gardens. In 1890, she sank at her moorings, and remained there for five years until her remains were blown up on Defence Department instructions.

It was also 1.00am nearly two years later when another Black Ball clipper, the well-known *Lightning*, suffered the same fate as her former sister ship, the *City of Melbourne*. The *Lightning* was well-named and had become renowned for her speed, still being recognised as the fastest-ever ship under sail long after her demise. It would be 30 years before steamships were able to equal her record-breaking performances. All her glory came to an end, however, alongside the Yarra Pier at Geelong in the early morning of 31st of October, 1869.

Like her sister, she had loaded much of her outward cargo of wool, hides and tallow when smoke was seen issuing from her forepart. Before long she was ablaze there, and the ship's pumps were brought into operation to flood the burning hold. Crews quickly gathered from the *Aboukir*, the *Argo* and the *Lanarkshire* which were anchored in the vicinity, forming bucket chains to cast more water into the inferno. After an hour during which their efforts seemed to be having little effect, the tug *Resolute* was called in to shift the blazing ship away from the pier, but this was hardly under way when a number of fire engines arrived. The ship was swung back to allow the fire engines full effect, but after a further 90 minutes without real results, the *Lightning* was towed out from the pier so that attempts could be made to scuttle her.

While carpenters worked to cut into her hull, stevedores were brought in to begin unloading what wool bales they could reach into lighters, with whatever ship's fittings and furnishings they might also be able to save. Now that efforts to extinguish the flames from the pier had ceased, the fire leaped and roared with increasing intensity, an incandescent hell. This continued until the metal foremast melted in the heat and brought down a tangle of spars and blazing rigging onto the deck. For the men still on board it was time to retreat. This they did around 9.00am, after throwing overboard all the bales that had been pulled from the holds. The irony then was that the removal of some 400 heavy bales had buoyed the hull above the line of holes which had been cut to sink her.

As a last resort the local militia were called in to use artillery to sink the ship, but although three guns were employed, they ran out of powder after loosing off 50 salvoes without achieving a result. No shots had struck below the waterline. The ship was therefore left to burn, which she did for the rest of the day until she sank around 6.00pm. Later salvage efforts recovered most of the remaining cargo, but the wreck remains were not finally removed until June 1871.

As well as being known for her performance as the fastest amongst the growing clipper fleet, the *Lightning* was also renowned for her associations with the best-known of all Black Ball skippers, Captain James 'Bully' Forbes. On her delivery voyage from the USA in 1854, Captain Forbes drove the *Lightning* at speeds that were to set the pace for later voyages. A former skipper of another well-known clipper, the *Marco Polo*, Captain Forbes was notorious as a man who pressed his ships and crews hard, caring little for the comfort of his passengers in his quest for speed. Captain Forbes left the *Lightning* in 1855 to take command of the latest Black Ball acquisition, the luxuriously-appointed clipper, *Schomberg*. On her maiden voyage to Australia in October–December 1855, however, about which he boasted, 'Hell or Melbourne in sixty days!', he wrecked both the *Schomberg* and his reputation by running her aground, soon to become a total loss, near Peterborough on Victoria's 'shipwreck coast'.

In complete contrast with the fate of these ocean-going clippers, the Murray River paddle steamer *Rodney* was also a fire victim, but in quite unique circumstances. It was the time of the 1894 shearers' strike, and the paddle steamer *Rodney* had been contracted to take 45 free labourers up the Darling River to work in the wool shed of the Tolarno district. In an effort to prevent such movements, unionists were camped at various points along the river, and were prepared to go to any lengths to achieve their aim.

Sometime around the middle of August, the *Rodney*'s skipper, Captain Dickson, had been advised that a number of unionists were camped at the Polia wool shed, and were prepared to stop any vessels carrying non-union labourers from proceeding upstream. Thus forewarned, on 26th of August he stopped and tied up for the night in an area of swampy lakes and braided river courses, feeling secure in the knowledge that an approach through such terrain would be almost impossible in the darkness. Just to be certain, he rostered a number of guards around the *Rodney*, then settled down for the night.

His precautions were all in vain, for it appeared the unionists knew the convoluted river system better than he did. Word certainly reached the unionists by some means that a boat-load of scab labour was trying to sneak through their lines. At 4.00am or thereabouts, over 100 armed men boarded the *Rodney*, held her crew at gun point and scattered the labourers to the four winds, some naked, others clad only in their long underwear, and more than a few having first been thrown overboard.

The raiders then set the *Rodney* alight. When she was blazing well the crew were allowed to move onto the barge that the paddle steamer towed in her wake, but Captain Dickson was held until all hope of saving his vessel was gone. After the raiders had left he made a desperate attempt to scuttle her but was unsuccessful. By that time the flames had become so fierce that he had to make his own escape, which he did by means of a small boat he kept tied to the stern.

After several hours the *Rodney* had burned out and sank. All that remained worth salvaging was her boiler. Shortly after the blaze a number of men were arrested, but their trial was inconclusive and they were released. Some time afterwards another man was arrested and tried in connection with the loss of the *Rodney*. He was subsequently jailed, though many believed he was merely a scapegoat and that the real perpetrators were never caught. Though the *Rodney* had been insured, because of the strike situation in which she was burned the insurers refused to pay out.

In Melbourne meanwhile, fire destroyed the cargo vessel *Habitant* on 8th of June, 1894, in her berth at South Wharf on the Yarra River. The incident happened in the early hours of the morning, and though arson was suspected, it was never proved. It was no doubt a most spectacular blaze for those who witnessed it.

The *Habitant* finished the unloading of some 28 000 cases of kerosene only a few hours before the outbreak. As a cargo vessel, large quantities of the fuel had been carried on previous occasions, and she was due to leave for Newcastle next day to pick up a cargo of coal for the Philippines. Such cargoes were highly flammable and even after ships had been unloaded, dangerous residues would often remain to soak into their timbers or accumulate in spaces between decks.

About 5.00am a passing river pilot noticed fire aboard the *Habitant* and immediately raised the alarm. The *Habitant*'s master, Captain Potter, quickly roused his wife and children who were aboard with him, and then the crew. With the flames clearly taking a firm hold, he hurried everyone off the ship before returning to gather up the ship's papers and what personal belongings he was able to save.

The fire brigade took 30 minutes to reach the dockside, by which time the *Habitant* was well alight. Her hatches had burned through by then, which gave new strength to the flames. More than 40 firefighters had assembled to help combat the blaze, but their efforts were constantly hampered by billowing smoke which welled up thickly from below. In addition, it soon became obvious that the fire was a deep-seated one and therefore difficult to reach, even though the ship was in ballast in preparation for her trip to Newcastle and had only dunnage in her holds. Suspicions were thus aroused that the conflagration may have started as an act of incendiarism, though little was likely to remain to elicit the truth.

As there was also the danger of flames spreading to other vessels, the *Jenny Harkness* was shifted from immediately astern of the *Habitant* for fear her own cargo of kerosene might suffer in the same way as her empty neighbour. With 30 000 cases of the volatile oil still lying in her holds, the port authorities had to act quickly to move her away to safety, so preventing the possibility of a wider and perhaps more explosive conflagration. Eventually the fire burned itself out after holes had been cut in the hull. The *Habitant*'s remains were later raised and converted into a floating dock, which remained in use in nearby Williamstown for another 60 years.

Perhaps the most dramatic fire episode in human terms was that which destroyed the *Hilaria*, sister ship to the *Habitant*, on 7th of July, 1895. It was certainly one of the most heroic. The scene was again set amongst the Melbourne wharves, and once more a volatile cargo was involved, in this instance 2000 cases of kerosene and 500 barrels of resin.

As a portent of her ultimate fate, the *Hilaria* had suffered a small fire only a few days earlier. The decisive actions of Deputy Chief Officer O'Brien of the attendant fire brigade had the outbreak extinguished quickly after he was lowered into the burning hold to aim hoses directly into the source of the flames. On the second occasion, shortly after midnight, the ship was burning fiercely by the time the fire brigade arrived, and with her cargo already a flaming mass the fire fighters were to be hard-pressed in trying to save her.

For a while all seemed to be going reasonably well as the large quantities of water being poured into the stricken ship appeared to be keeping the fire contained. Soon though, a rising wind began to bear on the ship, causing her to list under the volume of water aboard and to poise her blazing rigging over the wharf and the people beneath. It was a dangerous situation. Because several other vessels were moored nearby, a decision was made to move the *Hilaria* out into Port Phillip Bay, but while the tug *Albatross* was undertaking the task Superintendent Gee, one of the fire chiefs, fell head first down a hatch into the depths of the burning ship.

Deputy Chief Officer O'Brien was again on the scene. Donning a protective smoke-jacket, he quickly descended into the smoke-filled hold in search of the unfortunate Gee. Some 15 minutes passed with mounting concern that O'Brien himself was lost, but feeling a tug on his safety line, others of his party hauled him up—feet first! His harness had slipped and he appeared to be dead, but he was nevertheless able to gasp out that he had found Gee and tied him to his other line. His bravery was to earn him the Humane Society Medal.

No time was wasted in hauling the badly-injured Superintendent out of the hold. However, his condition was such that with a fractured skull and brain injuries, he died later without having recovered consciousness. Throughout all this, all ongoing attempts to quell the fire had failed. Burning fiercely from stem to stern the *Hilaria* was abandoned, then subjected to artillery fire from a gun brought from HMVS *Nelson* on a barge. When this also failed, a number of explosive charges were fixed and fired under her hull. The resulting holes quickly sank the blazing hulk, whose remains were later raised and broken up.

Chapter 11

LOCH ARD

1878

Castle Tower Rock, Loch Ard Gorge.

'Fearing the approach of unfriendly Aborigines, whose calls she had
thought were war-cries, she had crawled away to hide in the darkening
scrub, and had only been discovered when one of the searchers ...
heard her terrified moans ...'

I n the leathered comfort of the first class lounge of the clipper *Loch Ard*, Dr Evory Carmichael lingered over a last glass of port before turning in, looking back over a voyage from London that had been pleasantly fulfilling, and quietly contemplating their arrival in Melbourne tomorrow, 2nd of June 1878.

At the urging of his eldest son William who had earlier settled in New South Wales, and prevailed upon by the rest of his family on health grounds, he had left a well-established medical practice in Ireland and brought them all out to begin a new life in Australia, where they would be arriving next day. Already asleep in their cabins, having enjoyed a small farewell party with the other passengers on this final night at sea, were his wife, four daughters and his two younger sons. They had much to look forward to in this young, burgeoning country if all William had said was true.

The voyage itself had had a promising start, with fair weather, only one gale when nearing the Cape, and the excitement of a race with the clipper *John Kerr* to see which ship would reach Melbourne first. This was an uneventful passage, totally unlike her maiden voyage to Australia four years before when she had been dismasted twice and had to cover the last 4500 miles to Melbourne under jury rig! But Captain Gibbs, in relating the story, had assured his passengers that such teething troubles had long been resolved, and that all promised well for a safe arrival.

Unusually, the captain had declined to join the evening's party. Dr Carmichael had noted a certain anxiety about the man now that they were nearing their destination. He was aware that this was Captain Gibbs' first trip to Australia, having spoken with him many times over dinner at the captain's table. What he did not know, however, was Captain Gibbs' concern over the accuracy of his compasses—but all would no doubt be well on such a tried and tested route, especially as the hazards of the Bass Strait entrance were marked now by permanent lighthouses.

Even so, his mind still slipped momentarily to the foreboding expressed by that fellow Reg Jones, a passenger who had been telling his daughter Eva that he felt he would never set foot in their new country. Dr Carmichael shrugged and drained his glass. Some people were born pessimists. The *Loch Ard* was forging along steadily under full sail, about 100 miles south west of the Cape Otway light. He rose stiffly, adjusting his gait to the heel of the ship, and carefully made his way to bed.

———

As it happened, Reginald Jones' pessimism so long ago was fully justified. His body now lies buried on a windswept clifftop within sight of Victoria's Twelve Apostles, alongside others of the Carmichael family who sailed on the ill-fated *Loch Ard*. Many others died in the tragedy, but their bodies were never recovered. Only two people were to survive her loss.

Captain Gibbs' unspoken anxieties were also justified. All that night he remained on deck, searching, looking ahead, checking his ship. After midnight the wind strengthened and before three o'clock the first sails had been furled. Though a heavy mist lay out where the Cape Otway light was expected, the sea was clear and stars were visible. A lookout ascended the foremast at regular intervals to look for the light, until the shrouding fog closed in. Then, around 4.00am, the mists parted to reveal looming cliffs close to hand, and very little room in which to try to sheer away.

All hands were called on deck, and orders were quickly given to hoist sail in a desperate attempt to bring the *Loch Ard* about, but with insufficient sail set in such restricted waters the ship missed stays, lost momentum, and wallowed head to wind. With a lee shore so close to hand the *Loch Ard* was in dire straits. The wind began to press her backwards towards the cliffs. Both anchors were let go to check her drift as land loomed perilously close, but these then failed to hold. In the turmoil of waters churning beneath the cliffs, the rise and fall of the ship lifted the anchors clear of the sea floor. Only 50 fathoms of chain were let out since more might have set them upon the rocks. This was to be their fate, even so, despite all the urgency of bracing the yards and setting enough sail to wear the ship out of danger.

Within minutes the *Loch Ard* fouled a rock ledge so close to the shore that her yards struck the perpendicular face of a nearby sea stack as she rolled. The shifting sea then began pounding the ship on her rock pinion, time and again, starting holes and buckling plates as alarm and distress spread amongst the passengers. Orders were given to lower the boats, people hurriedly donned life jackets, and panic threatened as the waning gloom revealed their plight. Heavy seas began breaking over the ship as she continued to swing against her underwater trap, drenching all. The *Loch Ard* was already settling lower amongst the seething waves. While the crew struggled with the boats, loose running gear, blocks and spars, and large pieces of stone started to fall, breaking away in collisions with the towering rock walls and causing many on the crowded decks, passengers and crew alike, to seek shelter again below. It was a fatal choice. There was little time left.

One of the six crewmen trying to launch the port lifeboat was 18-year old apprentice Tom Pearce. Though he had been at sea less than three years, he was already familiar with the perils they now faced, and the possible consequences. His first ship, the *Eliza Ramsden*, had suffered a similar fate to the *Loch Ard*. On only his second day aboard on the 24th of July 1875, she struck Corsair Rock while negotiating

Port Phillip Heads and later sank in Port Phillip Bay. Worse still though, only four months before that, he had lost his father, Captain R.G. Pearce, who was master of the steamer *Gothenburg* at the time she foundered after striking a reef off Townsville, Queensland, in February 1875. The sea rarely forgave the unwary.

The boat was released, carried away at first on the backwash from the cliffs. The men sought to hold onto the *Loch Ard* with grappling irons, but their boat capsized almost immediately as it surged into the stricken clipper. Tom Pearce went down, grasped at the upturned boat on surfacing, then slipped beneath it for a better hold while he regained his strength. When he emerged there was no sign of his shipmates, nor was there much else to see from amongst the floating wreckage but the soaring cliffs close by. The surging tide carried the capsized craft to and fro until by chance he spotted a gorge that cut into the cliff face only a short swim away. He let go of the boat and struck out for the sandy beach now becoming visible at the head of the gorge. Cold, wet and near exhaustion, he struggled ashore only to be faced with the chill realisation that he was alone. The *Loch Ard* had gone, and with her the rest of her complement. The sea was filled with flotsam that was already beginning to drift into the cove, but of survivors there was no sign. Numbly he staggered for shelter into a nearby cave.

Tom Pearce was lucky. The five men with him in the lifeboat were drowned when it overturned. Six or so others were carried away when the upper main topsail yard snapped on striking the cliffs, taking them with it. Captain Gibbs was last seen on the poop. Many were trapped below decks or had sought shelter there from falling debris, and so went down with the ship. The last prayers of those crying for deliverance went unanswered, save for a merciful death beneath the waves.

One small spark remained, however, despite the trauma of the wreck, the chill of the sea, and the fear of what might still befall. Eva Carmichael, who had listened to the premonitions of Reginald Jones while trying to lift his despondency, still clung to a spar she had somehow reached, though unable to swim, and now was only half alive after her frantic struggles and long immersion. For a while she shared the spar with two others, Reginald Jones of all people, and one named Arthur Mitchell. She had witnessed Jones attend the shivering plight of Mitchell, adding his own life-belt to that worn by his companion, before both swam away into oblivion. She was now alone.

How long she drifted she had no idea. Her own life-belt was lost when its ties parted. Sighting a rock she set out to reach it, but the sea dashed her against it, bruising her badly and almost drowning her as she strove valiantly to survive. Despair filled her being and her strength was near-gone when, around the rock, she glimpsed a figure on the distant strand. Shouting as best she could and waving feebly, her relief was almost overpowering when she saw Tom Pearce turn, walk out into the water, then commence what became a desperate struggle first to reach her, then to take her to the safety of the sands.

Tom Pearce had rested in his cave for about an hour before hunger drove him out in search of food. It was then that he heard Eva Carmichael's cry for help, and spied her clinging to the spar about 200 yards from where he stood. He waded out as far as he could, then struck out again to reach the fast-fading girl whom he quickly recognised, despite her bedraggled state, as one of the Carmichael family. Almost as soon as he reached her she fainted away, but he managed to hold on to her clothing with his teeth as he drew her unconscious form back towards the beach.

Once there he could only marvel at the girl's slender hold on life, as badly bruised and chilled through as she was, and wearing only a nightdress and jacket. Though it was now approaching midday, the air was cold and her bluish pallor told him that shelter was essential if she was to remain alive. The young apprentice therefore carried her over to a larger cave he had seen, where he made her as comfortable as he could on a bed of vegetation. From amongst the flotsam at the water's edge he collected a case of brandy, some of which he plied her with when she regained a measure of consciousness. The brandy, the shelter and a massaging of limbs helped to restore something of her natural colour, but after she had succumbed to her exhaustion once more, he knew that he would need to get help soon if she was to further survive her ordeal. Before that though, he needed to rest . . .

Where to get help? Where were they? Looking out onto the cove a while later, Tom could see that it was enclosed by high cliffs topped with a heavy kind of shrub, without any obvious means of ascent. How to climb them, and where to go then? He remembered that around mid-afternoon the previous day, Mr Baxter, the second mate, had said they were 150 miles or so south-west of Cape Otway. Having at no time seen the light there, he felt they had been wrecked some way to the west of the Cape still, therefore a long way yet from Melbourne. The coast they had seen appeared barren and rocky, as was evident to him now. Surviving the wreck was clearly one thing—continuing to survive promised to be quite another. With a last check on Eva's sleeping form, he set out to try and find a way up the cliffs.

His first efforts were frustrating failures. The rock faces were steep and the sandstone mass offered few hand- or foot-holds. In desperation and increasing fatigue, he looked about for a gully, a water-course or some other crevice up which he could climb, to conserve his energies for the journey that would follow. At last, however, he was able to haul himself over the edge of the cliff where he paused to regain his breath, only to be confronted then by a dense sea of waist-high coastal scrub, broken here and there by thickets of taller vegetation, forbiddingly impenetrable and almost impossible to traverse. But he had to try.

The landscape was bleak and uninhabited. The scrub tore at his clothes and scratched his skin, and more than once he had to banish the thought of returning to the security of the cave. He pushed his way forward through the short abrasive bushes, swearing and sobbing occasionally as the day wore on, without a sign of civilisation. Then, by chance, he came upon a beaten track and was instantly encouraged to go on, heartened by this first sign of humanity amongst the surrounding desolation. His persistence and fortitude paid off. Before long he was hailed by two men on horses, who saw before them a ragged, wild-looking youth, bleeding from hands and feet, who smelled of brandy but who also gasped out a tale about a shipwreck and a dying girl somewhere off to the west.

George Ford and William Till were mustering sheep from nearby 'Glenample' station when they saw Tom Pearce approaching. Having told the men his story, describing the wreck site as best he could and asking them to ride for help, he stoically declined an offer of food and fresh footwear, and turned back to the cliff-top, fearful of Eva's reaction should she wake and find him gone. The two drovers reached the station where food and drink were quickly packed by Mrs Gibson, the station-owner's wife, while Hugh Gibson himself saddled horses to make up a rescue party.

Gibson and his drovers found a bloodied Tom Pearce in a state of acute distress when they reached the head of the cliffs in the late afternoon, seeing him caught amongst the heavy scrub and near to tears. On scrambling down to see what was amiss, they freed the young man then went round to the cave, only to find it empty. The group split up and searched all around the cove, looking for Eva who was nowhere to be found! 'She's gone, she's drowned herself,' the youth cried in anguish, and he immediately fell in a faint, such was his tiredness and the depth of his concern.

Evening was fast approaching, being early winter, and the need to find the missing girl was becoming urgent. Gibson and his men continued the search until nightfall, having sent William Till back to the station for lanterns, more helpers, and a lightweight buggy to transport the girl when she was found. It was nine o'clock before he returned with four others and the buggy, but by then Eva had been located, just at the point where they were to call off the search. On awaking she had missed Tom, hearing instead the strange calls of people moving about the nearby cliffs and beaches. Fearing the approach of unfriendly Aborigines, whose calls she had thought were war-cries, she had crawled away to hide in the darkening scrub, and had only been discovered when one of the searchers, coo-eeing to others of the party, heard her terrified moans issuing from a clump of bushes.

Blankets were produced, a fire was made of wreckage from the ship, and the food and coffee prepared earlier was given to the two grateful castaways. Then began the task of getting both up the cliff to safety, a difficult task in the ill-lit darkness with the girl still suffering from the effects of her ordeal, and grieving the almost certain loss of her family. When the weary party arrived back at the 'Glenample' homestead it was past 2.00am. The shocked girl was fussed over, warmed through and put to bed, though she remained semi-delirious throughout the night. Meanwhile young Tom Pearce, his heroic task complete, collapsed into a sleep of utter fatigue. The day was not over for George Ford, however, the drover who had first spotted Tom Pearce. As soon as the girl was found, Hugh Gibson sent him away to ride the 50 miles to Camperdown to break the news of the *Loch Ard* disaster.

The following day a sombre party made its way back to the wreck site in the faint hope of finding other people alive. According to Tom Pearce, now recovered from his exertions, up to 50 people might have perished in the wreck. Arriving at the cove they found wreckage piled all along the waterline. Of the ship, only a single mast stood a little way off the islet, now called Mutton Bird Island, to mark the scene of the tragedy.

The first bodies they found were Eva's mother, Rebecca, and her sister Raby. Tom Pearce's feelings became evident when he remarked, 'Of all on the ship, this girl is the one I would like to have saved.' Shortly afterwards they found the bodies of the two men who had briefly shared a spar with Eva, Reginald Jones and Arthur Mitchell. Eleven more bodies were sighted from the rim of a blowhole, but there was no way of reaching them from the cliffs. There were no other survivors.

Many local people attended the burial of the *Loch Ard* victims at the place on the wind-swept bluff chosen by Eva Carmichael, within sight of the wreck. It was attended by police and customs officials who were already there to supervise the first salvage operations, safeguard the cargo, and deter the pilfering that had been reported. Others came from around the district and assisted this work. Several newspaper reporters were also present. The Gibsons of 'Glenample' were there with Tom and Eva, together with the men who had rescued them. Coffins had been made from piano cases washed ashore from the wreck, and the preacher from Heytesbury, a village nearby, conducted the service.

After the burial, serious thought had to be given to the enormous quantities of wreckage being washed into the gorge and piling up on the sands, much of which came from a cargo valued at more than £50 000. The wreck was auctioned and sold to a Geelong company for £1200, and the new owners were quickly on the scene to assess the task. Teams of horses and gangs of men were organised to sort through the heaps, arrange stacks of like salvage and begin the work of hauling it up the sheer cliffs. The amount of cargo to be salvaged promised to yield a fair profit when suddenly, despite locals' warnings, a heavy storm blew up during which big seas filled the gorge, reclaimed the stacked goods, and swept them out to sea.

Undeterred, the salvage merchants then chartered the steamer *Napier* to carry divers out to the wreck to undertake further salvage there. On returning to her base at Port Campbell on her aborted third trip, however, the *Napier* was forced onto rocks by a rising swell, damaging a propeller and holing her near the bow. The steamer's captain quickly sent three boats off to lay an anchor with which to kedge her off the rocks, but conditions were such that two were immediately stove-in. Though further efforts were arranged to refloat the *Napier* in calmer weather, including the use of a pump ordered from Melbourne, the steamer had become a total wreck before it could be delivered. All salvage prospects were then abandoned.

Throughout this time, Tom and Eva stayed with the Gibsons for two months while they recovered fully from the tragedy. In Melbourne, Tom attended an inquiry into the circumstances of the wreck where he was afterwards presented with a gold watch and chain by the Governor of Victoria. Next day he was presented with the first gold medal of the Royal Humane Society of Victoria in recognition of his heroism. By public acclaim Tom was indeed seen as a hero, though he modestly felt he had only done what was right at the time. The people of Warrnambool collected £100 to give him new clothes and pocket money. Later, at a public reception in Sydney, he was presented with a set of nautical instruments and navigation references as suitably befitting the seaman he was. In addition, a trust was established to receive the substantial sum subscribed by the Victorian and New South Wales public for his personal use, either on coming of age or on assuming command of his first ship.

Back at 'Glenample' meanwhile, a closeness and affection had developed between the two young people, no doubt encouraged by Jane Shields, a local girl of Eva's age with whom she had become friends. As Eva recovered her natural vitality, she would often embarrass the young seaman by throwing her arms about him and proclaiming him, 'My saviour!' Their relationship might have held all the promise of contemporary Victorian romance and melodrama, for this was how many viewed it, but it was not to be. In spite of the warmth of her care and attention amongst new friends, she was alone in a strange land. And public subscriptions on her behalf had raised enough for her to be able to return to others of her family in Ireland. In August 1878, therefore, she was seen off aboard the SS *Sanjore* by Tom Pearce and her friends from 'Glenample'. She would never see either Tom or Australia again. A few years later she married T.A. Townshend of Bedford, England, where she lived and raised a family in the years that followed.

Tom Pearce himself went to Sydney shortly afterwards, and there joined the crew of the *Loch Sunart* on her maiden voyage from England. His adventures at sea were by no means over. On her next voyage to Australia the *Loch Sunart* sailed into Skulmartin Rock off the coast of Ireland, and became another total loss. The crew, including young Tom, were all saved. Tom Pearce eventually married and raised his own family. He rose to become a captain with the Royal Mail Steam Packet service until he retired on the grounds of ill-health, and died in 1908.

Tragedy continued to dog Tom's footsteps even after he had left his employ with the Loch Line. In 1905, one of his sons was lost in the wreck of the *Loch Vennacher*, which sank off Kangaroo Island, South Australia, in September of that year. The Loch Line had an unfortunate record amongst its many vessels, despite the fact that the company itself was very successful, and the clipper ships they operated were often the latest in speed and comfort. No fewer than 17 of their ships were lost at sea between 1871 and 1918, 11 of them whilst still under Loch Line ownership. Of these 11, 6 were lost off the Australian coast. Besides the *Loch Ard* and *Loch Vennacher*, the others included: *Loch Leven*, which became a total wreck on King Island in 1871; *Loch Maree*, which disappeared after leaving Geelong for London in 1881; *Loch Sloy*, wrecked on Kangaroo Island in 1889 with the loss of 31 lives; and *Loch Katrine*, which became a coal hulk in Sydney following a misadventure in the Tasman Sea in 1910.

The grave of the *Loch Ard* lay undiscovered until 1967, when her remains were found close to Mutton Bird Island by a local diver. Controversy surrounded the ownership of the wreck for some time, during which the *Loch Ard* became the focus of a fossicking frenzy by treasure hunters, with as many as 30 divers pulling pieces from the wreck on one occasion, according to a plaintive article written for a dive club newsletter at the time. Some items were later recovered under the terms of the *Navigation Act* 1911, while others were recorded as part of the 1993 amnesty which allowed for declarations of ownership of wreck relics without fear of prosecution.

This amnesty was devised and administered to locate and record relics, not to confiscate them, and so many of the items from the *Loch Ard* are still in private hands. Owners may not dispose of such relics without a permit, but meanwhile there is no guarantee that the care, conservation and security of privately-owned artefacts is either adequate or appropriate. The best location for such artefacts is undeniably a conservation laboratory or an accredited maritime museum. Unfortunately, the Flagstaff Hill Maritime Museum at nearby Warrnambool still has relatively few relics, though it does hold some sheets of copper and large numbers of lead ingots, as well as the magnificent Minton peacock which was destined for display at the Great Melbourne Exhibition of 1880.

Chapter 12

QUETTA
1890

RMS *Quetta*.

'The suction of the sinking ship takes a hold and drags many into the depths, where only the strongest or most determined kick and struggle to the surface through a tangle of flailing arms and legs ...'

For the passengers aboard the steamer RMS *Quetta* on the evening of 28th of February, 1890, off the north Queensland coast, the night held promise of another warm tropical calm on a glass-like ocean. Many of them had chosen to remain on deck after dinner as they sailed north towards Torres Strait, in order to escape the stifling heat that filled the accommodation below. The cooling breeze that accompanied the ship's passage offered some relief from the humid warmth. It was pleasant, anyway, to meet up with new friends for a drink or a chat, or perhaps to dally at the rail with a lady at the end of this, their eleventh day at sea. The pink and purple light of the dying day still showed off to port where lay the low outline of the Australian coast. Apart from Thursday Island next day, for many it would be almost the last glimpse of their homeland as they journeyed off to Britain and other exciting destinations overseas.

About 9.00pm the *Quetta's* master, Captain Sanders and Captain Keatinge, his Torres Strait pilot, made the first turn into the Adolphus Channel to round Cape York for Thursday Island. Navigation at night could be tricky amongst the northern shoals and coral reefs, but pilot Keatinge was well-experienced, the weather was fine and visibility was good in the rising moonlight. All the local navigation points were where they were expected. Then, at 9.14pm, the *Quetta* struck an uncharted rock near the middle of the channel, the collision ripping away a large number of plates from her bow to the engine room amidships, leaving a yawning gap into which the seas thundered unchecked.

For a shocked moment few realised what was amiss. But as the *Quetta* slowed and began to settle, horror dawned unbelievingly on those still on deck. For those who had turned in below, there was already little hope. The seas flooded in mightily, engulfing all. In less than five minutes—some said only three—the *Quetta* was gone, along with nearly half of those on board. Her last voyage had just become the worst maritime disaster in Queensland's history.

The RMS *Quetta* was one of the British India Line fleet which plied regularly between various ports in England, India and the Far East. In 1880, an extension of their services to Queensland had been negotiated by the Queensland Government in a move to speed the passage of mail and passengers directly to and from Brisbane to the United Kingdom, rather than via Sydney or Melbourne as previously. The *Quetta* was specially built for the run to Australia, being fitted with refrigerated cargo spaces in anticipation of a profitable frozen meat trade. Launched in March 1881, she made her first voyage to Brisbane in 1883 as part of the Queensland Royal Mail Line service, hence the letters RMS (Royal Mail Ship) before her name.

Quetta was fitted out with all the comforts of her class at the time, along the lines of her sister ships *Manora* and *Merkara*, the latter of which undertook the initial run from London to Queensland. At 380 feet long, 40 feet wide, and 30 feet deep, her gross tonnage was 3300 tons and her measured speed over 13 knots. She was designed to carry 72 first class (saloon) and 32 second class (steerage) passengers, though her accommodation was later altered to carry fewer saloon passengers in favour of larger numbers of migrants—with a strict division to opposite ends of the ship between single males and single females! On her last voyage from England in December 1889, she carried only 21 saloon passengers, but more than 350 migrants in cabins that were now uncomfortably cramped.

In addition she had the capacity for almost 1500 tons of mail and cargo, and over 500 tons of coal as fuel.

The *Quetta* had completed 11 round trips between London and Brisbane during her five-and-a-half years on the service, and had become a popular ship amongst the well-to-do, if not amongst the migrants. Even so, many a new Queenslander had cause to bless the *Quetta* as their vehicle to a fresh start in life. *Quetta*'s voyage to oblivion was the uncompleted second leg of her twelfth round trip.

On this passage *Quetta*'s crew numbered 121, comprising 15 European officers and 14 other trades, the remainder being made up of 92 lascars who were seamen (oilers, stokers, firemen and saloon boys) from India. Before leaving Brisbane she embarked 26 saloon passengers and 34 for steerage, and expected to pick up 42 others at various Queensland ports on the journey north. On this particular trip also, some temporary deck-houses had been installed near the stern to accommodate a group of 70 Javanese who had been working out three-year contracts in the cane fields and were now returning home via Batavia. They were to be embarked at Mourilyan. Only one person would disembark before the ship left Australia. A total of 292 people were thus aboard the *Quetta* as she steamed at 12 knots towards the fateful rock in the Adolphus Channel— one of them a stowaway who had come aboard with like-minded friends from Townsville, and had remained undiscovered when the others were found and put ashore.

Imagine then, the stark transition between the comfort, security and peace of one moment as the ship sails serenely northwards on what, for many, should be the trip of a lifetime, and the rising fear and apprehension a few short moments later when the ship is holed and sinking rapidly. Imagine the horror knowing that people trapped below, some of them loved ones, are already dead or being drowned. Confusion reigns in the disbelief that this is really happening. Then the deck tilts frighteningly as

Quetta takes on a sharp list to port. Her officers are heard shouting orders to 'Lower the lifeboats!' and 'Break out the lifebelts!' while at the same time asking for calm. People begin to move fearfully in all directions, panic barely subdued in their efforts to seize the proffered lifejackets, to reach the boats, to look for relatives, to stay together while scrambling up the tilting deck, or contemplating a leap into the darkening sea. Reality is still slow in taking hold, for the glancing collision itself was barely felt.

In the first instant of the strike, however, the entire boiler room and engine room crews have been wiped out as the sea surges in, some scalded to death by boiling water or escaping steam, some drowned, others hurled against machinery or flung against bulkheads. Those asleep in their bunks are overwhelmed where they lie, or drown in the confusion of crowded cabins. Numbed disbelief slows reactions. Others who have escaped into the corridors find their way blocked by struggling people on narrow ladders and companionways, while the flooding waters rush in to smother all. Few escape from below decks, and those who do are confronted by the melee above as the ship slips further into the waves. The screams and cries of the desperate are all around, while people hurrying nowhere add to the frenzy. Others stand in stunned silence, terrified of the unknown.

Less than two minutes have passed and already the ship is well down by the head, her stern beginning to lift clear of the waves. The tilt is becoming menacing, with sea water surging along the decks, rising higher each second as the vessel continues to sink. When the first boat hits the water it is immediately swamped by a host of screaming, leaping people— the deck-housed Javanese. Efforts to launch a second boat come to naught as the tilt makes a launch impossible, the falls give way, and the people already in it are tossed into the sea. Others have jumped overboard. The water is a thrashing, grasping scene of struggling, drowning people who seek to cling to anything or anyone within reach. Any hope of keeping order has gone. Survival is paramount.

The sounds of the sinking ship defeat the cries of those in the water and those wailing in terror still on board. The bursting boilers are voiding steam through the funnel in a raucous, screaming roar. Pent-up air below decks is being forced out in bubbling shrieks through open portholes, while hatch covers give way explosively above the mounting pressure from beneath. Fittings on deck begin to shift and tumble to the sounds of mounting distress amongst the stricken passengers, and machinery within the hull crashes and thuds against straining bulkheads. The lights flicker and go out, come on again, then are extinguished forever. Only the dim moonlight remains to reflect the phosphorescent splashing of those in the foaming surge below. The soft glow illuminates the horror on the faces of those who have remained on the tilting stern, who suddenly realise they are about to be trapped, as beneath a giant hand, by the canvas awnings still spread as protection from a sun that many will never see again.

In the water non-swimmers quickly drown, often impeding the movements of those who can swim and drowning them too. The suction of the sinking ship takes a hold and drags many into the depths, where only the strongest or most determined kick and struggle to the surface through a tangle of flailing arms and legs, broken ropes and rigging, and a mess of flotsam that once was a ship—spars, deckchairs, oars, gratings, rafts and drowned livestock from the pens on deck. Above them the hull of the doomed *Quetta* poises darkly against a dark sky in moonlit silhouette before the last rush into the deep. Her stern is momentarily checked as her stem cleaves the sea-bed before it, too, disappears in a gushing, bubbling swirl with the last group clinging still to hope. In just three minutes or so from the time of the collision, *Quetta* is gone, taking about a third of her complement with her. The rest are left to fight for their lives in the water, though already their numbers are diminishing as the weakest succumb to shock, exhaustion and exposure. For a short while the night is rent by harrowing calls to lost loved ones, by cries of distress and despair.

Only one lifeboat had survived the wreck, upturned and badly damaged. The ship's cutter had floated clear, but it too was capsized. Even so, it offered some small security to a large group of Javanese and lascar seamen, and mayhem reigned as they fought and struggled to grasp and climb aboard the upturned craft. Unintentionally their combined weights served to right the boat, albeit half full of water, which was then once more swamped by the sheer numbers trying to scramble aboard. Fortunately the ship's quartermaster, James Oates, was on hand to order most people out so that the cutter could be baled, before allowing them all back in to row to the distant shore.

Number 1 starboard lifeboat had meanwhile attracted a similar crowd, though one more orderly, controlled by Third Officer Thomas Babb. The craft was righted and baled out, but was found to be so much damaged that it served as little more than a floating support, largely awash, for the people clinging on and around it. Nevertheless, a drifting spar was added thwart-wise as a makeshift seat for some of the occupants. Then, with the help of the only pair of oars at hand and the determination of the survivors, this boat also headed towards the land, picking more people up on the way, including Captain Sanders.

Others in the water had to make do with what they came across in the darkness as a means of support, though youth and vigour played a notable part in the remarkable survival of two of the younger passengers. Alice Nicklin, 19, had been parted from her parents when her father stayed to help one of the ladies, while she herself was sucked into the depths when the ship foundered. A strong swimmer, Alice fought and struggled back to the crowded surface almost totally exhausted. Soon she found a wooden grating, but others were clutching it too, threatening to render it ineffective. Shedding her impeding skirt, she swam away to find some other form of support, for a while being thankful for the company of a dead sheep to which she was able to cling. Shortly afterwards she bumped into a thick timber hatch-board to which she attached herself by means of an iron ring for the rest of the night.

Emily Lacy, 17, was writing letters in the saloon when she felt the collision and the shudder which followed. As young as she was, she was immediately alert to some likely danger. Without a second's thought, she ran down to her cabin to rouse her sleeping younger sister May, and hurried her back on deck where their uncle, Tom Hall, was looking for them. As the *Quetta* began her downward plunge, they struggled aft up the canting deck to avoid being trapped beneath the sun awning, and there stepped over the outside of the rail to avoid being crushed by the press of people. They saw one of the boats being stampeded by Javanese, but another appeared nearby, capsized, onto which they tried to jump. At this point they became separated—sister May managed to reach the upturned craft, but was drowned when it was righted by the sheer weight of numbers. Uncle Tom was seen by others later wearing a lifebelt but dead nevertheless.

Emily meanwhile had also fought her way to the surface, having been drawn down by the sinking ship. Her calls brought no response, however. To swim more freely she was able to strip off most of her clothing, and very soon came across the grating that Alice Nicklin had abandoned shortly before. Emily decided to stay with it, and was able to call across to Alice who floated nearby on her hatch-board before the groups drifted apart. When a larger raft appeared, Emily swam over to join those aboard, but its Javanese passengers would not let her on. This happened again twice the next day, so each time Emily had to return to the grating. On the last occasion the grating had drifted away with the others, leaving her alone in the sea.

For those aboard the cutter and the damaged lifeboat, progress was much more encouraging despite the overloading, the effort needed to overcome the currents, and the difficulties of moving the boats at all. Around midnight the two boats had come together, and so arrangements were made for the cutter to land its people on the nearest island and return for some of those from the lifeboat. This way, both boats made the shore, whereupon Captain Sanders sent the cutter back to the wreck site with Second Officer Scott to search for more survivors. They were lucky in finding a cowshed that had been on *Quetta*'s deck to which clung six survivors, as well as a number of others still singly afloat. By the time dawn broke, a group of 98 survivors had been brought together on one of the Little Adolphus Island group. There, preparations were soon in hand to ready the cutter for a trip to Somerset on the mainland, 10 miles away, to break the news of the *Quetta*'s demise.

Dawn found Alice Nicklin within sight of two islands, a small one relatively close to hand, a larger one more distant. Feeling that her chances of rescue would be better if she could reach the larger island, she was heading that way, still holding onto her hatch-board, when her attention was caught by two Javanese survivors nearby who were calling to her and gesturing towards the smaller island. There on the beach was a man, who waved in response to their calls. This was Aconeih Islet, which lay on the other side of Mount Adolphus Island from the main group of survivors. Nevertheless it was still welcomed by Alice who was so tired after her ordeal that she could barely stand on reaching the beach. The man she had seen, himself a survivor, waded out into the shallows to help her, following which she slept where she lay. Her ordeal continued on waking, however, when she found that there was neither shade nor water on their refuge. To limit sunburn and stave off thirst, both survivors spent much of their time in the water, waiting for rescue, which would not come until the end of the day.

By then a rescue operation was in full swing. Captain Sanders and the crew of the cutter had left the main survivor group before 6.00am that morning. They had struggled against currents, without shade or water save for a rest on Albany Island, until they arrived at the Somerset home of Frank Jardine at 10.30am. Having told him of the tragedy, a detailed message was sent to Thursday Island by telegraph. By good fortune the steamers *Albatross* and *Merrie England* were lying in Thursday Island's Port Kennedy, the former waiting for the arrival of the *Quetta*. On receipt of the telegram, the *Albatross* was quickly dispatched to pick up the main group, while the *Merrie England* was readied to follow. Preparations were also started to receive survivors when the boats returned. On Little Adolphus Island the main group of castaways had spent a cold miserable night, then a hot blistering day, without food or water. It was after sunset before they were rescued by the *Albatross*.

Other people were not so lucky, and spent yet another night of uncertainty about the waters of the Adolphus Channel. The precise number of those who lived to welcome the second day cannot be known, but one of these was Emily Lacy, still in the water, still swimming, but without support since losing the grating late the day before. She was sighted around 9.00am on 2nd of March, near naked, very badly sunburned, and more than a little distracted when she was lifted aboard the *Albatross*. Her survival in the water for 36 hours was an amazing story of endurance. Her swimming motions were said to have continued aboard the rescue craft until she fainted. The search then continued all that day and on into the next, but the plucky teenager was one of the last to be found alive.

At the final count the number of survivors from the *Quetta* disaster was 158 (54 percent of the total number of people on board). Many suffered exposure, dehydration and severe sunburn from their plight, and most had lost everything except the scant clothing they were found in. The local community rallied to their cause, however, and as well as attention to their immediate comfort and condition, a public appeal raised enough money to give all of the shipwreck victims, and some of their dependants, some small compensation. The *Quetta*'s owners, the British India Line, also ensured that everyone would be moved on to their original destinations, or back to their homes in Queensland or elsewhere if that was their wish.

But while so many had been saved, almost as many had died. Casualties from the wreck totalled 134, including all of the ship's engineers and a large number of the lascar crew who were serving as oilers and firemen in the engine and boiler rooms at the time of the collision. They would have perished in a very short time as the seas imploded through the massive gap left by plates sheared away on the unyielding rock pinnacle. Dying quickly too would have been those passengers who had turned in early, particularly steerage passengers (86 percent of them, in fact) berthed on the ship's lower deck, and all the children who had been put to bed, along with their mothers. Several entire families were thus lost: Brightman (3); Coombe (3); Copland (3); Davidson (4); Giffen (3); Jackson (6); McGladdery (5); Willet (3); and Williams (5). Some men had not accompanied their families on this fateful voyage. Several had lost their wives and children, surviving themselves by being somewhere else in the ship at the time of the sinking. Still others, such as husbands and wives, were known to have deliberately sacrificed their own chances by staying and dying with their loved ones.

The more fortunate were those on deck or in the higher accommodation, or those who knew exactly what to do in an emergency. The Javanese party were housed as outer deck passengers and for this reason many (79 percent) survived, though records show that most of them panicked, rushed and swamped the boats, refused to allow others onto rafts, and so perhaps reduced the chances of more being saved overall. The lascar crew on the other hand, both on and off watch, immediately went to their emergency stations around the ship where they were seen to be steadfastly carrying out their duties as required, and thus also surviving in large numbers (78 percent). But while the saloon passengers had cabins on the upper deck, many still died (81 percent), particularly those who were older or less able. In both passenger classes, most of those over the age of 40 appear to have perished. Questions were afterwards asked about the disproportionate representation amongst those lost and saved, but these were the stark facts.

Other questions were asked by the Government, the press and the community as to why the wreck occurred in the first place. Was there really an uncharted rock in the Adolphus Channel as Captain Sanders and the pilot claimed, or was there a case of negligence or incompetence to answer? Could there be another cause for such a ship to sink so quickly, as some suggested? An explosive cargo, a burst boiler, sabotage and bombs placed amongst the coal were all conjectured and rejected. An uncharted rock was indeed soon found, the result of a false report concerning a boat-load of survivors away to the south, beyond the range of the first searches. This report sent the *Albatross* and the *Merrie England* out again as rescuers. No survivors were found, but on her return journey the *Albatross* took soundings and located the suspect rock about a half-mile from where the *Quetta* finally sank.

Before long divers were sent down to the wreck to assess the prospects for salvage. *Quetta* was found to be lying over on her port side. On her starboard side, some 12 feet out from the keel, a massive gap 4 to 12 feet wide was noted where the plates were missing, extending from a point near the bow all the way back to the engine room—half the length of the ship. It was therefore not surprising that the *Quetta* went down so quickly. No bodies were to be seen. On the salvage prospects, the divers noted that in the difficult tidal conditions encountered, recovery of cargo could only be undertaken using explosives, at a cost likely to be uneconomic for the owners. Salvage work was started some months later, though the quantities recovered were not great. Personal items that were found and identified were returned to their owners or their families. A number of relics raised then and later now decorate the Quetta Memorial Church, consecrated in 1893, on Thursday Island.

One question remained unanswered after all the investigations on the *Quetta* ceased. A small girl, aged about two years old, had been snatched out of the steerage cabins by a steward. In the flurry surrounding the righting of the upturned cutter, the child was thrust aboard and taken by one of the off-duty engine room crew, who looked after her through all that followed until she was rescued from Little Adolphus along with the other 97 survivors there. Soon the question was asked, 'Who is she?', but there was no answer. No one knew for certain. When her future was debated, several claimants sought to adopt her, including the crewman from the boat. After much consideration she was eventually adopted by Captain Edmund Brown and his wife, a childless couple resident on Thursday Island.

When Edmund died in 1899, she was taken in by relatives of the Browns in Brisbane where she eventually married, twice, within the extended Brown clan. Though given the name Cecil Lechmere Brown, within her adopted family she was always known as Cissy, while on Thursday Island she would forever be remembered as Quetta Brown. There was some supposition that the child was Mary, the younger daughter of the Copland family who had perished in the wreck—though one or two other identities were possible amongst those who were lost. Quetta Brown died in 1949, but the sea was never to give up its secret as to who she really was.

Chapter 13

STORM VICTIMS

1850–1974

The *Koombana*.

*'Huge seas soon began to overwhelm the ship, flooding down below,
extinguishing the boiler fires and leaving the steamer wallowing
helplessly without power. The first lifeboat to be launched was instantly
swamped, drowning all within.'*

One hundred years ago, on the night of the 4th and 5th of March, 1899, a violent storm struck Cape York Peninsula, northern Queensland, in the vicinity of Cape Melville. The coastal region over a range of 200 kilometres, from Port Stewart to the west of Cape Melville to Cape Flattery in the east, was devastated. Shortly before midnight, without visible signs or warning, the storm roared in from the Coral Sea on the back of what until then had been a moderate south-easterly breeze. For the next 10 hours it battered the coast and hinterland with hurricane force winds and tumultuous seas, before receding to the south-west the following morning. This was Cyclone Mahina, said to have been the worst tropical cyclone in Australia's history.

Fortunately that part of the Queensland coast was not heavily populated—but the storm still took its toll. Anchored in Princess Charlotte Bay, in the adjacent Bathurst Bay and a number of coves in the area were large numbers of pearling luggers. Because it was the weekend nearly 100 of these craft were coming together with their mother ships to off-load their catches, take on fresh provisions, and carry out repairs in anticipation of another busy week. Since it was close to midnight when the storm blew up, few would have been awake to notice the brooding cloud masses building overhead, while those filling the north-eastern horizon would have remained darkly hidden.

Overnight, therefore, the assembled fleet was near annihilated as the little vessels leapt and rolled amongst the thunderous winds and waves, dragging their anchors, turning turtle, smashing into each other and being

177

driven ashore. What the raging weather and seas failed to destroy in the first few hours, a surging tidal wave finished off as it crashed ashore. In all, 54 pearling luggers were entirely lost, including some as far away as Thursday Island. Twelve others were driven ashore, five larger craft were sunk, more than forty other vessels and a lightship foundered, and over 300 from amongst their crews were drowned. It was a maritime disaster of immense proportions at the time—and there were few means of knowing when or where the next marauding storm might occur.

The pearling fleets around northern Australia had been prone to such losses ever since they began gathering there in the second half of the 19th century. The oyster beds were seen as a resource to be exploited, just as seals and whales had been exploited in southern waters during the first half of the century, and gold from the 1850s onwards. Such natural resources were seen as rich pickings for anyone able to become involved, and so the pearling industry drew large numbers to waters around the north of Western Australia and off northern Queensland. For the most part the profits came cheaply by using sailing craft manned by island divers, many of whom were Malays. From time to time, however, when the winds and sea held sway, there was a heavy price to pay in the loss of boats and the lives of their crews.

The complex weather patterns in this part of the world were little understood in those days. Strong winds, gales and thunderstorms might occasionally be expected in what was recognised as the northern Wet Season, but their formation was regarded as a matter of chance rather than part of a timeless pattern. So, on Christmas Eve, 1875, the pearling vessels working out of Exmouth Gulf, Western Australia, were caught without warning and beaten by the fury of the ensuing storm when hurricane-force winds descended on the coast. Boats were capsized, dismasted, forced ashore or sunk. Four were entirely lost, more were damaged, and 59 of their combined crews died.

The pearling fleets of Western Australia continued to experience such storms during the northern summer, which soon became referred to as tropical cyclones. The craft which went there to load guano from the islands offshore suffered similarly. In February 1877, ten vessels were so engaged at the Lacepede Islands north of Broome when they were overtaken by heavy weather. It was a portent of worse to come. The winds gathered strength over the course of four days until cyclonic conditions which generated storm-force winds, torrential rain and mountainous seas prevailed. Some of the larger ships put to sea to ride out the storm, while others were driven wildly ashore, a number having deliberately slipped their anchors in the hope of saving the crews. Several substantial vessels were wrecked, but more than 70 of their crews were saved.

Before many years had passed it was realised that tropical cyclones were a regular, albeit unpredictable, hazard on the north-western coast of Western Australia. Even so, the profits to be had from pearling and the gathering of pearl shell proved to be stronger than fears of the risks at sea, and so the work continued. In February 1881, a cyclone in the vicinity of Barrow Island wrecked five vessels and damaged six others. Six years later two cyclones which struck the Port Hedland and Eighty Mile Beach areas wrecked, sunk or damaged up to 50 working luggers and drowned 145 men. Cyclones hit the district around Cossack and Roebourne twice in January 1894, wrecking many small vessels and leaving 50 dead. Then in April and December 1908, and again in November 1910, cyclones struck Broome itself, devastating the pearling fleets assembled there, wrecking or driving ashore nearly 100 luggers over the three occasions, and claiming more than 140 lives in the process.

Cyclones have continued to visit this part of Australia's coast, though the loss of vessels at sea and the lives of their crews has much diminished. The last cyclone to wreak havoc amongst the hardy luggers occurred in March 1935, when one of the worst storms to afflict Broome sank 20 pearl boats off the Lacepede Islands with the loss of 141 of their crews. By then the industry which had peaked in 1914, when around 400 luggers were working the oyster beds of the north-west, was in the last stages of decline. It was an enterprise soon to be overtaken by plastics and pearl cultivation. No longer would such large fleets of vulnerable craft congregate in critical areas.

Since the war years too, constant improvements to our weather warning systems now give notice of gathering storms well in advance, to warn all seafarers to steer clear of their paths. We should not become complacent about the vast powers of nature, even so. Despite all the warnings, Cyclone Tracy flattened Darwin in six hours early on Christmas Day 1974, killing 49 people. Ten vessels were wrecked in and around Darwin harbour, and at least 16 lives were lost at sea.

Bad weather, gale force winds and high seas have always been some of the worst hazards to contend with in mastering the oceans. As inescapable features of the universal maritime environment, they have been no less frequent in Australian waters than elsewhere, as the shipwreck tales related here have shown. We have an extensive, often inhospitable continental coastline, and our latitudes range from the treacherous shoals and cyclone dangers of Torres Strait, through the island and atoll maze of the Great Barrier Reef, to the navigational hazards of Bass Strait and the Southern Ocean's winter gales. It might therefore be argued that the early mariners faced greater dangers in approaching Australia in adverse conditions than anywhere else in the world.

Storms were a perennial danger along our shores in these early days, especially around the coast of south-eastern Australia. From Portland, Victoria, through Bass Strait or around Tasmania, then north beyond Cape Howe as far as Newcastle and Port Stephens, the shipwreck records are a testimony to the turbulent seas to be encountered there. The wildness of the ocean around the eastern end of Bass Strait even in summer was amply demonstrated during the 1998 Sydney–Hobart yacht race, when seven yachts were lost and six of their crew died. And 200 years earlier, in the summer of 1797, it was a hurricane off the east coast of Tasmania that brought about the loss of the *Sydney Cove*, one of the first traders sent out to establish commercial connections with the new colony.

The coasts of New South Wales have been particularly prone to violent storms over the years, and the 19th century catalogue of wrecks is full of victims lost to the raging elements. At first the record is largely one of small vessels plying out of Sydney—whalers, schooners, cutters, smacks— which were overcome by sudden squalls or gales the prudent skipper might have sheltered from, or waited for their passing. As the number of settlements like Newcastle, Eden, Port Stephens and Port Macquarie grew, a coastal trade developed which brought bigger craft in larger numbers into more exposed waters, with the risk of being caught on a lee shore or between points of shelter. Many vessels were lost in the waters north of Sydney.

As the 19th century progressed the volume of shipping increased, and with it came a commensurate rise in the number of vessels lost or wrecked. The inflow of new settlers, the exploitation of cedar forests and coal deposits, growing intercolonial trade and the discoveries of gold from mid-century onwards—all added to the demands on the available ships. The pressures to shift cargoes and to move people grew throughout the world around this time, peaking with the scramble to reach the goldfields, first to California, then back to Victoria and New South Wales, then over to New Zealand. The demands were such that all types of ships, most of which came from overseas, were pressed into service. Not all were seaworthy, many became overloaded, and some had masters who were of dubious character and qualification. Adverse weather conditions off New South Wales were always a severe test of a ship's weaknesses, probing the seams of old vessels, pressing them to extremes, and trying the skills of the unworthy. Many failed.

Two often ferocious weather systems that periodically frequent the coast of New South Wales are the so-called 'southerly buster', and a phenomenon known in meteorological terms as an extra-tropical cyclone, or East Coast Low. The first is the result of the interaction between a strong, cool southerly airflow and the Australian Alps, which confine its northward surge to the coast, producing sharp squalls, gale force winds and piling seas. The second occurs when air pressures near the coast fall in association with the marked temperature gradients. A vortex forms in the manner of a small cyclone, usually generating hurricane force winds, heavy rain and violent seas within a short time. Both can pass relatively quickly—but woe betide any sailing ship caught unprepared in their path!

From April to July 1836, these coastal disturbances gave rise to a series of storms and gales that were remarkable enough to destroy several craft in the vicinity of Port Stephens. Some of their remains were later observed far out to sea. Worse was to follow in this particular area, however, when the coast between Newcastle and Port Macquarie seemed to become a protracted storm focus during the 1860s. This part of New South Wales had been subject to destructive gales on a number of occasions, but these intensified in the 1860s to bring major storms on no fewer than six occasions. Large numbers of ships were lost, wrecked or driven ashore with the loss of many lives.

The year 1864 proved to be a particularly bad one at sea. First, the coasters *Gazelle*, *Julia*, *Rainbow*, *Waratah* and *Woolloomooloo* were wrecked by severe gales on the north coast in early June. In September fierce gales in the same area destroyed seven similar ships and damaged many others. Meanwhile gales had also battered the south coast between Jervis Bay and Wollongong in mid-June, sending five vessels ashore at the height of their fury. A total of 17 ships were lost in the three incidents, together with many of their crew. Given the severity of the conditions, others were fortunate to be saved.

Then in July 1866 came the Great Gale, believed to have been the worst in Australia's maritime history. Again seemingly focussed on Newcastle and moving north towards Port Macquarie, it raged for two days during which 15 ships came to grief off various points along the coast. Large numbers of craft were caught at sea by the onset of the storm. Those in the vicinity of Newcastle immediately tried to reach the safety of the Hunter River, but the shallowing seas were piling high on the bar by the time they arrived. The river entrance is guarded by the notorious Oyster Bank onto which several of the vessels seeking refuge were cast, in full view of the horrified townsfolk. Their presence saved the lives of several who managed to struggle ashore, but many others were to die in the raging surf out of reach of any assistance.

The worst victim of all was the 550-ton paddle steamer, *Cawarra*. Her master, Captain Chatfield, had hoped to reach Newcastle before the storm was fully developed, but he too found the river mouth a maelstrom of sweeping seas and driving rain. In trying to negotiate the entrance huge seas soon began to overwhelm the ship, flooding down below, extinguishing the boiler fires and leaving the steamer wallowing helplessly without power. The first lifeboat to be launched was instantly swamped, drowning all within. Then the funnel collapsed as the ship began to settle, taking with it a number of passengers who were clinging to its stays. Shortly afterwards the foremast went the same way with the same result, until the *Cawarra* herself sank three hours after her quest for safety began. By a strange coincidence there was one survivor, a seaman by the name of Fred Hedges, who was pulled into a boat piloted by none other than James Johnson, who himself had been the sole survivor of the *Dunbar*, which had foundered outside Sydney Heads in similar circumstances nine years earlier.

Of the 60 people lost from the *Cawarra*, only 41 had been recovered for burial a week after the storm. Several other vessels were lost together with their passengers and crews along the coast to the north, though a number were able to slip their anchors and allow themselves to be driven ashore, where their people were saved. In the aftermath, search parties up and down the coast found human remains and many animal carcasses from the lost ships along with broken cargoes strewn along the beaches, but no other survivors. In February 1868, the Sydney–Newcastle coast was again beset by wild weather and gales that claimed 11 ships, from whose crews at least 30 died. The following year two violent gales wrought further destruction, one in February which destroyed four sailing craft leaving at least eight dead, and another in May, dubbed the Second Great Gale, which left nine ships as wrecks and a large number of people drowned.

The total number of dead amongst all of these storm losses has never been known for certain since they included some unknown wrecks whose identities were never established, and several ships which had simply disappeared without trace. One of the largest amongst those which have never been found, in terms of both tonnage and the number of lives lost, was the steamer *Koombana* which vanished between Port Hedland and Broome on the 20th of March 1912. Of 3800 tons and owned by the Adelaide Steamship Company, she was carrying 138 passengers and crew at the time she sailed off into a north-east gale, the precursor of a gathering cyclone from which she never emerged. What happened to the *Koombana* is still a mystery, though the remains of what could have been a substantial shipwreck were noted in 1973, in deep water some 35 kilometres out from Eighty Mile Beach.

The perils of seafaring around our shores continued throughout the rest of the 19th century and on into the 20th century. Even today we are not wholly free of the enduring risks, with the ever-present prospect of sudden squalls capsizing small craft, disabling larger vessels and driving others onto lee shores or unexpected reefs. The overall threat has been considerably diminished, nevertheless, with the total disappearance of commercial sailing ships, a greater awareness of sea safety, improved engine types, better communications, and more effective weather monitoring and forecasting. But still the threat remains . . .

———————

The most notable shipwrecks of yesteryear would often shock nations on account of their circumstances, their severity and their losses. In the 20th century alone, the sinking of the *Titanic* in 1912, the torpedoing of the *Lusitania* in 1915 and the *Athenia* in 1939, and even the fire loss of the old *Queen Elizabeth* in 1972 have all stirred the emotions in various ways as a measure of their impact on society at the time. However, by virtue of the relative shortness of human memory, the constant shifts in human values, and the gradual transition of time into history, yesterday's disasters have often become the focus of today's education, entertainment and leisure. The rediscovery of the *Titanic* in recent years may be the best-known example of this.

Though of no comparison, one of Australia's worst maritime disasters of this century involved the storm victim SS *Yongala*, sister ship to the *Koombana*, another storm victim referred to earlier. Lost in 1911, the *Yongala* was for many years the subject of one of this country's most intriguing sea mysteries. Rediscovered in 1958, her remains today have become known as the most spectacular wreck dive in Australia.

In the early afternoon of 23rd of March 1911, the Adelaide Steamship Company's SS *Yongala* raised steam for the last time, dragged her anchor up from the bottom and slowly moved away from her stopover at Mackay, Queensland, en route for Townsville, her next port of call. The ship was a popular one on the Melbourne to Cairns service at a time when, without a rail link, she offered the easiest and most comfortable way of reaching the isolated coastal towns of north Queensland.

Built in 1903 in Newcastle, England, at 3664 tons the *Yongala* was a well-found ship in all departments. She was said to be well-balanced and stable at sea, well-provisioned in her galley and dining rooms, and capable of a fast 15 knots from the triple expansion engines that drove her single screw. She was fitted to provide comfortable accommodation for 110 first class and 130 second class passengers, and carried a crew of 70 or so. Her master was Captain William Knight, who had a sound record at sea—but oddly, shortly before the ship left Mackay that day, he had puzzled a friend by remarking that this would be his last trip on the *Yongala*, but no one would ever part him from her. Since he was not to change ships or retire, and the company had no plans to replace him, the comment was puzzling indeed.

The *Yongala* had been scheduled to arrive in Townsville the following morning. When she didn't, port officials and friends and relatives waiting to meet her passengers were alarmed and concerned for her safety. Shortly after the *Yongala* had left Mackay, the Meteorological Office had issued a warning that a cyclone was advancing from the Coral Sea and might be encountered by shipping north of the Whitsunday Group in the course of the next 24 hours. Unfortunately there was no way of warning the *Yongala*, who would be sailing directly for the storm since she was still not equipped with a radio. On later voyages, it was planned, she would be, as they had already been shipped from England. On this voyage though she would be deaf to any warnings, and later that night she would be equally blind to any signs.

When, after a day, the *Yongala* had still not arrived in Townsville, ships journeying south were asked to keep a lookout for any signs of the missing steamer. The weather overnight had produced strong winds and rough seas, but the thinking even then was that the *Yongala* had either broken down or been forced to seek shelter. Several ships had reported being slowed by the cyclone's impact, but what was most disturbing was that they had been sailing behind the *Yongala* and had seen nothing of her before arriving in Townsville themselves. Neither had any other ships seen her, as they were soon to report.

So where was she? How could such a modern vessel just disappear? There was a reluctance to believe the worst—but she was still missing. The only positive news at that point came from the keeper of the Dent Island lighthouse, who reported having seen her negotiating the Whitsunday Passage around 6.30pm on 23rd of March, the day she left Mackay. The weather then was already creating mountainous seas, with a wind strength of force 7 to 9—nearly a strong gale. The news was not encouraging . . .

The search was intensified as boats went out to comb the southern coastline for any signs of a mishap. After a day or two the first word began to filter back that some flotsam and minor wreckage had been recovered along the shore, but from a source unknown. Then a pillow and a lifebuoy were found bearing the 'ASCo.' mark of the Adelaide Steamship Company. As apprehension grew, the final evidence was discovered in the form of a shark-eaten carcass of a horse, found near Cape Bowling Green some 35 miles due east of Townsville. It was that of the racehorse 'Moonshine', the loading of which had delayed *Yongala*'s departure from Brisbane just a few days earlier. There could be no more doubt that the *Yongala* was gone. Townsville was in shock and went on to mourn the loss, but of the ship and her passengers and crew no further trace was found—until 1943.

In the years after her sinking the *Yongala* became something of a local legend, a mystery ship that some swore still frequented the Mackay–Townsville shipping route, to be seen on occasions in the form of a rusty old freighter, a ghost ship. Whatever the source of such apparitions, more tangible evidence of her whereabouts came in 1943 when a minesweeper of the Royal Australian Navy (RAN) snagged what appeared to be a wreck or a reef some distance to sea off Cape Bowling Green. The RAN followed up the report in 1947, when the survey ship HMAS *Lachlan* confirmed the presence of a wreck some 12 miles from the Cape. It was not until 1958, however, that the wreck was identified as the lost storm victim, *Yongala*, after divers had reached her and retrieved her safe.

The *Yongala* had lain untouched for almost 50 years, during which time her remains had been transformed into an artificial reef by the abundant sea life. The ship lay intact on her starboard side, her bow still pointing towards Townsville. Her funnel was gone, all the timberwork of her bridge, decks, masts, rails and hatches had been eaten away, but her metal framework remained as the refuge of millions of fish and the home of a vast array of other marine fauna and flora. It appeared from her location that she had been overwhelmed by the cyclone not far from Townsville in the pre-dawn of the day she was due to arrive, but why was not clear.

Many theories were advanced as to why she had succumbed to the storm, from a collision with a coral reef to an internal boiler explosion. Three men who were living in the vicinity of the wreck claimed to have heard a loud whistle and an explosion on the day she disappeared, but her boilers were found to be intact, and the only reef off that part of the coast was the *Yongala* herself. Her sinking had apparently been sudden, for her lifeboat davits were still in the inboard position. Her missing funnel suggested that it may have been carried away, with a sudden inrush of water that extinguished her boiler fires and upset her stability. There were some who already believed that the *Yongala* and her sister ship *Grantala* were top-heavy and might readily capsize in rough seas. Whatever the cause, however, no one knows for certain.

For a while the *Yongala* was subject to the attention of treasure-seeking divers, but the passing of Commonwealth shipwreck legislation has curbed such activities. The wreck is now preserved within a 500-metre protected zone, thereby creating what is now widely acknowledged as Australia's most spectacular wreck dive. As noted earlier the wreck has taken on the form of a tropical reef, and as the only one in a very wide area, it has attracted a far greater variety of marine life than most other places on the nearby Barrier Reef. The top of the wreck lies within 12 metres of the surface, falling to a depth of 30 metres on the sandy bottom. The wreck has been rapturously described as an oasis in a submarine desert, a diver's dream, a marine biologist's paradise, an underwater photographer's delight.

On the surface above the wreck visitors are likely to encounter first the turtles and sea snakes that have taken up residence amongst the *Yongala*'s remains. Then to see the wreck they descend through clouds of bait fish, hardyheads and a myriad others that sweep and dash amongst the less frantic movements of angel fish, batfish, turrum, trevally, sweetlips and barracuda. It is a kaleidoscope of shifting shapes and colour. Hovering around the fringe of visibility their peripheral vision might pick up the shadow-like movements of large manta rays which silently swoop and glide, or whalers that seem to be keeping a suspicious eye on intruders.

But then might come the distraction of a bottle-nose dolphin or a curious turtle, and very soon the wreck itself. Parrotfish, damselfish, moorish idols and red emperor cluster around in colourful welcome over a carpet of assorted corals and coral trees, and the hosts of ascidians and bivalves, sponges and sea whips, crinoids and gorgonians, whose brilliance is revealed in artificial light. From the wreck itself peer coral trout and cleaner wrasse, while those venturing into its depths can expect, quite literally, a much bigger welcome from the metre-long Maori wrasse, the larger cod, and finally the awesomely huge Queensland grouper moving serenely about their business—unless, that is, the visitors have come prepared to feed the residents. A feeding frenzy amongst so many fish of all shapes and sizes can be both exciting and injurious. Be prepared to be bashed, bruised and buffeted as the water boils with life. And especially beware of the species which seem unable to distinguish between the proffered titbits and the proffering fingers!

Chapter 14

HMAS *Sydney* & HSK *Kormoran* 1941

HMAS *Sydney*.

'The loss of the HMAS Sydney *shocked and embarrassed the nation.
For many it seemed inconceivable that such a well-armed, well-
armoured warship as HMAS* Sydney *could fall prey to a German
merchant raider, even by means of trickery and deception.'*

On Monday, 17th of November, 1941, the European War seemed very remote to the officers and men of HMAS *Sydney*, the 6830-ton Australian light cruiser, as they waved a cheerful farewell to those aboard the troopship *Zealandia*. For the past week they had escorted her from Fremantle, Western Australia, to the Sunda Strait between Java and Sumatra, and there handed her over to a Royal Navy escort, HMS *Durban*, for the final leg to Singapore. It was time to go home.

Sure, there was always the prospect of meeting one of Germany's roving armed merchant cruisers in this part of the world—ships that stalked the wider oceans as wolves in sheep's clothing in search of their prey. The *Pinguin* was known to have worked in waters both east and west of Australia before she was sunk, and now the *Komet* had been reported as operating somewhere in the South Pacific together with a supply ship. There might also be the odd Nazi U-boat around, though that prospect was more remote. This wasn't their theatre, they would be a long way from home, and anyway the German Navy had better things to do with its warships and U-boats out in the North Atlantic. Not much chance of meeting an Italian either, who were fully occupied in the Mediterranean.

The North Atlantic, the Med—one a maelstrom of freezing winds and mountainous seas at this time of year, the other a virtual hornets' nest on Europe's doorstep. Neither was a place you would choose to be with U-boat packs decimating the Atlantic convoys, while submarines and dive-bombers constantly harried those trying to bring aid to beleaguered Malta. Many aboard HMAS *Sydney* remembered their service in the Mediterranean the previous year, where they had been luckier than most. They had been in Alexandria when Italy entered the war in June 1940, and so were instrumental in sinking the destroyer *Espero* and the cruiser *Bartolomeo Colleoni*, and badly damaging another cruiser, the *Giovanni delle Bande Nere*. They had claimed first blood, with only a hole in a funnel themselves. It was exciting stuff, though later patrol and convoy escort duties kept up a state of nervous tension amongst those on board, ever aware of the menacing U-boats and frequently subjected to aerial bombardment.

But here, close to home—well, this was Paradise by comparison, a shake down cruise for all the new lads from the Flinders Naval Depot. Another easy escort job completed today, then back to happy-go-lucky Perth by the end of the week. They waved a final farewell, flashed a last rude message on the Aldis lamp, and settled back into normal patrol routine as the *Sydney* turned once more towards Australia. With any luck they would still be on the coast at Christmas, and so might get a spot of home leave. That would be good for many of the youngsters aboard, especially those from Western Australia, for God only knew where they'd be next Christmas . . .

———

At about the same time as HMAS *Sydney* turned for home, a rather nondescript-looking ship was steaming steadily towards the coast of Western Australia from the south-west, aiming for the bulge where the coast and the Tropic of Capricorn cross. Ostensibly she was the *Straat Malakka*, a Dutch freighter bound for the Netherlands East Indies. Her drab black and brown colouring, relieved only by a yellow band around her funnel, was actually designed to make her appear ordinary and inconspicuous, and unlikely to draw attention. Her captain, Theodor Anton Detmers, had her painted this way so he could go about his business as unobtrusively as possible. Only a few days earlier, on rendezvous with another vessel in the Indian Ocean, his ship had been equally drab, though her superstructure was then white, her name had been *Matthew*

Luckenbach, and she flew the American flag. It was just one of her many disguises.

Straat Malakka was thus no ordinary ship, and her role was never that of an ordinary freighter. Beneath her dull paintwork she was a highly efficient fighting machine. Behind various camouflage screens on deck were hidden six 5.9-inch naval guns and a formidable array of support weapons. Below decks she carried torpedoes for her six torpedo tubes and up to 360 mines, as well as an Arado spotter plane and a fast motor launch. She was provisioned for long periods at sea. And like her captain, her crew were not Dutch but members of the German Navy, for the inconspicuous *Straat Malakka* was nothing less than a German *Handelstorkreuzer* (HSK) or auxiliary cruiser, a commerce raider soon to be more widely known as the *Kormoran*. Having sunk 11 ships in forays in the South Atlantic and Indian Ocean on this, her first operation, she was now on her way to lay mines off Shark Bay, Western Australia, in the vicinity of Carnarvon.

Kormoran's commander was a man seeking glory and recognition. In June 1940, Captain Detmers had been given Germany's latest, biggest and fastest raider, the former Hamburg–Amerika liner *Steiermark*, to crown his 20 years in the German Navy. By December 1940, however, when his now-converted Ship No. 41 or Raider G was ready to sail, he was already a late starter in this particular field. His previous command had been an ageing destroyer in which he had nevertheless served with distinction, but other raider captains had been active much longer in the distant oceans, with enviable sums of tonnage sunk as a result. It therefore rankled that on this cruise his own successes totalled a mere 68 000 tons compared with records exceeding 100 000 tons amongst his contemporaries. And since he already had the Iron Cross (First Class), he was also becoming obsessed with the possibility of earning a Knight's Cross of the Iron Cross and the acclaim that would go with it—provided he could boost his record accordingly. Successes of late had been few and far between, however, and he was due to return to Germany by the end of May, 1942.

As HSK *Kormoran* sailed on towards the north-east and the shallow waters off Shark Bay, HMAS *Sydney* was heading south for the Australian coast on her passage back to Fremantle. It was almost inevitable, therefore, with clear visibility and moderate seas, that they should meet. In the action that followed, as is well known, both ships were lost in circumstances that only one side could later relate. A total of 317 from the *Kormoran's* officers and crew were subsequently picked up at sea or captured on the mainland, though no one appeared to have survived the sinking of the cruiser, HMAS *Sydney*. The story of the encounter, the ensuing gun-battle and the fate of the two ships off Carnarvon therefore emerged only slowly, from careful analysis and cross-checks of detail from repeated interviews with captive Germans recounting their version of events. As a result, and largely because a number of unresolved inconsistencies and contradictions were later compounded by baseless narrative, opinion and wartime suspicions, many Australians feel that the loss of HMAS *Sydney* has never been satisfactorily explained, even today. We can be sure of only the broadest outlines of this fateful engagement, which was to lead to such a disastrous outcome for Australia.

Shortly before 4.00pm on Wednesday 19th of November, 1941, at a position 26° 34' South, 111° East, lookouts aboard HSK *Kormoran* reported what appeared to be a sailing ship below the horizon on the port bow. There was apparently some thought that the vessel might be the square-rigged barque, *Pamir*, known to be in Australian waters, but very soon the image manifested itself as the much more menacing hull and upperworks of a rapidly-approaching Perth-class cruiser, one seemingly fully intent on challenging the *Kormoran* on her identity. It was a situation Captain Detmers had to avoid at all costs, being considerably out-gunned in the event of conflict.

As the *Sydney* charged on, challenging lights already flickering from her bridge, a quick decision was needed, but since bluff was probably out of the question his only real options were flight or fight. Detmers opted for the first to gain time, but hastily prepared for the second. As it was late in the afternoon there was a slim chance that they might just escape with darkness, laying a smokescreen as necessary to blind and confuse their enemy. With his main engines full ahead, Detmers swung the *Kormoran* about from a course of 025 to one of 250, heading away west of south west and into the lowering sun.

Those aboard the *Sydney* were presented with the sight of an unidentified merchant vessel suddenly turning away at their approach, making off at full speed in the opposite direction and beginning to make smoke which obscured her movements. It was not the action of a guiltless ship. Suspicions were understandably raised that this might be a German raider, for if the fleeing ship had been a friendly vessel so close to Australia, they would have had nothing to fear. At full speed the *Sydney* took off in pursuit of the unknown quarry, expecting soon to overhaul her with a much superior speed. Meanwhile, both commanders called their full crews to action stations.

The Australian cruiser was capable of more than 30 knots on full power, whereas Captain Detmers was told soon after the chase began that a piston in number 4 engine was running hot, which reduced his own full speed capability from 18 to 14 knots. At that time of day the difference may have been critical in seeking to avoid the threatened detention. The chase therefore lasted around half an hour while HMAS *Sydney* closed on the fleeing ship, which had lately hoisted the Dutch flag and signal letters identifying her as *Straat Malakka* in response to the *Sydney*'s insistent challenges.

With the two ships steadily closing, the *Kormoran*'s captain resorted to a number of ruses in order to gain more time and to stave off closer contact. An emergency 'QQQ' signal was transmitted with the position and adopted name in the hope that the cruiser would pick it up and perhaps ease off the chase. Detmers intended it also to mean to anyone listening that a Dutch ship was being threatened by a possible hostile enemy. He later said he also deliberately misread or ignored signals from the *Sydney* in the pretence of not knowing their meaning, or bungled his responses, thereby gaining time while prolonging the uncertainty aboard the Australian ship. He is also said to have shown a large white flag for a while.

Throughout all of this the *Kormoran* had not slackened speed, maintaining 14 knots as the cruiser gradually drew abreast to starboard. At this point HMAS *Sydney* was preparing to lower a boat, and her Walrus aircraft was also being readied for launching while her main armament covered the suspect. The distance between the two ships was variously reported to be a mile or less, well within range of their respective guns. Tensions and excitement ran high aboard the raider, whose crew had already trained their loaded guns and torpedo tubes onto particular targets aboard the approaching warship from behind the camouflage screens—the *Sydney*'s bridge, her vulnerable bow and stern, the threatening forward gun turrets, and the fully-fuelled Walrus to spread fire amidships. At this range they could hardly miss—and they still held the vital element of surprise. All they needed was the order to de-camouflage, drop the screens, and fire. The fate of both ships and their crews would be determined in the next few minutes.

What thoughts and preparations were in the minds of the Captain Joseph Burnett and his officers on *Sydney*'s bridge can never be known. Why he exposed his ship broadside-on, at such short range, to what could still prove to be a German raider is impossible to comprehend. He must clearly have had no idea what he was dealing with in approaching so closely, whereas Captain Detmers, appraising the enemy warship from his own bridge, just as clearly did. Shortly after 4.30pm, with an armed boarding party ready to cross between the ships, the cruiser signalled the 'Dutch' suspect to stop engines and to hoist her secret callsign—that is, the other two-letter flags of the real *Straat Malakka*'s official four-letter code, in response to the two being flown from the *Sydney*'s signal hoist. For Captain Detmers the game was decidedly up—he did not know them. Now he could either surrender ignominiously, or fight. He chose the latter.

According to German accounts, and all within the space of seconds, the Dutch flag dropped as a German battle ensign broke free, counter-weighted screens clanged down and each pre-aimed gun opened fire, to be followed soon after by torpedoes from *Kormoran*'s underwater tubes. Surprise was apparently complete, though there is some doubt as to which ship fired first. Captain Detmers later stated that the *Sydney* may have fired first by just half a second, alerted perhaps by sudden activity aboard the raider. In the ensuing confusion the first salvoes from both vessels were thought to have missed their marks. Corrections aboard the German vessel were fast enough, however, to knock out the *Sydney*'s bridge and both her forward turrets, 'A' and 'B' in successive salvoes. A large fire burst out between the cruiser's funnels where the Walrus amphibian had stood, and seconds later a single torpedo exploded between 'B' turret and the bow.

Despite the shock attack, the initial hammering from the disguised raider and the severe damage that was immediately inflicted, the Australian cruiser was able to fight back, though only from her 'X' and 'Y' turrets aft. Her forepart was devastated. The central gunnery director tower had also been destroyed, so the *Sydney*'s aft turrets took on the raider under local control, scoring vital hits on her engine room and elsewhere. They proved to be just as crippling to the German as those she had received herself. All subsequent actions by one ship to defeat the other were therefore constrained by the damage each had sustained.

The cruiser was on fire around the forward funnel and amidships, but nevertheless attempted to ram her opponent, launching four torpedoes at the German vessel soon afterwards while maintaining fire from turrets 'X' and 'Y'. Captain Detmers managed to avoid the *Sydney*'s fan of torpedoes by turning towards them, but then efforts to swing his ship further to bring more of his own guns to bear were frustrated when the *Kormoran*'s engines failed and the ship lost way as a result of the *Sydney*'s successful gunfire. And still the two ships continued to blast each other as they began to draw apart, though both had been badly mauled in the engagement and their efforts were less intense.

Just how long the battle lasted is a matter of doubt and contradiction, even amongst the German survivors. Estimates range up to 90 minutes, though the main action was fiercest during the first 15 minutes when the two ships were at their closest and the heaviest damage and associated casualties were being inflicted. Thereafter the *Kormoran* lay stopped in the water, bereft of power and burning in places but still able to harass her opponent with shell fire and torpedoes, while the *Sydney* slowly turned away southward, ablaze from stem to stern and intent now only on reaching the safety of an Australian port. Official reports by the RAN have assessed the encounter as lasting an hour, with 25 minutes of actual combat. How many men were lost during this time can hardly be guessed at.

The *Kormoran* ceased fire as the distance between the ships increased to six miles. She had her own problems to attend to, though those aboard HMAS *Sydney* could have been no less. The German crew had no friendly haven, however, their ship was crippled and blazing fiercely now, and with the loss of power they had no means of extinguishing the spreading flames. They also had a special problem in the 360 mines they were carrying which might blow them all to hell before very long unless action was taken first. Their only real option was to set scuttling charges, then take to the ship's lifeboats and hope that they would be sufficiently clear of the ship before she exploded. Darkness was falling and speed was essential in preparing to abandon ship.

While all efforts were being made to provision and launch the lifeboats, Captain Detmers was able to note the distant progress of his stricken adversary as she steamed slowly south-east in the gathering dusk, a blazing wreck limping over the horizon. Close to midnight the last boat moved away from the abandoned raider, charges having been set to explode an hour later. About this time the fate of the *Sydney* appeared to be sealed when, according to some survivors, the bright flare of an explosion was seen beyond the south-eastern horizon. Others denied such a sighting, suggesting instead that the crippled cruiser had been torpedoed. The German ship exploded and sank at 1.00am on 20th of November 1941, destroyed by her own mines. The last position of either ship has never been known for certain.

———————

News of the possible loss of HMAS *Sydney* did not reach the authorities for nearly a week after the incident. In the interim there was considerable anxiety that the ship was overdue, since she had been expected back in Fremantle the day after her unsuspected encounter with the German raider. The first indication of something amiss off Western Australia came early on the morning of Sunday, 23rd of November, when the military transport *Aquitania* picked up 26 sailors from a raft about 100 miles west of Carnarvon. Fearing the presence of an enemy warship and obviously not being enlightened by the castaways, the *Aquitania* maintained radio silence as she continued on her way to Sydney. All naval signals to the missing cruiser meanwhile had not been acknowledged. An air search was mounted and a Dutch cruiser, the *Tromp*, was asked to search the area of the earlier rendezvous with HMS *Durban*.

Late on 24th of November, the tanker *Trocas* picked up 25 more survivors to the north-west of Carnarvon, who were definitely identified as German. This was radioed to the Australian authorities who intensified the air search in this region in response. A later message from the *Trocas* said that their German captives were claiming to have sunk the *Sydney* in a fight with their own ship, the raider *Kormoran*. Fears for the men aboard the cruiser reached new heights. More aircraft were brought in to search the seas around the alleged battle zone, and very soon five lifeboats were sighted which raised hopes that large numbers of Australian sailors might have survived the conflict. Such hopes were dashed when the first boats reached the Australian coast, and their occupants were also found to be German.

More enemy sailors were picked up at sunset on 26th of November by the passenger ship *Koolinda*, while later that night flares were sighted by the Blue Funnel ship *Centaur* (see Chapter 15), which guided her to a lifeboat containing 61 others of the *Kormoran*'s crew. On being allowed aboard the *Centaur* to report their situation, the raider's First Lieutenant claimed to be a Norwegian seaman whose ship had been sunk by an Allied warship. Captain Dark of the *Centaur* was astute enough to recognise him as a German naval officer, however, and bluntly told him so. Not wanting his ship to be taken over by so many men of the German *Kriegsmarine* (Navy), Captain Dark insisted on towing their lifeboat overnight, only to find it near-submerged early next day. Suspecting trickery, and having lost two other ships to enemy action in the Atlantic, he lowered two of the *Centaur*'s lifeboats to the luckless Germans with the comment, 'If they manage to sink these two, they can swim to Carnarvon!'

More than 300 of the raider's crew were eventually rescued from the seas off Western Australia, though alarmingly none from the missing Australian cruiser, now feared lost. As the larger German contingent were gathered together in Carnarvon, naval officers from Fremantle started their interrogations in an attempt to reconstruct the tragedy that had claimed so many, while others in Canberra began the grim task of compiling casualty lists and preparing telegrams to break the dreadful news to relatives of the dead.

No formal announcement was made concerning the *Sydney*'s loss until Sunday, 30th of November, nearly a fortnight after the event. In the interim the search for possible survivors continued, with diminishing hope as the days wore on. Small items were found by a number of search vessels, though little of substance other than two damaged lifebelts which revealed nothing. The largest item was a damaged RAN carley float which then seemed only to confirm the worst, but which would be the source of much later speculation on the likely fate of survivors. Another float recovered with a body off Christmas Island some twelve weeks after the *Sydney–Kormoran* incident gave rise to similar conjecture, but while the float seemed to be of Australian origin, no firm link with the lost cruiser was ever established.

The *Sydney* herself would yield nothing further to enlighten subsequent research or inquiry. She lay with her broken adversary in Indian Ocean waters up to 5000 metres deep, a war grave shielding her dead. While the nation grieved her disappearance and the loss of her entire complement, those responsible for her sinking were moved across country to prisoner-of-war camps near Murchison in Victoria. Transported separately, the officers were interned in the nearby 'Dhurringile' homestead for the duration of the war. While there, Captain Detmers learned that he had indeed been awarded the Knight's Cross of the Iron Cross for his exploit, with decorations for others of his crew. Returning home after the end of the war, in 1947, he was revered as a hero up to his death in 1976, and his success may well have seemed an adequate recompense to some for the destruction of the raider *Emden* by an earlier HMAS *Sydney* in 1914, during the first months of the First World War.

The loss of the HMAS *Sydney* shocked and embarrassed the nation. For many it seemed inconceivable that such a well-armed, well-armoured warship as HMAS *Sydney* could fall prey to a German merchant raider, even by means of trickery and deception. The fact that there were no survivors to assert the truth thus gave rise to speculation and rumours that more than one enemy vessel had been involved, that all the Australian survivors had been machine-gunned in the water by one or other of the enemy to ensure their silence, and that there may well have been a Japanese submarine in the area in association with the *Kormoran* as well, to add to the mystery.

Evidence has never been forthcoming to support any such claims, however, either in contemporary eye-witness reports, or in the wartime records of either side which were examined in later years. The official story, after all the available evidence was examined and all subsequent inquiries were complete (including the most recent Joint Parliamentary Inquiry, which commenced in late 1997), was that both ships were lost as a result of their mutual destruction, and that no other vessels took part in the engagement. Regrettably, all those aboard the Australian cruiser perished in the affray, 645 in total, with little evidence to suggest what finally happened, and where the ship went down.

But the rumours have persisted nevertheless. The disbelief and concern following the loss has been steadily fuelled by the lack of any complete and acceptable explanation. Theories and allegations have mounted to the point where accusations of an official cover-up were made, which persist to this day. Books have been written around all the available facts, while others have fanned a burgeoning controversy with bitterness, conjecture and unsubstantiated 'revelations' and opinion. Still others have been published analysing the development of the controversy itself. The situation has not been helped by clumsy attempts by persons unknown to manufacture 'evidence' purporting to 'set the record straight', thereby generating further controversy.

In one particular example from the early 1980s, a canvas-wrapped box apparently washed ashore near Kalbarri, Western Australia, purported to contain papers relating to events leading up to and following the clash between HMAS *Sydney* and the raider *Kormoran*. A carefully-typed Letter of Proceedings giving a narrative of the encounter seemed to indicate that the package originated on the *Sydney* herself, and had been prepared by a wounded junior officer, Sub-Lieutenant B.A. Elder, who had taken command of the ship following the death of all other senior officers. Its declared purpose was to serve as a record in case the ship foundered—a fortuitous letter for posterity! Also enclosed were several meticulously-typed alphabetical lists of the 645 men aboard the cruiser, and their casualty states after the engagement.

These two principal items, by themselves, might just have convinced the authorities of their authenticity. They look and feel authentic. Even so, it would still have been fair to ask how an injured 23-year old with only eight months service as a naval officer could take charge of a severely damaged warship, bring the burning vessel and its 210 remaining crew into some form of working entity, then sit down to dictate an almost faultless 5-page situation report and 15 pages of a detailed and equally faultless casualty list—all within the space of five hours before enemy witnesses noted the cruiser's demise.

The material in question is held in the archives of the Australian War Memorial, Canberra. What jars with the examiner is the miscellany of other material which accompanied the find—old letters, postcards, photographs, coins, address books, maps and technical manuals, and a variety of other odds and ends, much of which is clearly pre-1941, but which also prompts the question, 'Why this?' Why was such a mixed collection assembled, what was its purpose, and how could it have survived nearly 40 years in the sea in legible form? This question is particularly important in light of the fact that the metal items are rusted through, while the ink on the letters has not even smudged.

The collection has been described as a 'magpie's nest', for that is the impression created, along with a distinct feeling that someone has tried very hard to convince the finders that since all the dated items pre-date the loss of HMAS *Sydney*, they must be genuine. Forensic examinations of the box and the canvas bag which contained it have cast strong doubt on their supposed provenance, however, even if the contents themselves might not. One entry in the narrative states that at 1459 hours (2.59pm) on 19th of November 1941, just one hour before the *Kormoran* was sighted, a Japanese 'I'-Class long-range submarine was seen and identified by those on the cruiser's bridge, and noted as heading SSW (ie towards the *Kormoran*'s position) and diving. Were that to be true—and the perpetrators obviously wanted it to appear that way—the loss of HMAS *Sydney* only 19 days before the Japanese attack on Pearl Harbour would take on an entirely new and highly sensitive perspective. Fortunately for posterity and our international relations, the attempt to plant such inflammatory 'evidence' was most clearly a hoax.

Although the Joint Parliamentary Inquiry referred to earlier has now completed its task, it has shed little extra light on many unresolved issues arising from the sinking of HMAS *Sydney*, despite 19 volumes of submissions and hearings all over Australia. The loss of the cruiser is still hotly debated, with much sharp anger directed at the Royal Australian Navy, defence bureaucrats, and the government.

Emerging from the Inquiry is the promulgation of 18 recommendations. Some things the Inquiry panel advocates are: the release of all World War II documents for public scrutiny; subjecting the recovered Carley floats to close scientific analysis; locating the lone sailor's grave on Christmas Island, and exhuming his remains for examination and identification; sponsoring a search for the two vessels involved; and the subsequent protection and management of the wrecks.

Chapter 15

AHS CENTAUR
1943

AHS *Centaur.*

'Those who were saved told of blast effects and shock-waves, of a fiery inferno, of in-rushing seas, flame-lit darkness, a scramble along tilting decks ... They reported tales of miraculous escapes, of heroism and sacrifice, of unbelieving horror followed by bleak despair.'

Amidst all the barbarity of war, particularly throughout this last century, one symbol has stood out above all the horrors of martial conflict to give a measure of hope and succour to its victims—the Red Cross. For over 130 years, it has served as a universally recognised symbol of relief from suffering, as a refuge for the wounded, the sick and the dying, and as a promise of peace away from the carnage of battle-fronts and disaster areas. In situations such as these, red crosses have often appeared as umblemished symbols of humanitarianism adorning the sides of field ambulances, hospital ships and evacuation aircraft.

Behind the scenes the Red Cross and its representatives have been ever-present in dealing impartially with belligerents, in acting as a means of communication and negotiation, a go-between for warring parties. For those unfortunate enough to be taken by an enemy, the Red Cross has been there as a channel for correspondence and provisions for prisoners of war, and as a means of monitoring the treatment of such prisoners. At sea, Red Cross officials sometimes travelled on merchant vessels and hospital ships to observe, amongst other things, the proceedings laid down under the Hague and Geneva Conventions for the conduct of hostilities against merchantmen.

The symbol of the Red Cross still carries a message of non-violence even today, when most of us are more familiar with its annual funding appeals, its network of blood banks, its presence in the aftermath of disasters, or its work with refugees. But in the distant theatres of war and the sporadic local conflicts which continue to plague our civilisation, a red cross continues to be a symbol of aid and protection for its bearers, exempting them from involvement in the killing, and providing an internationally acknowledged shield behind which the suffering of war might be assuaged by its wearers engaged on errands of mercy. In a word, the Red Cross signifies immunity.

All this counted for nothing, however, early on the morning of 14th of May, 1943. Off the Queensland coast to the south of Brisbane, in the calm of the pre-dawn darkness, a brightly-lit ship sailed from Sydney north-bound to Cairns. Her bright lights, her white hull and upperworks, and the green band and red crosses on both all served to mark her for what she was—a hospital ship. The broad green band and the red crosses of her calling were all directly illuminated to indicate her purpose, as was required under the Geneva Convention. From Cairns she would move on to New Guinea to bring home wounded Australian soldiers who were struggling to resist the Japanese invasion of the islands to our north.

Lurking in the vicinity of Moreton Island was a Japanese submarine, stealing through the darkness like a jackal preying on the weak and, especially in this case, the defenceless. As fate would have it, this particular submarine's captain had enjoyed little success during this last mission, and was soon to return to his base at Truk, one of the Caroline Islands. There he would face the wrath of his superiors unless his scores could be improved beforehand. Any kind of ship would therefore do to show that his mission had not been a waste of time—warship, merchantman or coastal craft, all of which had eluded his search, or did not exist in this remote sector of a world at war.

Even a hospital ship would be a difficult target to resist, which was what he had just observed through the submarine's periscope. He could not have been unaware that such ships existed or what the approaching target was, for only they went about their business like peace-time liners, with all lights burning to illuminate their special colour-schemes as an indication of their protected role, notwithstanding the usual wartime blackouts. In any case, all belligerents regularly passed information to each other through the offices of the neutral Swiss to help identify these ships and their spheres of operation. All enemy warships and aircraft would therefore have surely known of this one—the Australian Hospital Ship (AHS) *Centaur.*

If the submarine commander reasoned his actions at all, since all the vessel's signs declared her immunity from attack, he may well have thought that as she was heading north she would not be carrying wounded troops. This would never have legitimated her as a military target, for she was still a hospital ship and thereby one protected from hostilities or interference by international agreement. But the submarine's record in shipping destroyed had still been a poor one, and her captain knew he would be obliged to explain this to his angry superiors in a few days' time.

———————

At the start of the war the MV *Centaur* was just another ship of the Blue Funnel Line on the Indian Ocean, plying her regular run between Singapore, Fremantle and other Western Australian ports, just as she had since being signed out from the Scottish shipyard which built her in 1924. There was nothing fancy or outstanding about the *Centaur*, though she was well-appointed. At 3200 tons gross, she had been conservatively built for the Ocean Steam Ship Company of Liverpool, owners of the Blue Funnel fleet, as a vessel designed to carry general cargo and livestock as well as 50 first class and 22 second class passengers. For the latter she was to provide a feeder service connecting with other Blue Funnel ships on the Liverpool–China run, via Singapore. For the former, she would be a maid-of-all-work on the Australian coast. Her name *Centaur* came from Greek mythology, like those of others in the Blue Funnel fleet. Over the course of almost 20 years she was to become a familiar sight in this part of the world.

The routine of her passages was barely interrupted by the outbreak of war in 1939, though she did come under the nominal control of Britain's Admiralty from that time. Far from the dangers of war in the North Atlantic, however, where merchant convoys came under regular attack and destruction by German U-boats, *Centaur* carried on as before save for some minor changes in the cargoes she carried. Occasional German commerce raiders posed the greatest and most unpredictable risk to life at sea, and several vessels were so far known to have been sunk by mines laid off New Zealand, and in Bass Strait.

For all that, the war remained remote. Even so, as a simple precaution her black and white colour-scheme with its distinctive blue funnel eventually gave way to a battleship-grey camouflage. Her routes and destinations were sometimes changed at short notice, and gradually she took aboard light defensive armaments and the men to use them as the war progressed. For over two years she continued in much of her former role—until suddenly, on the morning of 26th of November, 1941, she was diverted by a search aircraft of the Royal Australian Air Force (RAAF) to the scene of a naval engagement off Carnarvon, Western Australia, to pick up survivors from a number of rafts and lifeboats that had been sighted.

The survivors came from a battle that had taken place at dusk a week earlier between HMAS *Sydney* and the German raider *Kormoran* (see Chapter 14). In a desperate close-quarters action, both ships had been sunk. All the survivors were found to be German, for not one of the *Sydney*'s 645-man crew had been recovered, alive or dead. The news stunned Australia. *Centaur*'s usual master, Captain George Murray, had been relieved by Captain Walter Dark for a period of leave. Since the latter had already lost two ships to German submarines, he was disinclined to risk the safety of his ship, his passengers and crew to so many of the enemy he found adrift later that night. Instead he took a lifeboat with more than 50 men aboard in tow to Carnarvon, refusing even to bring them aboard *Centaur* when their boat appeared to be sinking. He ordered his captives into two of *Centaur*'s own boats, then after landing them at Carnarvon stayed in port long enough to transport most of the *Kormoran* prisoners under guard to Fremantle. The war had finally caught up with *Centaur*.

From there on hostilities increased rapidly. Within a week of the *Kormoran* rescue the American naval base at Pearl Harbor, Hawaii, was subject to a surprise air attack by the Japanese. On 19th of February, 1942, a similar assault was made on Darwin. Singapore fell the same month, putting an end to *Centaur*'s long-standing visits there. The Japanese steamroller was thrusting down through the island chains to Australia's north, and soon threatened the mainland. The war had come to our doorstep, and Australian troops were hard-pressed to resist the enemy's advance. In New Guinea, casualties were already being evacuated by three hospital ships which had been withdrawn from the Middle East. These were the *Manunda*, the *Oranje*, and the *Wanganella*, but as pressures grew towards the end of 1942, it became clear that there would soon be a need for another such ship, particularly as the others were at risk despite their protected status. AHS *Manunda* had already been attacked and damaged during the raid on Darwin, and had later been under threat from Japanese warships attacking New Guinea's Milne Bay.

Two Australian ships met the requirements set down for readily-convertible merchant vessels at this time—the *Centaur* and the *Koolinda*. Aboard each there was ample passenger accommodation and open decks for livestock, which could easily be converted into medical facilities and spacious wards for 200, and later 252 wounded evacuees, at minimal cost and effort. *Centaur* was working the coastal routes around Australia, having sailed once in convoy to Port Moresby, when she was selected for conversion as a hospital ship. On 6th of January, 1943, therefore, *Centaur* arrived at Victoria's Williamstown Naval Dockyard to begin the process that would soon change her identity—and also seal her fate.

Centaur's conversion to her new role took two months of intensive effort, during which time she had her original fittings stripped out, and the resounding spaces scrubbed and scoured in preparation for the installation of wards and operating theatres and all the ancillary equipment space a hospital needs for the care of its patients. A range of new accommodation was built for all manner of additional personnel, from extra cooks to the padre, all of whom needed better toilet, bathroom and ventilation facilities than those dating from the 1920s, when there had not even been piped hot water. Teams of doctors and nurses came aboard shortly to ensure all their stores requirements had been met and were correctly placed, and that the ship would work as a floating hospital in all anticipated situations.

There were also changes to the crew as her Asian complement was paid off and Australian merchant seamen took over the sailing of the ship. Lastly, she was painted in the distinctive colours demanded under the Geneva Convention for recognition as a hospital ship: white hull and upperworks; a 1.2-metre wide green band along each side of the hull, broken at three places by red crosses 2×2-metres square; a yellow funnel with red crosses 2×2-metres square on either side; and the ship's identity number, '47', stencilled in white on a black ground on both sides of the bow. Her deck was also emblazoned with two huge red crosses for recognition from the air, while she would fly the Red Cross flag from her foremast. At night, she would be brightly illuminated to ensure that all would know her for what she was.

AHS *Centaur* was to make just three voyages in her new guise before her fateful meeting with the enemy submarine off Moreton Island. On only her second voyage, she was to visit Port Moresby, out and return from Brisbane between the 8th and 18th of April 1943, having picked up 200 Australian and American wounded, and 10 wounded Japanese. She returned to Sydney on 8th of May to prepare for her next trip to New Guinea, via Cairns. On this occasion the *Centaur* would embark 220 men of the 2/12 Field Ambulance—ambulance drivers, medical orderlies and attached Army Service Corps (ASC) personnel—together with their arms and personal equipment. Their embarkation and later appearance on the deck in khaki uniform caused a considerable amount of consternation amongst observers, including some of the *Centaur*'s officers and medical staff, and more than a few wharf workers engaged on loading the ship for departure. What was going on aboard a hospital ship?

One of the Articles derived from the *Adaption of the Principles of the Geneva Convention to Maritime Warfare* states that vessels designated as hospital ships should not be used for any military purpose. To do so would be to infringe such a vessel's immunity from attack. To watchers on the Darling Harbour wharf that day, the presence of armed and uniformed troops about to go aboard AHS *Centaur* seemed to indicate a total contravention of her status. The ship's officers hurried down the gangway to halt the embarkation, and to seek an explanation for the soldiers being there, and especially soldiers with weapons.

After a number of telephone calls, the soldiers and their weapons were allowed on board, following assurances from the appropriate authorities that such weapons (i.e. rifles and revolvers) were a valid part of an ambulance driver's kit for defending the sick and wounded as determined by a further Article from the Principles of the Geneva Convention. Though the soldiers and their weapons were to be shipped north, the others aboard were assured they were not carrying ammunition. This was not enough for the attendant wharfies, however. Rumours were rife regarding the significance of armed troops aboard a hospital ship and the likelihood, therefore, of associated military equipment. Union delegates gathered to discuss the matter. Not until further assurances were given by Captain Murray, together with an invitation to inspect the ship's holds—which they did—were union representatives satisfied that the soldiers were who they were supposed to be, and that nothing beyond their legitimate personal arms had been taken aboard *Centaur*.

AHS *Centaur* left Sydney for the last time around mid-morning on Wednesday, 12th of May, 1943. It was a bright autumn day which saw her resplendent in white and green livery with the bright red crosses and her decks lined with uniformed troops as she passed beneath the bridge and out along Sydney Harbour. While only the military had been present when she cast off at the wharf, ferries and excursion boats saluted her passing and the role she clearly played in the war. But who knows who else saw her departure and wondered at her uniformed passengers, dressed now in jungle green and apparently bound for combat? Investigations after her sinking failed to determine why she was selected as a target. Even the identity of the submarine and her guilty captain remain circumspect despite intensive inquiries made in Japan after the war. In the absence of clear evidence to the contrary, actions by enemy agents and fifth column sympathisers can never be dismissed as contributing factors to the fate of the *Centaur*. Of the 332 people aboard that day, including 12 nurses of the medical contingent, only 64 would survive the torpedo attack which took place a week later.

That the *Centaur* was at some risk in going about her mission was understood. Indeed, the Geneva Convention itself acknowledged a degree of risk and peril during her voyages, though hardly, one would have thought, so close to home and as brilliantly conspicuous as she was. About this time, however, Japanese submarines had been seen off the Queensland coast, and four ships were known to have been recently sunk. Much was therefore riding on the significance of *Centaur*'s paintwork, and the trust that the Japanese would honour its symbolism. This was seen shortly as a vain hope.

The torpedo which sped out of the darkness at 4.10am on Friday, 14th of May, struck the hospital ship squarely on the port side between bridge and bow, blasting into the forward holds and cargo spaces (now converted to open wards) above and below the water line. One man, Corporal Albert Taylor, glimpsed the wake of the lunging missile from the ship's rail barely seconds before it exploded. Three minutes later the ship was gone, taking with her 45 of her officers and crew, 179 men from the 2/12 Field Ambulance and the ASC, 33 of the male medical staff, and all but one of the 12 nurses. But for a brief glare on the eastern horizon that was noted by soldiers guarding a new gun emplacement on Moreton Island, nothing was seen from the mainland to mark her passing. Not even the submarine's commander would have witnessed her demise, having no doubt dived his boat to escape detection after launching his torpedoes, listening instead for the dull percussion which would signal success.

The shock and carnage within the stricken ship in the brief moments remaining is almost impossible to imagine. The single torpedo had smashed into the vessel's side at the most vulnerable point, igniting and exploding *Centaur*'s tanks of diesel fuel with all the force of a second torpedo. Blast waves and fire swept through the holds and engine room in an instant, stunning and incinerating their occupants, then on through the open wards of the upper and lower decks where the Field Ambulance personnel were bedded down. Few escaped. Most of those who did would have been quickly overwhelmed by the flooding rush as the sea thundered inboard under pressure from the sinking ship, drowning men who were still incapable of helping themselves. Others were lost as the vessel began to break up around them. Only those on watch, or close to the outer decks, or those who were extremely lucky below decks, stood any real chance of survival.

Those who were saved told of blast effects and shock-waves, of a fiery inferno, of in-rushing seas, flame-lit darkness, a scramble along tilting decks, and the rain of debris and blazing oil which met them there before plunging into the sea. They reported tales of miraculous escapes, of heroism and sacrifice, of unbelieving horror followed by bleak despair. Friends, colleagues and even brothers were separated and lost in the sudden jolt from deep sleep to the desperate struggle for existence, seconds only amidst the mind-turning confusion of noise, billowing smoke, roaring flame, hurtling bodies on steepening decks, uncertainty, panic, and swirling rising waters. For those who had come through the first stunning impact, the course of life or death was to be instantly determined by individual actions and directions in darkness and fear—whether in the disorientating gloom a companionway was this way or that, whether a way out was clear or blocked by debris, whether there was time . . .

For many there was not. In three minutes the *Centaur* had surged beneath the waves, a blazing, disintegrating wreck. Three minutes—the time required to listen to a tune on the radio, watch a commercial break on television, or make a cup of tea. Mundane aspects of one's everyday life, but all that was left of life for most aboard the doomed ship early that morning. For the remaining few, there were still the horrors at the surface to be faced, in darkness, loneliness, and often in pain, grasping for any means of staying afloat, choking for breath in the cold shock of the pre-dawn. The last light from the searing fires showed a shifting sea of broken bodies, while others struggled away from the grasp of the sinking ship as she canted high for a final plunge, roaring and spuming, still shedding debris. Then she was gone. All around could be heard pitiful cries of distress and helplessness amongst pools of burning oil and the flotsam now beginning to surface from the *Centaur*'s grave.

Good fortune, presence of mind, or their particular place in the ship saved 64 people that dark morning—less than a fifth of her complement.

Some of the crew who had just come off watch had not yet turned in, and so were most alert and aware of escape routes, even in the dark, when the first blast came. Those furthest from the explosion, especially on the starboard side or aft, were also able to escape on deck. Sailors in wartime half-expected their ships to be sunk. As their life jackets were always handy, they thus comprised nearly half the survivors at the final count. Amongst the medical staff, Sister Ellen Savage, the one surviving nurse, owed her survival to the life jacket she had casually tossed onto her bunk after the last boat drill, and which she hastily grabbed up on leaving her cabin. Even so, two of her jacket-clad colleagues died on being struck by falling debris in the water, while Colonel Manson, their Commanding Officer, lost his life while attending to the safety of the ladies.

Of the soldiers, only 14 were left alive from the 193 who had marched aboard in Sydney, most in the prime of their manhood. Pure chance allowed a handful to live, while fate took the rest. A dazed few grabbed life jackets as they fled from the flames. Driver George McGrath and Corporal Albert Taylor, the man who saw the incoming torpedo, had just answered nature's call at that time of the morning. Private Percy Kelly owed his sleeplessness to a vivid warning dream. Sergeant Bill Cornell was swept out of the ship by the waters surging within. Tongues of fire literally chased others away from their bunks and up stairways, including the 67-year-old Torres Strait Pilot, Captain 'Jock' Salt, who soaked some of his bedding in water to escape through the flames. There was no time to launch lifeboats, or even to release rafts. The ship sank fast beneath those still struggling in the attempt.

As dawn broke, two hours after the sinking, the exhausted survivors looked about them for companions in their ordeal. Some were injured, bruised or burned. Many were alone and afraid. Most were ill-clad, if not naked and covered in oil, and all were cold, hungry and already suffering from thirst. As the sun rose, its then welcome warmth would eventually give way to relentless sunburn to add to their woes. Fortunately there were enough rafts and an assortment of substantial debris afloat—hatch-boards, spars, barrels and drums, and even the wheelhouse roof—to offer some form of security and rest from their struggles. But there was no shelter. One of the rafts was a large one which soon had 30 men aboard or clinging to its grab-lines. About this the others slowly gathered as the daylight strengthened and the extent of the devastation unfolded, though a number would remain adrift and alone.

During the last hours of darkness, some of the survivors later reported seeing the dim outline of a submarine surface amongst the flotsam, but they had held their silence, fearing the enemy. The submarine soon departed without a sound or acknowledgement, leaving the survivors to their fate. Perhaps they had not been seen. If her captain had indeed been merciful, he had not had them shot in the water, for they were only 25 miles or so from the coast. Accusers aboard he did not want . . .

Though the survivors were glad to be left alone, they were still in a sorry state. By a stroke of luck, however, a broken lifeboat later proved to be heaven-sent in providing them with some very basic foodstuffs and a minimal supply of water—but it was better than nothing. Sister Savage quickly took charge of their scant rations and despite her own injuries, she was able to keep up the spirits of her male companions with sing-songs and prayers, to which others added until rescue came.

The chances of rescue were on everyone's mind. The ship's officers realised that radio silence had been the order of the day, and that there had hardly been time to send a distress signal, even had the duty operator and his transmitter survived the collapse of the bridge. They kept their own silence though, in the interests of morale. Rescue would therefore depend on a chance sighting by a passing ship or aircraft, but that assumed others would be looking out, which was probably unlikely. They had flares from the broken lifeboat with which to attract attention, as well as some picked up from the sea, but the ships and aircraft they spotted were either too far away to bring hope, or simply did not see them. Morale sank with every failed sighting, added to which they faced the threat of attacks by sharks which began to gather around their floating platforms as the day progressed. Survival then became a matter of fighting them off as they nudged the rafts and tried to charge aboard to grab what they could. This was the lot of the *Centaur*'s survivors as the hours lengthened, and no rescue came.

Night fell, and with it the hope that they might soon be seen and saved. Darkness brought other problems of cold discomfort and inability to tend to the wounded, though they huddled together for mutual warmth. At one point in the early morning, those who were awake were startled to hear the sounds of nearby engine noises, once more with the dark silhouette of a surfaced submarine! A call from the craft was ignored, even though it might have meant rescue. It might also have meant imprisonment, or worse. After a while the submarine left, to everyone's relief. With daylight hopes rose again that rescue would come soon, but it also became clear their numbers were starting to shrink. Driver Jack Walder, horrifically burned, died in the night and was buried at sea with the dawn. Others were drifting away elsewhere, lifeless and unseen, never having been part of a group.

When rescue finally came in the early afternoon that day, 15th of May, it was almost overwhelmingly sudden. More aircraft had been seen that morning which had not seen them, and morale was once more in retreat. There was concern for the food and water remaining, and the prospect of surviving another night at sea. To add to their problems they were drifting north-eastwards on the currents, away from the coast. Soon after they had seen two ships in the distance and released yet another flare to signal their predicament, they heard the welcome roar of a patrolling

Anson of the RAAF which had spotted the flare, then the *Centaur*'s oil slick and debris field, and then the groups of survivors. At about the same time, lookouts aboard the American destroyer *Mugford*, one of the distant ships, saw what appeared to be a raft on the sea. This was quickly confirmed by the Anson as it flew overhead to direct them towards *Centaur*'s survivors. Rescue was finally at hand.

The USS *Mugford* had left Brisbane early that morning to carry out escort duties in the vicinity of Moreton Bay. The Americans were therefore soon on the scene to pick up the shipwrecked Australians, search the area for any other survivors, and convey them back to Brisbane. For the 64 who had escaped with their lives, their ordeal was over save for a spell in hospital. The shock, horror and anger over the sinking of a hospital ship was about to rock the nation. The investigations to find the truth, and the Allied protests to follow, were soon to begin. It would be years before the matter was finally laid to rest, with many questions still unanswered, including which submarine sank AHS *Centaur*, who was her captain, and why did he commit such a callous act?

Continuing conjecture, post-war interviews in Japan and searches amongst Japanese records, together with a process of careful elimination of suspects, finally concluded that the slayer of the *Centaur*, against all the international rules of war, was one Lieutenant-Commander Hajime Nakagawa, captain at the time of submarine *I-177*. His war record was notorious for cold, sadistic acts in pursuing instructions from the Naval General Staff. In particular he had been identified as the perpetrator of known atrocities in the Indian Ocean, when the survivors of several British ships he had sunk were machine-gunned in their lifeboats and in the water, while others had been killed using sledge-hammers and Samurai swords. To balance accounts, he also had the unique distinction of sinking another Japanese submarine with all her crew on surface trials in 1939.

Nakagawa persistently denied his guilt, just as the Imperial Japanese

Navy had denied any association with the loss of an Allied hospital ship. The former submariner was nevertheless found guilty as one of the lesser war criminals, mainly on account of his treatment of the British seamen since proof of his connection with the *Centaur* was impossible to obtain. In 1948 he was sentenced to eight years hard labour, of which he served less then six. He died in 1986, aged 84.

The remains of the *Centaur* lay on the seabed for more than 50 years before they were rediscovered, quite by accident, by a group of divers in March 1995. The divers were looking for wartime aircraft dumped off Brisbane after the war ended, but instead they came across a wreck lying in two pieces in 180 metres of water, which a remote camera module soon identified as that of the ill-fated hospital ship from both its name and its registration number, AHS 47. To help resolve the claim that the ship may have been carrying munitions, none were seen on the images brought from the depths. The wreck is located 9.3 nautical miles east of the Cape Moreton lighthouse, in depths out of reach of conventional scuba-divers—which will help to preserve the remains as a war grave, and the memory of those who died in the course of their humanitarian duties.

Chapter 16

THE MAHOGANY SHIP

A typical Portuguese caravel, *The Voyage of Christovao de Mendonca* by Philip J. Gray.

'So what was the wreck? ... What was it doing there, a decade at least
before Captain Cook discovered this land, and years before its first
formal settlement? There were no answers from its mute timbers.'

Somewhere in the sand dunes between Warrnambool and Port Fairy in western Victoria lie the remains of the Mahogany Ship, a fabled wreck discovered in 1836 soon after the first settlers arrived in the district. The wreck was examined by a number of witnesses for most of the next half-century. It was then lost to view in the 1880s, never to be seen again. Without doubt, this is truly Australia's mystery ship—as enigmatic as the *Mary Celeste* and as elusive as the 'Flying Dutchman' of maritime legend.

This wreck has posed a riddle that has been pondered periodically, with varying degrees of intensity, for as long as the State of Victoria has existed. Historians suspect that this so-called 'Mahogany' Ship, if it still exists, might well hold the answers to the question of which European people first discovered Australia—the Dutch, the Portuguese or the Spaniards? Such answers would indeed lead to a rewriting of the history books. But we are no nearer determining the origins or the whereabouts of the wreck today, despite a number of systematic and increasingly scientific searches, than we were when it was first discovered.

The saga—for it has become no less—begins in January 1836, around the start of the Victorian whaling season. At the time, a party of three comprising Messrs Gibbs, Wilson and Captain Smith were operating out of Port Fairy, then called Belfast, and were looking for seals in the vicinity of present-day Warrnambool when their boat capsized in the surf near the mouth of the Hopkins River. Conditions were such that Captain Smith drowned, but the other two managed to stagger ashore barely alive.

Near-naked and without provisions, they were forced to walk the 15 or so miles back along the beach to Port Fairy to report the loss of Captain Smith and the boat. They carried sticks across their shoulders in imitation of firearms so as to frighten away natives who were said to be very numerous in the district.

Approximately half way through their journey, they came across the wreck of an old ship lying high amongst the sand dunes. The vessel appeared to have been there many years, as it was almost buried in the dunes, but enough of its dark timbers were exposed for them to distinguish the remains of quite a substantial craft, which they also reported on their arrival back in Port Fairy. Shortly afterwards, Captain John Mills, his brother Charles, a local identity by the name of Hugh Donnelly and one or two others took a whale boat out to retrieve the sealing party's capsized craft. They also intended to stop by the place described to examine the reported wreck.

What they found sticking up from the scrub and sand were the ribs and planking of a largish ship, built from a dark reddish timber similar to either cedar or mahogany, but bleached in a way that told of exposure to the elements over many years. The wreck lay nearly parallel to the shoreline, without masts, spars, rudder or rigging, but with enough decking remaining to suggest a vessel of some capacity below decks. What type of vessel she had been no one could say, though her lines would soon be taken for those of a long-lost Spanish ship after others visited the spot.

Of her immediate location, Hugh Donnelly remarked: 'She lay well up on the beach, fast in the brow of the loose dry sand on the edge of the natural verdure, almost broadside on with her bow towards Port Fairy, her stern a trifle more seaward.' From his first impressions, Captain John Mills said, 'I stood on her deck, not knowing what timber she was built of, and tried to cut a splinter out of her timbers, but my clasp knife glanced over them as if they were bars of iron.' Nevertheless, they were able to take some measurements from the deck planking, which Captain Mills said would be ideal for building a whale carcass ramp on Port Fairy's Griffith Island. After calculating the number of horses and wagons needed to cart the lumber away, the party went back to their boats.

Over the days following their return to Port Fairy, a number of people questioned local Aborigines about the wreck. They asked what was known of it, how long it had been there, and what caused it to lie where it did, but the Aborigines' answer was always, 'She all time longa here.' Even the oldest amongst them, aged about 80 or so, said the same thing, with the implication that the wreck must have occurred before 1760. Though certain Aboriginal tales recounted some early sightings of ships, they were without specific times and therefore inconclusive.

So what was the wreck? And where had it come from? What was it doing there, a decade at least before Captain Cook discovered this land, and years before its first formal settlement? There were no answers from its mute timbers. On a later visit Captain Mills, who was to become Port Fairy's first harbour master, scrambled to the top of the dunes to take what bearings he could from the featureless hummocks and the surrounding landscape. As more people learned of the sand-bound curiosity, it became something of a local landmark, and the beginnings of a legend. The notion that the wreck might be a lost Spanish treasure ship with a cargo of buried doubloons kept up the number of visitors, though no such treasures were found. Gradually, the wreck became just something to watch out for on rides between Port Fairy and Warrnambool, a point on the beach to walk to for recreation, or a feature people would later recall as a memory from their childhood or youth. But its origins still remained tantalisingly obscure.

The 'Old Wreck', as it became known, remained a place in the landscape for nearly half a century. It was visible from what was then the Hummock Road, merely a track along the base of the dunes used by riders and pedestrians before the opening of a formed road further inland between Warrnambool and Port Fairy. Amongst the passers-by, one Captain John Mason found the wreck interesting enough to record his observations. 'Riding along the beach from Port Fairy to Warrnambool in the summer of 1846', he recalled, 'my attention was attracted to the hull of a vessel embedded high and dry in the hummocks, far above the reach of any tide. It appeared to be a vessel of about 100 tons burthen, and from its bleached and weather-beaten appearance must have been there for many years. The spars and deck are gone, and the hull full of drift sand. The timber of which she was built had the appearance of either mahogany or cedar.' Such was his interest that he returned in 1847 accompanied by a ship-builder friend. Their joint opinion was that 'She had the appearance of a large lighter [a flat-bottomed vessel, or barge], but of a build which bespoke ignorance of the art of shipbuilding as we know it.' The mystery deepened.

In 1848 another witness, Mrs Thomas Manifold, who was the wife of a local magistrate, added further observations after coming upon the wreck, hidden from sight amongst the dunes. 'It was made of dark red wood', she said, 'but strangely designed and constructed. Instead of the familiar planks along its sides it had wooden panels.' It was thus noted and commented on by a number of people around this time, some of particular standing in the local community. Even Superintendent (later Governor) La Trobe reported seeing the wreck in 1849, in company with Thomas Manifold himself. These were reliable witnesses whose testimonies would carry the legend beyond the physical disappearance of the wreck.

Later observers also left their comments. As a Warrnambool schoolboy in the mid-1850s, Alex Rollo remembered walking out to the wreck with friends, and recalled feeling certain of its antiquity. In 1862, Francis Saul was erecting a fence for the Warrnambool Borough Council when he saw the remains from where he worked, 'About three chains east of the fence and four from the sea'. He told both his son and a local herdsman, Thomas Best, of its location, 'About a mile east of Gorman's Lane'. John Davies, a long-time local resident, set out with a friend some time before 1890 to seek clues to the wreck's identity. They confirmed Captain Mills' earlier bearings, as had Francis Saul, and cleared enough of the deck to assess the vessel as being of some 200 tons. With some difficulty they cut off a block of wood (now held in the National Library, Canberra) which they took back to Warrnambool, which many people examined but concluded only that, 'it was not unlike mahogany.'

Not all the visitors saw the wreck as a mere curio. At a time when dressed and seasoned timber was scarce and valuable, it was also viewed as a free resource. Captain Mills had already seen its usefulness as a whale ramp near Port Fairy. Alex Rollo, referred to previously, grew up to be a ship's carpenter and often walked out to the wreck, 'to secure a mahogany plank'. With one of these he is said to have made a mantelpiece for a cottage on Russell's Creek. Captain Mason noted that the flooring of Griffith's Farm was far superior than that usual for a bush building. He was told the timber 'had been obtained from the deck planks of an old wreck on the hummocks', just a short distance to the south. Similarly, when Charles MacGillivray remarked on the fineness of the interior fittings of 'Tara', a two-storey house on Gorman's Lane, he was told that the woodwork was made from timbers from the wreck.

Furniture is also said to have been produced from the ancient ship's timbers. A Dennington family by the name of Haberfield is said to be in possession of a chair, the 'J.W. Anderson chair', made by one Michael Bradshaw from material recovered from the Mahogany Ship. One of the items held in the Flagstaff Hill Museum, Warrnambool, is a roughly-made chest, said to be derived from timber found on Killarney beach, close to the wreck, which analysis revealed as being of tropical origin and resembling mahogany in its make up. Most recently there have been press reports of timbers from the wrecked vessel having once been used to construct local bridges.

As late as 1880 the remains of the wreck were still being plundered for what they would yield. Witness a report by one Thomas Paton, who stated that one Sunday afternoon in 1880, while on a brisk beach walk with his friend Samuel Avery, they came across a local farmer, Henry Lyfield, in the process of burning what was visible of the wreck. He had piled brushwood around the old timbers and fired it in the hope of recovering any bronze or copper fittings afterwards. The implication seems to be that the remains were still extensive enough to give encouragement to his actions. Whatever the outcome, by the following weekend all that remained was a heap of ash. These three individuals may have been the last people to lay eyes on the old wreck.

Nothing was seen of it after 1880, and the former existence of the so-called 'Mahogany Ship' passed into legend. The chronological reports of observers indicate a diminishing object anyway, Donnelly reporting a visible 12 to 15 feet of her timbers in 1846 when he last saw the wreck, compared with the 3 or 4 feet seen by Rollo the schoolboy 10 years later. It was locally believed that the wreck was fully covered by drifting sand. Certainly the introduction of grazing amongst the dunes about this time had set the sands once more in motion, pushed by the winds to bury anything in their path, while the fragile coast was being eaten back by the onslaught of the waves. This environmental degradation coupled with the steady removal of planking and the burning of the visible remains surely meant that anything left of the shipwreck was lost beneath the shifting sands, if not scattered by the tides. The very possibility became a prospect which continues to tease succeeding generations, even today.

Despite the early sightings and the many anecdotal reports, the wreck was not formally reported until 1870, and then only as the 'Old', 'Spanish' or 'Ancient Wreck'. The name 'Mahogany Ship' seems to have been adopted around 1890 when letters on the subject began to appear in the Warrnambool *Standard*, though its coining may be attributed to one Thomas Clark as early as 1860, after his (allegedly inaccurate) painting entitled *The Mahogany Ship*. Mr Joseph Archibald, curator of the Warrnambool museum, was a strong advocate for research on the vessel and its origins and was enthusiastic in his efforts to encourage a search for any of the wreck's remains.

Three searches were in fact made during 1890, the first of many conducted over the next 100 years. It thus became something of an irony that while the wreck was visible, no one was especially interested in an excavation to find out more about it. Once the ship had vanished, however, the fervour for a serious study mounted steadily, along with outpourings of opinion—some reasoned, some not—until the subject was taken seriously enough to investigate it further. The impetus for serious consideration grew from the question of who had discovered Australia first.

The rationale for earlier discoveries than those of Jansz, Hartog, Cook and others had been well argued and well documented in recent years by such writers as Kenneth McIntyre (*The Secret Discovery of Australia*) and Lawrence Fitzgerald (*Java la Grande—The Portuguese Discovery of Australia*). Their interpretation of ancient charts—the Portuguese Dieppe maps generally, and the so-called 'Dauphin Map' in particular—purporting to be of *Terra Australis Incognita* or the Great South Land, need not be discussed here. It is enough to say, digressing just a little, that extensive searches were being made throughout the 16th and early 17th centuries to find the fabled southern landmass that was thought to exist around the bottom of the globe. Such voyages were often made as legitimate adjuncts to trading ventures by the Spanish and the Dutch from their island possessions to the north, although the records of such ventures were kept hidden away from potential competitors.

The Portuguese were even more circumspect in their explorations, especially regarding their Spanish neighbours, since their presence in Australian waters would have been an unwarranted incursion—trespass, no less—into Spanish territory under the terms of the Papal Treaty of Tordesillas 1494. That year, in order to bring resolution to the rivalry between Spain and Portugal regarding their respective claims to new lands, rich trade resources and pagan peoples for conversion to Christianity, Pope Alexander VI devised a scheme whereby a line drawn down the Atlantic 350 leagues west of the Cape Verde Islands would effectively divide all non-Christian lands between the two nations—Portugal's share was to the east of the line, Spain's to the west.

To accommodate Spanish and Portuguese explorations on the other side of the world, the extent of the division, universally referred to as the 'Pope's Line' or the 'Line of Demarcation', ran all the way round the globe. This kept the Spanish and Portuguese apart, though with notable exceptions, for over 150 years. In the then unknown Australian context, the line demarcated the Indian Ocean as a Portuguese 'lake' as far east as today's Western Australian border. If the Mahogany Ship *had* been a Portuguese vessel, therefore, and one venturing as far east as the future city of Warrnambool, the Spanish would have been justifiably annoyed. The Portuguese would naturally have kept quiet about it, as they apparently did, but the possibility later excited a number of 19th century residents of Victoria. If not a Spanish treasure ship, *could* the Mahogany Ship perhaps have been Portuguese? Alas, we still don't know.

The first searches in 1890 were based on Captain Mills' rather imprecise bearings taken sometime after 1836, though several later observers had said they bore out the location of the visible wreck. According to Captain Mills' directions, remembered in 1890 by his friend Mr C. Lynar, the ship 'lay well to the east of Gorman's Lane. Proceed eastward along the beach', he had said, 'till you bring the point of land on which the old iron church stood in line with the highest point of Tower Hill Island.

The wreck would be almost in a straight line with those objects—well up in the hummocks.' During the third of these searches, notwithstanding the loss of the 'old iron church' as a key landmark, a number of intriguing artefacts were recovered. These comprised a quantity of 'rotten ship's ironwork'; 'the latch of a galley fire place, or oven'; 'a large spike nail'; a bronze bolt 'about six inches long, and evidently very old'; and 'a considerable quantity of what seems to have been massive hooping'. Despite the intensity of later searches, however, this handful of artefacts is the only tangible evidence of any wreck found so far. The nail, the bolt and the latch are kept at the Flagstaff Hill Museum, Warrnambool.

A few months after the last search, a paper from Joseph Archibald was read in Melbourne but there, for the time being, the matter rested. Archibald was unsuccessful in generating any greater interest in the whereabouts and origins of the wreck, and he eventually retired to New South Wales, disillusioned by community attitudes. Though the paper stimulated the fascination of one George Gordon McCrae for a year or two in the early part of this century, culminating in his own presentation to the Royal Geographic Society in Melbourne in 1910, it did nothing to raise interest in another search. After that, any serious consideration of the wreck seemed to lapse entirely for almost 60 years. Two world wars, some lesser conflicts, a stock market crash followed by a severe economic depression seemed to be greater preoccupations during this time.

It was not until the late 1960s that reawakened interest was sufficient to spark a new search. This was undertaken in 1969 by the Monash University Archaeological Club, though it was never regarded as a 'serious effort', and remained inconclusive. Soon afterwards, however, support for more serious investigations into the Mahogany Ship phenomenon was offered by none other than the National Trust of Victoria. As a result, two sites were selected for field explorations between 1974 and 1976, based on propositions made by McCrae and Archibald. Operation Mole probed the McCrae site during the 1974–75 season while Operation Wombat, on the Archibald site, followed a year later. Neither search unearthed fresh evidence, though one did lead to the other and eventually aided in the elimination of both.

It was during the latter search that a strong magnetic anomaly was located 'about two miles on the Belfast side of Warrnambool', near the site of another wreck once reported to be lying amongst the dunes. It had been noted as early as 1847 by a number of credible witnesses, and was assuredly seen at that time by author Richard Osburne, who described its position in his book, *The History of Warrnambool* (1887). It, too, had gradually become lost beneath the shifting sands. For a while therefore, and perhaps even now, discussions regarding the site of the Mahogany Ship were confused by apparently conflicting eye-witness statements. For this reason, this second wreck has not been mentioned up to this point. It seems clear though, that there *were* two unknown wrecks amongst the dunes about this time, both of which have since disappeared.

Detracting comments made by William Earle in his *History of Port Fairy* (1896) regarding the remains of a whalers' blubber punt (apparently the second wreck) seem to have become attached to the first, along with conflicting descriptions. But Captain Mason, who described the first Mahogany Ship wreck, also examined the second wreck in company with Mr A.C. Kell and dismissed it as of little significance, being apparently 'one of the old flat-bottomed punts built by whalers here in the forties'. Having seen both wrecks within six or seven years in different locations, the good captain is hardly likely to have confused the two. Local opinion now recognises the existence of a second wreck.

This immediately raises the question of which is which? Though in January 1975 the Warrnambool *Standard* went so far as to suggest the existence of two mahogany ships, the weight of contemporary testimony and later judgements clearly support the site nearer Port Fairy as that of the 'true', or at least the first, Mahogany Ship. Captain Mills' original bearings and most of the ensuing reports point to this. While there are fears in some quarters that the wreck may have been swept out to sea as a consequence of the lateral spread of a drainage channel dug through the dunes between 1868 and 1870 (Rutledge's Cut), there was clearly enough of it left for Farmer Lyfield to burn in 1880. More recent searches have therefore tended to concentrate on this area, specifically on a high sand ridge named Sandfly Rise.

Sandfly Rise was the focus of a further expedition under the National Trust's patronage, named 'Operation Sandfly' in 1981. It was conducted by the experienced leader of the two earlier investigations, Ian McKiggan, but again proved inconclusive in the time available, although several magnetic anomalies were recorded and a number of drill samples were recovered. Some of these contained basalt pebbles which may have come from a ship's ballast. On the other hand, basalt is a common substrate in the area and may have originated from nearby Tower Hill. Many experts have added their opinions to the search, and have clearly indicated where the wreck is *unlikely* to be on account of the age and structure of the surrounding terrain. Sandfly Rise remains the strongest contender as the Mahogany Ship's last resting place, but even the latest round of searches, in 1992, by technical teams from the universities and CSIRO using the most sophisticated electronic equipment, have still failed to find it. And so the mystery and intrigue continues.

In the absence of incontrovertible evidence, there has been endless speculation on the nature and origins of the Mahogany Ship. In the early years it was thought to be the wreck of a Spanish treasure ship, though this notion was apparently based on nothing more than wishful thinking. However, in 1595 a Spanish vessel, the *Santa Ysabel*, was lost overnight amongst the Solomon Islands from a flotilla commanded by General

Alvaro de Mendana, and never seen again. Could such a vessel have found its way from the island-strewn seas of the western Pacific to the southern shores of Australia, through unknown waters and much against prevailing winds and currents?

For a while another Spanish vessel was thought to be the Mahogany Ship. Taken as a prize by a privateer off Mexico, the *Santa Anna* was later employed as a whaler, working out of Sydney between 1806 and 1811. After being lost on a voyage to London in 1812, her remains were thought to be those found in the dunes between Port Fairy and Warrnambool in 1836, until subsequent research revealed that the *Santa Anna* had been wrecked in the Straits of Timor in 1812.

There was also a possibility, not entirely discounted, that the wreck might have been Dutch, in view of other Dutch shipwrecks found on the Australian coast. It is conceivable that a Dutch vessel following the southern Brouwer route from the Cape to the Indies might have been carried too far east by storms in the Southern Ocean, and been cast ashore on the present Victorian coast. Alternatively, such a vessel might have been engaged in charting more of the Australian coastline, following in the wake of François Thijssen and Abel Tasman. An Aboriginal story, told to one W.J. Murray in response to queries about the Mahogany Ship origins, says that two ships had called into the bay at Port Fairy at least 150 years earlier. The source was King Billy of the Merri tribe, then aged about 60, who went on to say that the local inhabitants would not go near them. After they had departed, however, a storm blew up and drove one of the ships ashore. If there was truth in this tale, at that time the mystery visitors would have appeared on the scene sometime before 1740.

Not all of the Dutch ships known to have been lost on voyages between Holland and Batavia in the 17th and 18th centuries have been traced. While four were later found to have been wrecked off the shores of Western Australia, at least three are still unaccounted for. These are the

Ridderschap van Holland, lost around 1684/5; the *Fortuyn*, lost in 1724; and the *Aagtekerke*, which went missing in 1726. Another said to be missing from the same period is the *Boor*. Since the Mahogany Ship has been variously estimated at between 100 and 300 tons burthen, any of these Dutch craft could match its identity. Coincidentally, the wood sample supposedly taken from the Mahogany Ship and later held in Canberra has been dated at between 270 and 320 years old, that is belonging to a ship most likely built between 1660 and 1710. A later analysis, however, states that the physical characteristics of the sample resemble species of Eucalypt.

But what of the Portuguese? One of the episodes of Portuguese and Spanish rivalry in the early part of the 16th century concerned Portuguese fears that Spain was planning to invade their lucrative holdings in the Spice Islands, part of the East Indies. When a convoy sailed from Spain in 1519 with this object, the Portuguese alerted their own naval craft, in three fleets, to intercept it. One of the officers of this armada was Cristovao de Mendonça, who was given three caravels with which to search for the Spaniards in the so-called 'Isles of Gold', the name by which Australia was then known to the Portuguese.

Mendonça missed his quarry having passed unknowingly through Torres Strait, whereafter Kenneth McIntyre, in *The Secret Discovery of Australia*, traces his voyage according to the Dieppe maps, down the east coast of Australia from Cape York and round as far as Warrnambool in the south. This route was via the site of Geelong where a set of keys (the 'Geelong Keys' found in 1847) was lost. Beyond Warrnambool, he claims, where the Dieppe maps end, de Mendonça turned about for reasons unknown—storms, ship damage, illness amongst the crew, etc. And here, he reasons, de Mendonça lost one of his three ships.

Current thinking is that the wreck found in 1836 may well be the remains of a Portuguese caravel, judging from its size and description, which perhaps was one of Mendonça's. Such a possibility is suggested by the view that the Portuguese were also secretly exploring the Australian coast in the 16th century, as suggested by interpretations of the Dieppe maps. McIntyre notes that an ancient wreck of a similar construction, said to have been uncovered in 1877 on Ruapuke Beach, on the west coast of New Zealand's North Island, may add further substance to the conjecture, particularly when this is linked to stories about pre-Dutch (1642) visitors leaving European facial characteristics amongst certain New Zealand Maori. But as yet, we cannot be sure.

For those favouring more prosaic or domestic origins, there is description enough amongst the notes of their observers to suggest that one of the wrecks found amongst the sand hills is little more than a locally-made boat of no specific design. Disregarding the discovery of the 'ancient' wreck in 1836, Earle was adamant that the remains were those of 'an old, flat-bottomed punt built by whaling parties here in the forties . . . to carry the blubber to the try-works'. Others have said the remains looked like a coal barge, or a local lighter. Even the timber sample reputedly taken from the Mahogany Ship is said to resemble Eucalyptus!

More recent opinion has suggested that the vessel may have been one built by convicts in which to escape from Tasmania: but one must then question how a party of convicts could build and hide a vessel of between 100 and 300 tons in the Tasmanian bush, unseen by their gaolers over a number of months, to the point where it was launched successfully and sailed to the Victorian coast. Even if their survival and arrival was then sheer luck, of all the options possible this seems the least likely.

On the other hand it might *not* be a vessel associated with Australia or Australian exploration at all. The beaches of far west Victoria abut the Southern Ocean in latitudes which reach down to the Roaring Forties and the so-called Furious Fifties of maritime lore. On either side of Bass Strait and Tasmania the oceans circulate almost unhindered, driven eastwards to New Zealand and beyond, by westerly gales passing below Africa's Cape of Good Hope, all the way from the southern spur of South America. Ships wrecked or disabled in any of these waters might drift long distances on the east-bound currents, to be cast up on shores half a world from the scene of their mishaps. It is well-known that islands in these regions became collecting grounds for flotsam, and early visitors to South Georgia, Kerguelen, Macquarie and Campbell Islands noted wreckage piled on the beaches as evidence of earlier, unknown sailing disasters. It is thus quite possible that the remains of the Mahogany Ship arrived on the remote Australian beach near Port Fairy the same way.

Having exhausted the most likely origins of this mysterious wreck, there remains one further possible explanation for the wreck's presence on that remote Australian beach. It is perhaps the most intriguing and not entirely unreasonable account, and one quite in keeping with the enigma of its later disappearance. In the 15th century, and in parallel with the maritime ventures of Spain and Portugal, China's Ming emperors embarked on a series of naval expeditions aimed at discovering more of the wider world, increasing trade, and bringing many of its lesser rulers to pay tribute at the Dragon Throne to the reigning Son of Heaven. The main proponent of this policy was the third Ming Emperor, Yung Lo, also called Zhu Di, who in 1403 ordered the construction of an imperial fleet of hundreds of assorted vessels, in anticipation of some major maritime enterprises.

As overall commander of the fleet, Yung Lo appointed Admiral Cheng Ho, also known as Zheng He, a 'three-jewelled court eunuch', who subsequently embarked on a series of exploratory voyages which ranged as far afield as modern Vietnam, Thailand and the Malay peninsula; Java, Sumatra, and other parts of what became the East Indies; India, Ceylon and the Persian Gulf; and the coast of Arabia, the Red Sea, and the east coast of Africa. In all, Cheng Ho took part in seven recorded voyages between 1405 and 1433, the largest of which comprised over 300 ships and some 27 000 men.

The Chinese at this time were said to be aware of the existence of *Terra Australis*, and even had a map on which it was depicted. Having spent some time at the port of Malacca and having sailed amongst the islands of the East Indies, it seems quite probable that the Chinese would have learned of the rumoured existence of *Terra Australis* amongst the Malaccans and Javanese, just as the Portuguese are said to have done a century or so later. If McIntyre argues that the mere rumour of such a land was enough to spark the Portuguese on their exploratory voyages, which he does, then why not the Chinese?

The late Jack Loney, in the introduction to his book *Wrecks in Australian Waters*, states in reference to the 'Great South Land' that, 'The Chinese knew this land existed in 1420, then in 1477 Emperor Ying Tsung produced a porcelain map of the coastline after Admiral Chang circum-navigated the continent with 62 ships.' Unfortunately his statement is not sourced and some of the detail appears to be wrong. The fact remains, however, that the Chinese were visiting our northern neighbours in large fleets. Many lesser voyages were no doubt made by smaller flotillas in pursuit of China's search for world knowledge. Could it be, therefore, that such a flotilla was ordered to investigate the stories of *Terra Australis* or the 'Great South Land', and to report their findings back to the Admiral and his Emperor? And might not just one vessel from such a flotilla have become lost and driven aground by the storms ever likely to be encountered off the southern-most shores?

In this kind of scenario, such a vessel—built 'like a coal barge' (W.J. Murray), in a way which 'bespoke ignorance of the art of shipbuilding as we know it' (Captain John Mason), and 'strangely designed and constructed' [so that] 'instead of the familiar planks along the length of its sides it had wooden panels' (Mrs T. Manifold)—would surely be a

Chinese sea-going junk? This type of vessel has been described as one of the most efficient and seaworthy vessels ever created, in spite of its rather cumbersome appearance. Of ancient origin, having regularly sailed the Indian Ocean since the 7th century, they were recognised as being far ahead of European shipbuilding throughout the Middle Ages. Constructed in a range of sizes up to 1250 tons, their mast and rudder configurations coupled with aerodynamically-panelled sails made them highly manoeuvrable, and their beamy, compartmented designs gave them capacious holds and a high safety factor. Chinese maritime history records many of these craft sailing the known world in large fleets during the 15th century.

In his enthusiasm for a Portuguese discovery, Fitzgerald declined to consider the possibility that Australia might have been sighted and surveyed by the Chinese as much as a century earlier. Experts who have studied the Mahogany Ship phenomenon over the years, however, have acknowledged a Chinese probability as 'justifiable'. For who were the 'yellow men' of local Aboriginal legend, the people who traditionally came amongst the area's Yangery tribe and left traces of 'some foreign strain' that were still recognisable by the early settlers? Similar 'foreign strains', referred to elsewhere, have been noted amongst the Aborigines of Western Australia's Shark Bay (probably Dutch), and certain Maori tribes in New Zealand (possibly Spanish or Portuguese).

Whatever the truth in this speculation, the other Aboriginal legend of ships visiting this area before the mid-18th century, coupled with the dating of timber said to have come from the Mahogany Ship and the known movements of the Dutch, all seem to suggest that the wreck was also Dutch. Equally though, for similar reasons, it may still be the Portuguese caravel of popular thinking. But it might just as easily have been a relic of a little-known Chinese admiral and his charge, caught in dire straits off a wild coast that has claimed so many other ships since European settlement. Unlikely? Implausible? Far-fetched? The fact is, we just don't know. Nor will we, until such times as the remains of this elusive wreck are found.

Appendix I

It will be apparent to readers by now that the loss of a vessel at sea, the sinking of a ship in coastal waters, or its break-up on rocks or reef is never the end of the story. Indeed, for every shipwreck, its loss is something of a new beginning - the end of one life and the start of another. Where once there was a modest workhorse plodding the coast, or a thing of beauty flying before the wind on the high seas (the loss of either of which might ruin its owners at the time of its demise), their wrecks often later preserve a special kind of wealth for future generations to find and appreciate. The most recent and spectacular example of this has been the discovery and subsequent exposition of the RMS Titanic, despite the depth of her Atlantic grave. Modern technology can reach and unravel such riches these days, which are only rarely present in the form of tangible treasure.

Shipwrecks offer much more than any intrinsic valuables they may contain. They are often described as time capsules, as was the case of the Mary Rose, the flagship of Henry VIII which sank off Portsmouth, England, in 1545 and was raised again in 1982. The Commonwealth Government, in enacting legislation to preserve Australia's most notable shipwrecks, has described them as 'gifts from the past' and 'museums beneath the sea'. Today, therefore, they represent archaeological, cultural, historical and technological resources which can be preserved, studied and analysed. Such wrecks represent valuable educational and recreational resources, as well as being a means of interpreting the past, bringing our ancestry to life or creating the foundation for new marine ecology sites.

But who owns these wrecks, these resources? What rights do finders have over 'their' shipwreck? Do they have an exclusive right to remove objects, either for their own benefit or for sale? Are known wrecks available to anyone who can reach them? Are they open to salvage or souvenir-hunting before the marine environment absorbs them for all time? Where are they? What condition are they in? Why are they important? If they can't be seen, why should we be concerned to keep them? These are understandable questions in what appears to be a convoluted area of Government policy.

Even though a vessel may have been totally wrecked by the violence of a storm, perhaps many years before its rediscovery, her ownership is still recognised as the prerogative of either the original owners or their heirs, or an insurance company, a salvage company or some other legal successor. In Australia, such ownership is dealt with under the Navigation Act 1912, whereby the Commonwealth Receiver of Wreck will take charge of any wreck or wreck material in Australian waters, and will consider any ensuing claims. Claims on a vessel or its cargo must be made within a year, after which anything not claimed becomes Commonwealth property. Shipwrecks thus do not belong to the finder. Fortunately for posterity, the time when shipwrecks were regarded as treasure troves for the diving community is largely past. Australians these days are much more aware of the heritage values of shipwrecks, as they are of older structures on land. Regrettably though, a few are still treated as private domains by some divers.

Past experience shows this can happen, the law notwithstanding. Within a month of its discovery off the South Australian coast in 1981, for instance, the 133-year old wreck of the Tigress had been devastated by fossickers. The William Salthouse lay as she had foundered when located in Port Phillip Bay the following year. A large part of her 1841 cargo of barrelled foodstuffs, wines and building materials was found intact in what remained of her hold, a unique snapshot of colonial provisioning in the mid-19th century. Within six months, however, divers had plundered the wreck, damaging both the historic cargo and the vessel's remains to such an extent that for a time diving on the wreck was prohibited. The Dunbar, lost off Sydney Heads in 1857, was an earlier target for treasure-seekers. But it was concern over the exploitation of 17th and 18th century Dutch shipwrecks off Western Australia in the 1960s that caused the Commonwealth Government to pass the Historic Shipwrecks Act in 1976 as the first attempt to identify and protect shipwrecks in Australian waters. Even so, it remains a fair assumption that not all wreck discoveries have been notified to the relevant authorities, and that damage continues in the meantime.

As a result of the 1976 legislation and that subsequently enacted by the States, the discoverers of shipwrecks have no automatic rights at all to disturb their fittings, or even to pick up loose items on a wreck with the intention of removing them from the site. This applies equally to items on known wrecks. Over the last 20 years or so, a system has been established to control diving on sensitive wrecks by means of permits and protection zones. Shipwrecks are now regarded as a valuable part of Australia's history - a finite, irreplaceable and often fragile cultural resource to be preserved wherever possible.

It is thus important that new wreck discoveries be notified to the appropriate State and Commonwealth authorities (see Appendix 3) so that essential research can be undertaken to establish their identity and their significance (usually assessed in relation to archaeological, historical, social, scientific or technological criteria) to Australia. It is equally important that known wrecks be cared for, by way of a suitable management plan if necessary, in order to minimise natural deterioration; to preserve their condition; to inform the public about their particular histories and attributes; and to discourage pilfering. Responsibility for most of these functions has been delegated to State heritage authorities by the Commonwealth Government under the terms of the Historic Shipwrecks Act 1976.

The 1976 Act applies to all Australian waters below the low water mark, and extends outward to the limits of the continental shelf. Most State authorities have enacted parallel legislation, like South Australia's Historic Shipwrecks Act 1981 or Victoria's Heritage Act 1995, which protect wrecks in inland waters and coastal waters above the low water mark. Originally the Commonwealth Act was designed to protect the Dutch wrecks off Western Australia and to declare certain other ship remains as 'historic', which were then to be the basis of a proposed Register of Historic Shipwrecks. In 1993, however, to streamline the administrative processes and to obviate delays in determining the significance and status of a particular wreck, the Act was amended to allow all shipwrecks over 75 years old to be automatically declared 'historic'. And rather than creating a central Register in, say, Canberra, each State has become responsible for its own input via a common format into an integrated computer system run by the Western Australian Maritime Museum in Fremantle. Today, the Historic Shipwrecks Register contains details of around 6000 wreck sites, including a large number which are less than 75 years old, but which are nevertheless deemed to be of special significance to the nation.

Under all of these Acts, the law reqires that anyone who finds the remains of a ship, or an article likely to have come from such a ship, shall inform the authorities of the find as soon as possible, and in enough detail to enable a follow-up investigation. Such Acts prohibit damage, interference, removal or destruction of a wreck or any associated articles, to the extent of imposing protected zones up to 200 hectares around historic shipwrecks in order to exclude divers, fishing boats, pleasure craft or any other activity likely to disturb their remains. Permits may still be granted to visit a shipwreck in a protected zone, depending on the purpose of such visits, but these are likely to be subject to supervisory conditions, and/or a requirement that any form of disturbance must follow recognised archaeological practices.

Though all of this may appear to impose irksome restrictions on the diving public, this is not really the case. Wrecks which become formally designated as 'historic shipwrecks' are a vital part of Australia's cultural and maritime heritage and need to be preserved intact, as far as possible, for future generations as well as our own. Protection zones are necessary within these provisions in order to protect fragile sites, or sites of special importance, which may also be subject to management plans designed to enhance such protection. Generally, people may visit most historic shipwreck sites without a permit, provided that they do not interfere with a wreck's material remains or any found in its vicinity. Wrecks which are not covered by protective legislation (i.e. most of the more recent sites) may be visited at any time without restriction, though it is always advisable to check before diving. The hope is that divers will still respect such wrecks as much as they would older ones. After all, today's curiosity may well be tomorrow's heritage, so the message to visitors is always one of 'Look, but please don't touch!'

Restrictions notwithstanding, community participation in maritime archaeology is actually encouraged by the authorities, and is frequently acknowledged as performing an important role in helping to find, identify, research and preserve our nation's sea-borne heritage. In these days of financial stringency, government budgets rarely provide sufficient funding to undertake the same level of effort as the many voluntary interest groups working in this field. However, there is usually enough in the kitty, as provided under the 1976 Act, to offer sometimes quite substantial rewards to the finders of new wrecks which are later declared 'historic'. The discovery of the bullion-ship Rapid (WA) drew the highest reward of $32 000. The finders of HMS Pandora (Qld) were paid $10 000. And $2000 went to the finders of William Salthouse (VIC), to name but three.

In recent times sport diving has become a multi-million dollar industry across Australia, both in terms of equipment sales and tourism income. More partic-ipants are taking up the sport year by year. Interest in wreck-diving has been particularly rapid over the last 15 or so years, reflecting a notable shift away from spear-fishing to underwater photography, or merely underwater sight-seeing. This has occurred in parallel with the development of a universal conservation-cum-heritage ethic. Wreck sites are ideal locations for marine life photography, as well as encounters with our maritime past. At the same time, technological advances in scuba gear have increased the possibilities for deeper dives, which in turn has meant more wreck discoveries.

The lore and mystery of shipwrecks is such that even the non-diving historian intent on sifting the archives, or members of the public viewing wreck remains in shallow water or on land, can play an equally important part in photographing sites, recording their locations and dimensions, researching historical facts or writing up descriptive notes. Most States support maritime archaeology associations as a focus for these activities.

Governments themselves, both Commonwealth and State, are active participants in promoting, rather than simply regulating, maritime history and archaeology. Most States have either a maritime museum or a maritime archaeology unit within an appropriate government agency - either planning, conservation or heritage - which records, researches and conserves shipwrecks and wreck artefacts. Sometimes, as in Victoria and New South Wales, there are both. These bodies, often in association with local councils, help to promote an understanding of maritime archaeology and the values inherent in our underwater heritage. They are involved not only in registration and conservation, but also in regular survey work, excavation and protection projects, interpretation and community education.

Perhaps the most exciting and meaningful development in recent years, however, has been the establishment of a series of shipwreck trails in the form of walks, drives and dives. These trails link shipwreck sites on both land and under water, and bring to the fore the value of these historical assets in terms of recreation, education and tourism. Several such trails now exist in New South Wales, Victoria, South Australia and Western Australia. Site information is usually provided at coastal car parks or lookout points opposite the wrecks. Increasingly, information is displayed on the seabed for divers in the form of plaques set up as wreck markers. Details on any of these trails and wreck sites can be obtained from the authorities listed in Appendix 3.

A National Research Plan for Historic Shipwrecks has now been devised by the Commonwealth Department of Communications and the Arts, which offers guidelines to all maritime archaeology agencies in pursuing their objectives of research, data base development, and public education and communication. The Plan seeks to convey the importance shipwrecks have in relation to Australia's wider history.

Appendix 2

LOCATIONS AND DIVE CONDITIONS OF WRECKS

NB. All the wrecks described below are designated historic shipwrecks under the provisions of the Commonwealth Historic Shipwrecks Act 1976, and related State shipwreck legislation.

NAME	BUILDER/ WHERE BUILT	DATE BUILT	VESSEL TYPE	TONNAGE	DATE LOST	LOCATION	DIVE CONDITIONS
SS *ADMELLA*	Laurence Hill & Co., Glasgow, Scotland	1857	Iron screw steamship	400 tons gross	6 August 1859	Carpenters Rocks, 27 km NW of Cape Northumberland, S.A.	Described as treacherous, requiring substantial experience on difficult dives, good seamanship and a strong element of luck. Little remains of the wreck, and what there is now lies scattered across the reef shallows. Not often visited.
BATAVIA	Holland	1628	Retour ship	600 tons burthen	4 June 1629	Morning Reef, Wallabi Group, Houtman Abrolhos, approx. 75 km off the coast of W.A.	Wreck remains found in a zone of heavy surf in water around 2 to 6 metres deep. Visibility is clear, though strong swells and surges will often prevent diving. Local conditions are difficult to predict, and can be dangerous. Experienced divers can best visit from November through May, though much of the site has now been cleared.
CATARAQUI	William Lampson, Quebec, Canada	1840	Ship	Registered 710 tons, burthen 802 tons	4 August 1845	North of Cataraqui Point, south-west coast of King Island, Tasmania	Rough seas and 'Roaring Forties' westerlies make this one of the most exposed wreck sites in Australia. Good dive opportunities are few, though at 100 metres the site can be reached from the shore. Little remains of the ship but cargo items might be found amongst the crags of the reef. Visibility is often limited by surge and tidal shifts.
CATHERINE ADAMSON	Aberdeen, Scotland	1855	Clipper	768 tons	23 October 1857	Below Old Man's Hat, Inner North Head, Sydney Harbour, NSW	Ground comprises large rocks and boulders which have fallen from the cliffs above. Any remains now lie amongst their crevices. Water depth is around 10 metres, max. 27 metres. Visibility depends on sea conditions, but is best on the flood tide. Swells and currents around the harbour entrance can make diving difficult.

NAME	BUILDER/ WHERE BUILT	DATE BUILT	VESSEL TYPE	TONNAGE	DATE LOST	LOCATION	DIVE CONDITIONS
AHS CENTAUR	Scott's Shipbuilding & Engineering Co., Greenock, Scotland	1924	Steel motor ship	3220 tons gross	14 May 1943	9.3 nautical miles east of the Cape Moreton light, Queensland,	Wreck was found in March 1995, and is said to be upright in two pieces in water 180-200 metres deep. Should be respected as a war grave. Historic Shipwrecks Act 1976 prohibits interference.
DUNBAR	James Laing, Sunderland, England	1853	Clipper	Registered 1321 tons, burthen 1980 tons	20 August 1857	Between The Gap and the Signal Station at Outer South Head, below Sydney Heads, NSW	A very exposed site subject to strong surges and undertow. Access and visibility depend on conditions - best times are during inshore calms accompanying periods of westerly winds and settled weather. Ground is rock and sand with kelp, and water depths around 10 metres. Salvors and souvenir hunters have removed much of Dunbar's remains.
LOCH ARD	Barklay, Curdie & Co., Charles Connell & Co., Glasgow	1873	Iron sailing ship	1693 tons gross	1 June 1878	Southern end of Mutton Bird Island, Loch Ard Gorge, Port Campbell National Park, Vic. Lat. 38°39'06"S, long. 143°03'30"E	The site is on a high energy coast and subject to heavy ocean swells and backwash from the cliffs. Divers are advised to access the wreck from Port Campbell by boat rather than a hazardous swim from the gorge. The outline of the wreck can be seen in waters 15-25 metres deep, though heavy looting has removed much of its substance.
THE MAHOGANY SHIP	Unknown	Unknown	Caravel?	Variously estimated c.100-200 tons	Before European settlement	Last seen in 1880 in dunes between Warrnambool and Port Fairy, Vic., east of the Gormans Lane access. There is a marked trail.	Not applicable
MARIA	Pembroke, Maine, USA	1848	Brig	156 tons	26 February 1872	Bramble Reef, Great Barrier Reef, Queensland	Conditions would be those of a typical shallow reef dive on the GBR. Nothing has been found of the wreck, which probably disintegrated quickly owing to the state of the vessel. Coral growth would cover any remaining artefacts, but the wreck is automatically protected from interference by the 1976 Historic Shipwrecks Act.
HMS PANDORA	Adams & Barnard, Deptford, England	1779	24-gun 6th-rate frigate	N/A	28 August 1791	Pandora Entrance, Great Barrier Reef, Queensland,	Diving is weather-and-sea dependant as the site is quite exposed. It features strong tidal movements at the surface and unpredictable currents at depth. Small reefs and coral bommies are additional hazards, while sharks are ever-present. The wreck lies in coarse coral sand at water depths around 30-33 metres, with visibility up to 50 metres on occasions. The Queensland Museum undertakes regular excavations on the site.

Name	Builder/ Where Built	Date Built	Vessel Type	Tonnage	Date Lost	Location	Dive Conditions
QUETTA	William Denney & Bros. Dumbarton, Scotland	1881	Steamship with barquentine rig	3302 tons gross	28 February 1890	Adolphus Channel, Cape York, Queensland	Wreck lies in approx. 24 metres at low tide, 45 metres at high tide. The hull is lying on its port side on an uneven bottom, with the bow facing ESE. Strong tidal flows make diving difficult, and occasionally dangerous. Visibility is often poor. Seas are calmest and the weather most favourable between October and January.
a) HMAS SYDNEY b) HSK KORMORAN	a) Swan Hunter Ltd., Wallsend-on-Tyne, England, as Phaeton b) Kiel, Germany, as Steiermark	a) 1934 b) 1939	a) Light cruiser, Modified Leander Class b) converted passenger ship	a) displacement 6830 tons b) 8736 tons gross	19-20 November 1941	Off Carnarvon/ Shark Bay, W.A., approx. lat. 26°1'S, long. 111°16'E. Precise positions of both wrecks are unknown.	Not applicable as the remains of both ships are likely to lie in oceanic waters 1000 metres and possibly up to 3000 metres deep.
DE VERGULDE DRAECK	Holland	1653?	Jacht	c.260 tons burthen	28 April 1656	Ledge Point, Cape Leschenault, W.A.	The wreck site lies off-shore in a situation and conditions similar to those of the Batavia and Zeewyk sites further north - exposure to huge Indian Ocean swells on a fragmented reef, producing difficult diving prospects on many days of the year. Most of the wreck material has been removed to the Western Australian Maritime Museum.
SS YONGALA	Armstrong Whitworth & Co Ltd., Newcastle-on-Tyne, England	1903	Steel steamship	3664 tons	23 March 1911	20 km. east of Cape Bowling Green, Central Queensland	This open water site is affected by wind, sea and current conditions, and is not always easy to locate The wreck lies at depths between 20 and 30 metres on a flat sandy bottom, but may be seen from the surface in good light. The wreck is renowned for its abundant marine life. Visibility is usually between 10 and 30 metres. Access within the ship is relatively free, but the dive is suitable for experienced divers only.
ZEEWYK	Hendrik Raas. Holland	1725	38-gun ship	280 tons burthen	9 June 1727	Half Moon Reef and Gun Island, Houtman Abrolhos, W.A.	Badly fragmented wreck remains may be found scattered in a shallow water surf zone in depths from 1 to 5 metres. Visibility is usually clear, though strong swells and surges may often impede diving. Local conditions are difficult to predict, and can be dangerous. Experienced divers can best visit from November through May.
ZUYTDORP	Penne. Holland	1701	40-gun ship	500 tons burthen	Mid-June 1712	Zuytdorp Cliffs, between Tamala and Murchison River mouth, lat. 27°11'10"S, long. 113°36'E.	This is a remote and very exposed site at the base of a 30-metre cliff, with heavy boulders bordering a narrow beach. Water depths inshore are 3-10 metres, with a wide surf zone and huge breaking swells. Diving conditions are mostly unfavourable, often being described as difficult to impossible. Local conditions are unpredictable. Most wreck material has been removed to the Western Australian Maritime Museum.

Appendix 3

COMMONWEALTH AND STATE AUTHORITIES
RESPONSIBLE FOR HISTORIC SHIPWRECK LEGISLATION

COMMONWEALTH

The Director
Cultural Development and
Heritage Branch
Department of Communications
and the Arts
GPO Box 2154
CANBERRA
Australian Capital Territory 2601
Tel. (02) 6271 1615
Fax. (02) 6271 1079

STATES

The Director
NSW Heritage Office
Department of Urban Affairs
and Planning
Locked Bag 5020
PARRAMATTA
New South Wales 2124
Tel. (02) 9635 6155
Fax. (02) 9891 4688

The Director
Museums and Art Galleries of
the Northern Territory
PO Box 4646
DARWIN
Northern Territory 0800
Tel. (08) 8999 8211
Fax. (08) 8999 8289

The Director
Queensland Museum
PO Box 3300
SOUTH BRISBANE
Queensland 4101
Tel. (07) 3840 7555
Fax. (07) 3846 1918

The Manager
State Heritage Branch
Department of Environment
and Natural Resources
GPO Box 1047
ADELAIDE
South Australia 5001
Tel. (08) 8204 9311
Fax. (08) 8204 9250

The Secretary
Department of Environment
and Land Management
GPO Box 44A
HOBART
Tasmania 7001
Tel. (03) 6233 8011
Fax. (03) 6224 2068

The Director
Western Australian Maritime
Museum
Cliff Street
FREMANTLE
Western Australia 6160
Tel. (08) 9431 8477
Fax. (08) 9336 6332

The Director
Heritage Victoria
Office of Planning and Heritage
Department of Infrastructure
GPO Box 2240T
MELBOURNE
Victoria 3001
Tel. (03) 9628 5033
Fax. (03) 9628 5650

References

Bates, D. *Passing of the Aborigines*, Murray, London, 1938

Bateson, C. *Australian Shipwrecks*, Vol. 1: 16221850, A.W. & A.H.Reed P/L, Frenchs Forest, NSW, 1982

Bennett, R. *A Narrative of the Wreck of the Ship* Loch Ard, T. Oakley, Warrnambool, Vic., 1890

Boyce, M. '*Pandora*'s Intrigue'. In *Sport Diving*, April/May 1990, pp. 78–83

Braydon, S. & Songhurst, R. (eds), *The Diary of Joseph Sams*, H.M.S.O., London, UK, 1982

Chaplin M. 'The HMS *Pandora* Excavation'. In *Skindiving*, April/May 1985, pp. 34–45

Charlwood, D. *The Long Farewell*, Penguin Books, Ringwood, Vic., 1983

Clark, T. 'The Queen of the Clipper Fleet'. In *Scuba Diver*, June –July 1988, pp. 73–6

Coleman, R. 'The Saga of *Pandora*'s Box'. In *Australian Sea Heritage*, February 1984, pp.11–15

Cornwell, E.L. (ed) *The Illustrated History of Ships*, Octopus Books Ltd., London, l979

Court, W.H.B. A *Concise Economic History of Great Britain*, Cambridge University Press, London, UK, 1967

Cropp, B. 'Lure of the Pearl', in *Scuba Diver*, August/September 1987, pp.40–8

Deas, W. 'Diving into the Past'. In *Scuba Diver*, Vol.3, No.2, 1984, pp. 9–15

de Burgh, W.J. & Henderson, G. *The Last Voyage of the* James Matthews, Western Australian Museum, Perth, WA, 1979

Domm, S. 'The Discovery of the *Pandora*'. In *Scuba Diving in Australia*, June/July 1978, pp. 28–30

Drake-Brockman, H. *Voyage to Disaster*, University of Western Australia Press, Nedlands, WA, 1995

Edwards, H. *The Wreck on the Half-Moon Reef*, Rigby Ltd., Sydney, NSW, 1970

Fitzgerald, L. *Java La Grande - the Portuguese discovery of Australia*, The Publishers P/L, Hobart, Tas., 1986

Foley, J.C.H. *The* Quetta *- Queensland's Worst Disaster*, Nairana Publications, Hendra, Qld., 1990

Foster, L. *The Wild Coast Wrecks*, Heritage Victoria, Melbourne, Vic., 1996

Frame, T. *HMAS* Sydney *- Loss and Controversy*, Hodder & Stoughton (Australia) P/L, Rydalmere, NSW, 1993

Gaastra, F.S. 'The Dutch East India Company - A Reluctant Discoverer'. In *The Great Circle*, Vol.19, No.2, 1997, pp. 109–23

Gerritsen, R. *And Their Ghosts May Be Heard . . .*, Fremantle Arts Centre Press, South Fremantle, WA, 1994

Goode, J. *The Rape of the Fly*, Thomas Nelson (Australia) Ltd., West Melbourne, Vic., 1977

Green, J.N. 'The VOC Ship *Batavia* wrecked in 1629 on the Houtman Abrolhos, Western Australia'. In *The International Journal of Nautical Archaeology and Underwater Exploration*, Vol.4, No.5, 1975, pp. 43–63 'Maritime Archaeology and the Indian Ocean'. In *The Great Circle*, Vol.2, No.1, April 1980, pp. 312

Green, J.N. et al. (eds) *The ANCODS Colloquium*, Special Publication No.3, Australian National Centre of Excellence for Maritime Archaeology, Western Australia Maritime Museum, Fremantle, WA, 1998

Henderson, G. *Unfinished Voyages - Western Australian Shipwrecks*

1622–1850, University of Western Australia Press, Nedlands, WA, 1980 'Three Early Post Australian Settlement Shipwreck Sites: HMS *Pandora* (1797), the *Sydney Cove* (1797), and a Site Near North West Cape'. In *The Great Circle*, Vol. 2, No.1, April 1980, pp.24–41

Henderson, G. et al. 'HMS *Pandora*: Lost and Found'. In *Archaeology*, January/February 1983, pp.27–35

Ingelman-Sundberg, C. *Relics from the Dutch East Indiaman*, Zeewijk, *Foundered in 1727*, Western Australian Museum, Perth, 1978

Jeffreys, M. *Wreck of the* Sydney Cove, New Holland Publishers P/L, Frenchs Forest, NSW, 1997

Kemp, P. (ed.) *The Oxford Companion to Ships and the Sea*, Oxford University Press, Oxford, UK, 1988

Langdon, R. *Elcano - The ship, the man, the mystery*, Spanish Embassy, Canberra, 1987

Lemon, A. & Morgan, M. *Poor Souls, They Perished*, Hargreen Publishing, North Melbourne, Vic., 1986

Loney, J. *Australian Shipwrecks, Vol.2: 1851 to 1871*, A.W. & A.H. Reed P/L,
Terrey Hills, NSW, 1980; *Australian Shipwrecks, Vol.3: 1871–1900*, List Publishing, Geelong, Vic., 1982; *Australian Shipwrecks, Vol.4: 1901–1986*, Marine History Publications, Port Arlington, Vic., 1987; *Ships and Seamen off the South Coast*, Neptune Press, Belmont, Vic., 1980; *Tall Ships and Sailormen*, Marine History Publications, Geelong, Vic.; *Wrecks in Australian Waters*, Australian Sports Publications, Newport, Vic.

MacKenzie, M.E. *Shipwrecks ... and more Shipwrecks*, MacKenzie, Peterborough, Vic., 1974

Mahogany Ship Committee. Proceedings of the First Australian Symposium on *The Mahogany Ship*. Mahogany Ship Committee, Warrnambool, Vic., 1985

Mawer, G.A. *Fast Company: The Lively Times and the Untimely End of the Clipper Ship* Walter Hood, Plainwords Press, Hughes, ACT, 1994

McIntyre, K.G. *The Secret Discovery of Australia*, Pan Books, Sydney, NSW, 1987

Mead, T. *The Fatal Lights*, Dolphin Books, Sydney, NSW, 1993

Milligan, C.S. & Foley, J.C.H. *Australian Hospital Ship* Centaur - *The Myth of Immunity*, Nairana Publications, Hendra, Qld., 1993

Muckelroy, K. (ed.) *Archaeology Under Water. An Atlas of the World's Submerged Sites*, McGraw-Hill Book Co., Maidenhead, UK, 1980

Pasrear, J. et al. 'Victims of the *Batavia* Mutiny: physical anthropological and forensic studies in the Beacon Island skeletons'. In *The Bulletin of the Australian Institute for Maritime Archaeology*, Vol. 22, 1998, pp.45–50

Playford, P.E. 'The Wreck of the *Zuytdorp* on the Western Australian Coast in 1712'. In *Journal and Proceedings of the Western Australian Historical Society*, 1959, Vol.5, Part 5, pp.5–41

Potter, B. (ed.) The Mahogany Ship - *Relic or Legend?*, Mahogany Ship Committee, Warrnambool, Vic., 1987

Simpson, D. 'The Treasure in the *Vergulde Draeck*: A Sample of V.O.C. Bullion Exports in the 17th Century'. In *The Great Circle*, Vol.2, No.1, April 1980, pp.13–17

Warwick, M. 'Nutmegeconomics and the White Tribe of Australia'. In *Sport Diving Magazines* February March 1997, pp.104–10

Unknown 'Men of Destiny'. In *Scuba Diver*, December 1988–January 1989, pp.20–7

Glossary and Abbreviations

Abeam off at right-angles to either side of the ship

Aft towards the rear of the ship

AHS Australian Hospital Ship

ASC Army Service Corps

Athwartships from side to side, at right-angles to a vessel's centre-line

Bare poles without sails, in storm conditions

Barque a three-masted sailing vessel, square-rigged on the fore and main-masts, fore-and-aft rigged on the mizzen

Barquentine a three-masted sailing vessel, square-rigged in the foremast, fore-and aft rigged on the main and mizzen-masts

Beam seas heavy seas approaching a craft side-on

Below below decks

Bilge the lowest part of a ship, where water collects

Bilge-pump a pump arranged to remove water from a vessel's bilges

Boatswain (bosun) a ship's officer responsible for sails, rigging, boats, anchors and flags

Bosun's mate see Boatswain

Bow the foremost part of a vessel

Bridge the platform from which the captain or officer of the watch navigates and steers a mechanically-propelled ship

Brig a two-masted square-rigged vessel

Brigantine a two-masted vessel, square-rigged in the foremast, fore and aft rigged on the mainmast

Brouwer route a route south from the Cape of Good Hope into latitudes of 40° or higher, to approach close to Australia on the prevailing westerly winds before turning north towards destinations in the East Indies

Bulkhead any wall which divides the space within a ship into compartments

Bulwark the sides of a ship raised above deck level for shelter and safety

Caravel a small, early three-masted Spanish or Portuguese trading vessel

Carrack a larger, more robust development of the caravel

Carry away the breaking away of a ship's masts, rigging or other parts as a result of storms

Carvel-built a method of fixing side-planking on a vessel edge-to-edge

Clinker-built a method of fixing side-planking on a vessel so the edges overlap

Commandeur on Dutch vessels of the VOC, the most senior officer in charge of all matters pertaining to a ship and its voyage, other than the actual sailing of the ship, which was the duty of the skipper

Companionway access way to the lower decks of a ship by means of stairs or ladders

Continental shelf the area of shallow seas fringing a landmass before they plunge steeply to oceanic depths

Course the direction in which a ship is steered to reach its objective; the largest, lowest sails on the masts of a sailing ship

Derrick a ship-board spar, pivoting on the lower end, for lifting heavy weights

Drop from yard a form of naval punishment in which the victim was dropped from a yard on a rope attached to his wrists bound behind his back

Dunnage mats or brushwood stowed around cargo to inhibit wetting, chafing or movement

Flotsam floating materials, wreckage, and so on

Flute a small Dutch supply vessel

Flyboat a flat-bottomed Dutch vessel with a high ornate stern, of the 16th to 19th centuries, used mainly for coastal trade

Fore-and-aft rigged sails rigged closely parallel to a vessel's fore to aft centre-line

Forecastle the high forepart of a ship which usually held the crew's living quarters

Galliot a small Dutch trading vessel, built like a barge with sails rigged fore and aft from a single mast

Gentlemen Seventeen (or XVII) the seventeen directors of the VOC, the Dutch East India Company

Halyards (haul yards) ropes or wires used to raise sails

HMAS His/Her Majesty's Australian Ship

HMS His/Her Majesty's Ship

HMVS Her Majesty's Victorian Ship

HSK (Handelstorkreuzer) a German commerce raider or merchant cruiser used during the two World Wars

Jacht a fast cargo ship of Dutch design

Jury rig sails temporarily rigged on a broken mast or span

Kedge a small ship's anchor; to haul a ship away from dangerous ground on an anchor positioned from a ship's boat

Keel-haul a method of naval punishment by which the victim was tied and dragged beneath the keel of a ship from one side to the other

Larboard a former term for the left-hand side of a ship facing forwards, now known as the port side

Lascar an Indian seaman

Lee shore one on a ship's sheltered side. A shore towards which the wind blows

Mizzen the hind-most mast of a three-masted ship

MV motor vessel

Poop the effect of a ship being overtaken at the stern by a boarding sea

Poop deck the highest deck on the stern of a sailing ship

Port the left-hand side of a ship facing forward

Predikant a minister or preacher; a Dutch Reformed preacher

Quarter the after sides of a ship, adjoining the stern

Quarterdeck in sailing ships, the after part of the main deck, sometimes raised, from which the vessel is navigated and controlled, and usually restricted to officers only

Quartering seas seas which approach a ship from left or right of the ship's stern

RAAF Royal Australian Air Force

RAN Royal Australian Navy

RMS Royal Mail Ship

RN Royal Navy

Roaring Forties the latitudes between 40;dg and 50;dg South which are often dominated by strong to gale-force westerly winds, and used to speed ships quickly between the Cape of Good Hope and Australia

Schuyt a Dutch flat-bottomed craft used in shallow waters, rivers, etc

Scuba Self-Contained Underwater Breathing Apparatus

Scuppers drain holes which pierce the bulwarks of a ship to allow water on deck to drain into the sea

Sea stack a pillar of rock left behind in the sea by receding cliffs, as in Victoria's Twelve Apostles

Ship a generic name for large craft, but also one applied specifically to three-masted vessels square-rigged on all three masts

Shrouds the standing rigging of a sailing vessel which gives lateral support to its masts

Spars the generic name for all masts, yards, spars, booms, or bowsprit aboard a sailing vessel

Square-rigged the use of large square sails attached to spars mounted on one or more masts of a sailing vessel

SS steam ship

Standard-bearer the lowest commissioned rank in the contemporary Dutch Marines equal to ensign or cornet. One who carries the flag or colours

Starboard the right-hand side of a ship, facing forward

Stays the standing rigging of a sailing vessel which gives fore-and-aft support to its masts

Stem the foremost timber or metal member attached to the keel which forms the leading edge of a ship's bow

Stern the hindmost part of a vessel; the rear

Sternpost the hindmost timber or metal member attached to the keel which forms the stern of a ship, and to which the rudder of a sailing ship was usually attached

Top gallant the third sail up from the decks of older sailing ships

Topsail the second sail up from the decks of older sailing ships

Uppermerchant the senior merchant or administrator aboard ships of the VOC, the Dutch East India Company

Uppersteersman the senior officer aboard VOC ships responsible for navigation, and the issue of directional instructions to the helmsman

Undermerchant the second most senior merchant or administrator aboard ships of the VOC, the Dutch East India Company

Understeersman a junior officer aboard VOC ships assisting the Upper-steersman in matters of navigation

USS United States Ship

VOC Vereenigde Oost-Indische Compagnie, Dutch United East India Company

Yards horizontal spars to which sails are attached, mounted at various points on the masts of square-rigged sailing vessels

Yawl a ship's jolly-boat with four or six oars

Picture Credits

Index